# THE
# CAMBRIDGE
# APOSTLES

# THE
# CAMBRIDGE
# APOSTLES

*A history of Cambridge University's élite intellectual secret society*

*Richard Deacon*

*Robert Royce Limited*

Published in Great Britain 1985 by
Robert Royce Limited,
93 Bedwardine Road
London SE19 3AY

British Library Cataloguing in Publication Data

Deacon, Richard
  The Cambridge Apostles: a history of Cambridge
  University's elite intellectual secret society.
  1. Cambridge Apostles—History
  I. Title
  378.426'59          LF129.5.C/

  ISBN 0-947728-13-9


Printed and bound in Great Britain by
Biddles Ltd., Guildford and King's Lynn

# CONTENTS

# ACKNOWLEDGEMENTS

Acknowledgement of permission to quote and for assistance and help is gratefully given to the following:

The Master and Fellows of Trinity College, Cambridge, for an extract from Add MS c 74[13] (letter from J. Spedding to W. H. Thompson, dated 4 November, 1833).

St John's College, Cambridge, for extracts from Henry J. Roby's privately printed *Reminiscences of My Life and Work: for my own family only* and the private papers of Hugh Sykes Davies.

The Senior Librarian, Miss S. Gates, of the Central Reference Library, Lincoln, for information on Lord Tennyson.

The *Cambridge Review* for quotations from Hugh Sykes Davies' article, *Apostolic Letter*, 7 May, 1982.

The *Cambridge Evening News* for assistance in researching their files.

Mr Michael Holroyd, author of *Lytton Strachey: A Critical Biography*; Professor Robert Skidelsky, author of *Maynard Keynes*.

The Archives of the Association of Scientific Workers, (formerly with the University of Sussex and now with the University of Warwick).

FBI and CIA material released under the Freedom of Information Act.

Finally, to all those many people who helped by information freely given in letters, conversations and even telephone calls, but who, understandably, wish to remain anonymous.


*Illustration Acknowledgements*

The photographs of Noel Annan Jonathan Miller and Peter Shore are reproduced by kind permission of Tophams Limited; all other photographs are reproduced by kind permission of Peter Lofts Limited, Cambridge.

# PREFACE

It was the brothers Goncourt who first made the observation that if two men who both spoke the English language were to be cast away on an uninhabited island, 'their first consideration would be the formation of a club.'

Possibly the golden age of club-life in its most imaginative and vital form ended with the eighteenth century, but it certainly flourishes in the universities of the 1980s. Nowhere does this apply more than in the University of Cambridge, England, where there are today scores of clubs to suit all tastes, ranging from debating societies, musical and literary clubs, to the Dungeons and Dragons Society and the Frugal McDougal Society to the Very Nice Society and the Sceptics, taking in *en route* such diverse societies as Virtue Without Terror and the Inter-Dits.

But the club known as the Society of the Apostles, founded at Cambridge University early in the last century and still functioning today, is rather special in that it keeps itself strictly to self-imposed rules of secrecy. It is not to be found listed, for instance, in the very long section on Cambridge societies in the *Varsity Handbook*. Yet over the years the influence of its members has been considerable on both sides of the Atlantic Ocean and in all spheres of life from administration to the arts, from philosophy to politics, from science to medicine. What is more, the life stories of many of its members are fascinatingly interesting.

One motivation for writing the history of the Society, originally known as the Conversazione Society, is that long ago I wrote a book entitled *The Hell-Fire Club: the story of the amorous Knights of Wycombe*. Not that the one club resembled the other; indeed, to members of the Society of Apostles it may sound frivolous to mention them in the same sentence.

Yet there are some curious parallels and even similarities between the two societies. Both were secretive and élitist, though the Knights of Wycombe were more hedonistic than philosophical. The Hell-Fire Club's true title was 'the Franciscans' and they dressed in the habit of monks, while the Cambridge society eventually became known as 'the Apostles'. So each had titles with what was, admittedly vaguely, a religious connotation. The Franciscans included among its members Cabinet Ministers, diplomats, scholars and bohemians. This is similar to the Apostles' membership over the years. Each society came into the news as a result of scandals. In the case of the Franciscans (so named after Sir Francis Dashwood, their founder) this was as a result of the prosecution of a member, none less than John Wilkes, for the alleged obscene libel of his *Essay on Women*. With the Cambridge Apostles it was caused by the revelations between 1979 and 1982 that some members of the Society had been agents of the Soviet Union.

In each instance the events which scandalised sections of public opinion both in the eighteenth and the twentieth centuries tended to give a totally erroneous picture of each of these societies. The Knights of Wycombe were not black magic addicts, as was suggested, and the Cambridge Apostles Society was not a subversive organisation.

Nevertheless, the fact that I had researched one secret society, discovered its wine-books and learned of some of the goings-on in those caves at West Wycombe, while useful experience, did not disguise the fact that to attempt to write a history of the Cambridge society was a task of almost awesome magnitude. For this was a society which, unlike the Franciscans, was still in existence and which had a code of secrecy which was even more highly respected today than it had been a hundred years earlier.

Then again, the Apostles was a society with a membership of some few hundreds over a period of 165 years, including such past celebrities as Tennyson, Bertrand Russell, Lytton Strachey and Roger Fry in an earlier age, and in more recent times Lord Keynes, Lord Rothschild, Lord Annan, Peter Shore and Dr Jonathan Miller. Not to mention scores of others who, though less well known, had made important contributions to politics, the arts, science and medicine.

It would be churlish indeed not to acknowledge that the task upon which I was embarking had already been undertaken to a limited extent by such writers as Paul Levy in his biography of the philosopher, G. E. Moore; by Professor Peter Allen, of Toronto University, in his meticulously researched work on the first ten years of the Society, and, bravely, if not always accurately, by Frances Brookfield in her own story, *The Cambridge Apostles*, published in 1905. Other members of the Society have from time to time broken the rules of secrecy to mention the Society in their memoirs.

Despite all this, there was still a strong case to be made out for attempting to bring up to date the history of the Society and, more importantly, to trace its changing face from one decade to another, and to show the influence its members had exerted in various spheres of activity. At the same time, as with the Knights of Wycombe, one had the feeling that some attempt needed to be made to put the record straight and to correct any distorted pictures such as have been perpetrated in some sections of the media.

In embarking on this adventure (for that is exactly what it has often seemed to resemble), I have delved into the lives of some hundreds of the Society's members between 1820 and the early 1980s. This alone has been a formidable quest. I have received help from very many people, including some living members, but in varying degrees. Much has depended upon the individual member's interpretation of the rules of secrecy. I have been supplied with lists of members and secretaries of the Society in great detail up to about 1950. Prior to that there have only been a few rather puzzling gaps in the lists (almost as though they have been censored). Some of the gaps I have been able to fill by diligent inquiry. From 1960 onwards the gaps in the lists have increased until one gets to the point where no lists at all are readily available. From this period onwards it has been much more difficult to ascertain who was, and who was not a member.

Naturally, there have been some members who have totally declined to assist in this task. Yet, even among these, there has been a hint of doubt as to whether this was the right course. One person, for example, wrote admitting he had been a member, but added:

'I am sorry to say that I don't wish to talk about the matter . . . If I have second thoughts I will let you know of them.' Another said: 'It happens that I do not nowadays agree with the convention of confidentiality which members of the group agree to observe. However, I *did* agree to it when I was an active member, and for that reason I don't feel at this stage I can break my promise by saying more.'

. Yet another stated: 'I hope you will forgive me if I say that I would not be prepared to talk to you about the Cambridge Apostles, although this does not mean a categorical refusal of cooperation. If, for example, there were any matters of fact on which you thought I might usefully be able to comment . . . I should be happy to do what I could.'

Such attitudes, however, politely phrased, and however much I personally understand them, have antagonised non-Apostles both at Cambridge and elsewhere. It is the combination of élitism and obsessive secrecy which they find offensive in a modern academic establishment. Yet this élitism and secrecy is only a reflection of what has long been a British disease – a compulsive desire to be secretive. The cult of secrecy in what is basically a university debating society hardly accords with twentieth century views on the need for freedom of information.

Undoubtedly the revelations made about Soviet agents among the membership have caused the Society to wish to avoid publicity for some years to come. The Security Services began to make their own inquiries about members – probably to an excessive degree. It is only three years ago that the furore about this died down. And, as one Apostle put it to me, 'there were good reasons for keeping silent and secretive. The motives of those wishing to know the membership list are not always pure.'

Yet, despite all this, what impresses one most is the way in which the high intellectual standards generally demanded of all new members has been maintained so well over the best part of two hundred years. This in itself is a considerable achievement. Secondly, there can be no doubt that a high percentage of the members have made valuable contributions to society generally in very many fields.

That is to speak of the past and the present. What of the future? The first American member of the Society joined in the middle of the last century. Since World War I there have been other close associations between the Apostles and the United States and Canada. This has been particularly true from the end of the 1930s, since when there has been a mutual exchange of ideas between such members and the American academics. One sees this slowly but surely flowering, not in any ostentatious way, but in a positive contribution to the development of ideas and theories in the English-speaking world.

I may be alone in stressing this as a pointer for the future. It is at present something intangible and yet inspiring. Maybe Cambridge University, England, would be either nonplussed or shocked at such a suggestion, but might not there be a case for Cambridge University, Massachusetts, establishing a similar society? Apostles Across the Ocean? It is a beguiling idea.

# 1

# CONVERSAZIONE

'The best of life is conversation,
and the greatest success is confidence'
(Ralph Waldo Emerson)

In an Emersonian sense, and with Emerson's implied corollary, that conversation inspired confidence, the Cambridge Conversazione Society was founded at Cambridge University in 1820.

Initially, it was a straightforward debating society, not so very different from other societies at the university. It was started largely through the influence of George Tomlinson, who later became Bishop of Gibraltar, and is credited with being its founder. However, there were actually twelve founder-members, according to the records, these being, in addition to Tomlinson, Edward Brice, Henry Thompson, Henry Harford, John Punnett, Thomas Ainger, Robert Henderson, George Shaw, Charles Wiseman, Richard Battersby, James Furnival and John Simpson. Despite various theories to the contrary, the probability is that the Society's nickname of 'The Apostles' derived from the fact that it had twelve founder-members.

Soon it became known by the abbreviated title of 'The Society'. Most of its early members were somewhat undistinguished students, though Tomlinson subsequently made a name for himself and took his doctorate in divinity. They were nearly all evangelical in that they sought to propagate the Gospels in some detail, but almost instinctive Tories in their political attitudes. It was their earnestness which held them together. The themes chosen for debate had strong analogies with the current literary scene, and they were also influenced by clerical opinion.

Perhaps the truth is that, if evangelical, one cannot for very long remain bogged down in the kind of Toryism which existed in the early nineteenth century. The evangelical Apostles of the New Testament, Matthew, Mark, Luke and John, were themselves anything but

1

nineteenth century Tories: 'Seek and ye shall find' was not the motto of Matthew alone.

In seeking and not always finding, these eager young clergymen of the future (nine of the first thirteen members took holy orders) gradually became faced with doubts. Not doubts about fundamental matters in religion, but doubts about methods and how best to present the Gospels. The more serious doubts were to follow at a much later date. The doubts led to more intensive, self-examining debates, to more daring choices of subjects for discussion.

Most of the early members came from St. John's College, including Tomlinson himself. He was the only one of the nine clergymen who rose to any prominence in the Church, and even he ended up as an unremarkable colonial bishop. His progress in the Church was aided by his having been tutor to the family of Sir Robert Peel, after which he became secretary of the Society for Promoting Christian Knowledge. His work for the SPCK and his campaign against atheism in the periodicals of the day led to his travelling to the Near East, after which he urged the creation of an Anglican bishopric covering the whole of the Mediterranean territories where the Church of England had any influence. Thus it was that the then Prime Minister, Sir Robert Peel, appointed Tomlinson as the first Bishop of Gibraltar. In fact, Tomlinson operated primarily from Malta.

He was rather a dull man and lacking in the diplomatic virtues which a newcomer as bishop ideally required in a vast area where there were far more Roman Catholics than Anglicans. After he died in 1863 his daughter offered to sell a portrait of her father to the Conversazione Society, but this proposal was declined, possibly because the members had nowhere to keep it, or they had lost interest in their founder.

It seems fairly certain that in the beginning there was nothing particularly secret about the Society, or its activities. As to its nickname, nobody seems sure whether the title 'Apostles' was used originally as a compliment to the twelve, or in a derogatory sense. Though to non-members the Conversazione Society was not considered as a secret body in the early years, and its existence was well known inside and outside the university, nevertheless it became increasingly conspiratorial. This was chiefly because the original twelve members insisted that the recruitment of new members to take the places of those leaving the university must be conducted with the utmost secrecy. Sir Arthur Helps, the author and barrister, who was an Apostle in the 1830s, spoke of the deliberations of members before a new nominee was accepted. 'Sometimes months were given to consideration of claims for membership,' he declared. John Mitchell Kemble, son of the famous actor, who later edited the *British and Foreign Review*, said that 'no one was elected until every member agreed he should be elected. One black ball was fatal. No one knew he had even been proposed until he was accepted.'

The rules for the conduct of business were simple enough. The Society met each Saturday night, usually at the rooms of a member, when one of them would read an essay on a topic chosen sometimes by, and sometimes for him, the previous week. Having delivered this, the subject of his essay (usually posed in the form of a question) was debated and at the end of the night a vote was taken for or against the question. Immediately afterwards lots were drawn for the following week's speaker and the subject of his essay was chosen by a common consent.

From the earliest years each member was obliged to attend every meeting when he was resident in Cambridge, except in the case of illness. This rule later on applied to graduates and dons who were also members. However, all those who wished for one reason or another (and such reasons had to be serious and not frivolous) to be relieved of the obligation could apply to the Society for a dispensation. Such a person then became an 'Angel', the whole process being referred to as 'taking wings'. Bertrand Russell (later Lord Russell) in his autobiography defined the taking of wings as 'being to retire from habitual presence at meetings of the Society, which was usually done in the man's fifth or sixth year.'[1] An 'Angel' could attend such meetings of the Society as he wished, as well as the annual dinner, at which all members were welcome.

The nickname 'Apostles' was formally accepted as the title for members quite early in the Society's history. Edward Fitzgerald, the translator of *The Rubaiyat of Omar Khayyam*, who was at Cambridge in the early days of the Apostles, but was not a member, suggested that the nickname came from the fact that the 'most academically incompetent members of the graduating class were termed Apostles when there were twelve of them.' This may, however, have been merely an indication of Fitzgerald's resentment that he was not chosen as an Apostle. First of all, there were not always as many as twelve 'incompetent' members of the graduating class, and, secondly, the original twelve members of the Society, though relatively undistinguished, were not academically incompetent. They all took degrees.

Perhaps a more relevant clue is to be found in a letter which John Punnett, one of the founder members, wrote to Bishop Tomlinson's daughter on her father's death and which she passed on to the Society. '"The Apostles" was the name we gave ourselves in secrecy, but I think it would be more becoming to describe ourselves as Apostolicans in that we were all evangelists. We were concerned to propagate and explain the Gospels and in doing this honestly and sincerely to resolve all doubts concerning our respective interpretations by debating them in secret.

3

There had been a tradition of secret societies in the University for very many years, but we maintained secrecy in order to resolve first and therefore not to confuse. We were mindful of the fact that there was an ancient society who called themselves the Apostolicans and some of us had examined their records with interest.'[2]

One wonders whether those records were looked up for any specific purpose, and if this led to the mystique with which the Society eventually surrounded itself. Punnett said no more on the subject. The Apostolicans were a secret sect combining Christianity with a form of pre-Marxian communism in the north of France in the thirteenth century. Nonetheless, whatever views some of the Apostles of the 1930s may have held, it should not for one moment be thought that those members of the 1820s held any similar views.

Punnett's reference to there having been a tradition of secret societies in the University is interesting. There had been both Jacobite and Jacobinical societies at Cambridge in the eighteenth and early nineteenth centuries. 'The Family', a society with positive Jacobite origins, so called from the toast to 'the family over the water', was a dining club to which most heads of colleges belonged. It was functioning in the 1830s and even in the 1920s.[3]

Both Oxford and Cambridge Universities had some unusual and semi-secret societies in the latter half of the eighteenth and the early part of the nineteenth centuries. At Oxford the most notorious was the Hell-Fire Club, founded at Brasenose College, and modelled on the society founded in the previous century at West Wycombe in Buckinghamshire which bore the name of the Knights of Wycombe, initiated originally by Sir Francis Dashwood, a Chancellor of the Exchequer and Postmaster-General. Yet another debating society at Oxford was the Oriel Noetics, while at Cambridge there has always been a wide variety of societies to suit almost every taste, and even the supposedly modern Herodoteans, specialists in Greek philosophy and Greek musical instruments, had its origins in the late eighteenth century.

As to the Jacobinical society at Cambridge, in 1793 one William Frend, a Fellow and Tutor of Jesus College, had been prosecuted for publishing a pamphlet entitled 'Peace and Union' recommended to the Associated bodies of Republicans and anti-Republicans.' Frend was alleged to have degraded the rites and doctrines of the Church of England and was expelled from the college. The Vice Chancellor of the University asserted that 'the expulsion of Frend was the ruin of the Jacobinical party as a *University thing*, so that the party is almost entirely confined to Trinity College.'[4]

Not entirely confined to Trinity, however, for the President of Queens' College, Isaac Milner, wrote a letter to William Wilberforce in 1801 which stated: 'At Queens' we happened unfortunately to have several clever Fellows, some time ago, who should have filled our offices of trust as Tutors etc., but were disqualified on account of their principles. I was positively determined to having nothing to do with Jacobins or infidels, and custom has placed in my power the appointment of the Tutors, provided they be Fellows of our own college. Our own being very unfit, we went out of the college, sorely against the wish of several; however, by determining to make no jobs of such things, but to take the very best men I could find, I carried the matter through in no less than three instances.'[5]

Now if St. John's was the college which monopolised the Society in its very earliest days, the majority of members were soon recruited from Trinity and elsewhere. Did Trinity pass on to the Society the Jacobinical influence? Did the secrecy of the Jacobins who, in this country, modelled themselves on the French revolutionary Jacobin Club become a fetish with the Apostles? One must remember Canning's phrase for the pro-Jacobin fellow-travellers of the latter part of the eighteenth century – 'the friend of every country but their own', at a time when there were crypto-Jacobins in high places. It is not insignificant that not many years elapsed before the Apostles were taking a revolutionary interest in countries other than their own.

There were many warnings in this period about the alleged dangers of secret societies. Some of them were somewhat melodramatic pleas such as those repeatedly made by Cardinal Manning. This convert from Anglicanism to Roman Catholicism went so far as to assert that 'on the day when all the armies of Europe will be engaged in an immense conflict, then, that day, the revolution which until now has been working secretly underground will have found the favourable moment to show itself in the light of day.'[6]

The phrase 'Apostolic' seems to have been in general use in Cambridge in reference to various functions long before the Conversazione Society was founded. Many years before there had been a regular supper meeting for the clergy at Christ's College, called 'the Apostolic'. There seems little doubt that the members of the Conversazione in the early 1820s regarded themselves as theological apologists and natural successors to the Apostolic Fathers of the second century A.D.

Gradually the Society developed its own jargon and indulged in a love of what they called 'coded language' (something which non-Apostles could not share). There was an element of the schoolboy about all this and letters of the period reveal how extremely immature the early Apostles were.

Later, as will be seen, the jargon became more sophisticated and today it would be almost unrecognisable. Here is a list of some of the Society's adopted phrases up to the early part of the twentieth century:

ANGEL   a member who is released from the obligation of attending meetings, but who remains a member for life and is free to attend when he wishes.

ARK   the trunk in which the Society kept its records.

BIRTH   the induction ceremony for a new member.

BRETHREN   members of the Society.

BROTHER   a member of the Society.

CHARISM   a vital quality for becoming an Apostle. The phrase 'Apostolic' was also used later on as applied to one who had the right qualities for membership.

EMBRYOS   those being considered for membership.

FATHER   a new member's sponsor.

HEARTHRUG   when a member delivered his essay he was said to be 'called to the hearthrug', from whence he spoke. The 'hearthrug' was the Apostles' equivalent of a pulpit or dais.

ILLUMERS   members who were especially good at illuming the truth about any subject discussed. This phrase appears to have gone out of circulation after the 1840s.

JACOBINICALS   radical members.

MODERATOR   the member giving his essay, or reading.

PHENOMENA   the rest of the world – i.e. all those who were not Apostles.

PHENOMENAL   non-Apostolic. John McTaggart, an Apostle of the latter half of the 19th century, referred to a fellow-member 'taking unto himself a phenomenal wife'.

REALITY   anything to do with the Society and its members and environment was arrogantly described as 'Reality'.

SIMONIANISM   this phrase owed its origin to the cult of Claude, Comte de Saint-Simon in France, and was an important thesis of some Apostles in the late 1820s and early 1830s in the sense that a new social order could only be established through spiritual regeneration.

STUMPS   apostolic term for Philistines.

TO TAKE WINGS   as previously explained, to become an 'Angel', i.e. a life member of the Society with a dispensation to attend meetings only when a member could and wished to do so.

UNAPOSTOLIC   anyone who did not possess the qualities required of an Apostle. This phrase has lasted well into the twentieth century.

WHALES   the nickname given to sardines on toast, the conventional fare at the Saturday night meetings.

FOOTPRINT   a reference to any Apostle who had made his mark in the world. This seems only to have been used for a brief period.

Many other phrases which were regarded as exclusively Apostolic were added in later years, and in the current century, certainly since World War II, more have been added and in some instances substituted. The phrases given above are those which more especially represent the spirit of the Society in the last century. It is not easy to analyse this spirit of the early years because it changed subtly and positively often without the members realising how rapidly this was happening. Earnest evangelical Toryism was always somewhat of a contradiction of itself. The urge to preach and teach led to both radicalism and doubts, religious doubts on the technicalities of the Church of England and especially some of the Thirty-Nine Articles. The trend away from Toryism to radicalism was imperceptible at first, but it soon gained ground.

However, it must be remembered that the founder members' influence on later members was minimal. Those founder members tended to choose people similar to themselves, from among those intending to take holy orders or to become teachers rather than imaginative innovators. Thus people such as Thackeray and Edward Fitzgerald were never recruited. Fitzgerald had attended King Edward VI's Grammar School at Bury St. Edmunds, which makes it all the more remarkable that he was not elected to the Society, for this school provided a high percentage of the early members. Ex-pupils of the school who became Apostles included W. B. Donne, Sydney Gedge, John Kemble, Edward Romilly, Henry Romilly, Frederick Malkin and James Spedding. Fitzgerald was a close friend of Spedding and Thackeray, but perhaps this talented poet was too much of a recluse for the Apostles. The school at Bury St. Edmunds owed much to the liberal influence of its headmaster, Dr. Benjamin Heath Malkin, who stressed the need for individual thought being more important than conventional knowledge. It was he who succeeded in sending so many of his pupils to Cambridge.

In the first ten years of the Society's existence some seventy-two members were elected. After that the selection of new members became subject to more cautious and sometimes pernickety assessment. Sometimes there would be only two, or at most three new members a year. In 1850, for example, no new member was elected.

The first Apostle really to stamp his personal influence on the Society was not one of the founders, but John Frederick Maurice, who has sometimes been wrongly described as a co-founder. This is chiefly due to the fact that Maurice's son in the official biography of his father stated that in 1834 at the annual dinner of the Apostles' Club they toasted his father 'as the author of the club.'[7]

Maurice was elected an Apostle in November, 1823, and his expression of some theological doubts just as much as his sometimes forthright views immediately had an impact. Arthur Hallam, who became a member in 1829, may have contributed to the idea that Maurice was a founder of the Society by a letter he wrote to W. E. Gladstone, the future Prime Minister, saying that the effect which Maurice had produced 'on the minds of many at Cambridge by the single creation of that Society of Apostles (for the spirit not the form, was created by him) is far greater than I dare calculate, and will be felt, both directly and indirectly, in the age that is upon us.'[8]

This letter must have had a considerable effect upon the young Gladstone as, shortly afterwards, he launched a debating society at Oxford which was similar to that of the Apostles. Indeed, he actually called it The Society, the name by which the Conversazione became known within a few years of its creation. But it never progressed, nor acquired the same widespread influence as the Cambridge society.

Maurice certainly revitalised the Apostles and gave them a new zest for learning and developing their own ideas. He stressed the need for friendship among members, for the encouragement of intimacy in an intellectual sense of frank probings into personal problems, doubts, philosophies and habits. True, there was much talk of 'spiritual regeneration', but the truth is that this phrase covered many matters which were non-spiritual. In many ways it was an attempt to give to the members a freedom of thought and action which some of their future clerical members would never dream of granting to their parishioners or co-religionists. The Apostles could air their doubts in cosy secrecy and this they called 'regeneration'. One cannot say that it was particularly healthy and it may have paved the way for much of the humbuggery of the Victorian Church of England. The Apostolic members of the clergy of the era would, of course, argue that they were taking a step forward from the squirearchical clergy of the eighteenth century.

Maurice's influence was to give the Society something of the nature of the Oxford Group of the 1930s, an urge to indulge in an orgy of confessions of members' sins and doubts, to share their innermost thoughts with one another and to debate and analyse them. It was the antithesis of conventional thinking of the period, which was increasingly inclined to stifle such thoughts, or keep them to oneself and avoid embarrassing topics.

Thus it was that members sometimes produced essays which were confessions of doubts about certain theological premises, or expressed anxieties as to whether such-and-such a course of action, habit, or even book or poem was immoral. Immorality appeared to be the one word which perpetually made them feel uneasy. Possibly this was a reaction to eighteenth century rationalism.

Frederick Maurice has been called the father of Christian socialism, though one doubts whether he would have described himself in this way. He came from a Nonconformist background which was liberal rather than Calvanist. His family, dominated by a preponderance of females, had suffered from all manner of religious arguments and matrimonial upsets. Yet he became by far the most prominent and influential of the early Apostles. At Cambridge he moved from Trinity to Trinity Hall and then on to Exeter College, Oxford, to prepare himself for the Church. During a chaplaincy at Guy's Hospital he worked for part of the time as a professor of English literature and history at London University. In 1853 he was sacked from this post on account of his unorthodox opinions upon the subject of eternal punishment. He had himself always been uneasy about many rigidly held beliefs in all the Churches, and so he encouraged his fellow Apostles to examine their own doubts and to see whether they should pronounce open disagreement on a number of cherished religious principles.

He returned to Cambridge as professor of moral philosophy in 1866. Maurice was forever playing alternate roles in life, at one moment that of God's Agent on earth and the next punishing himself by inflicting penances, such as when he decided to go to Oxford to complete his training. It was here that he was not only received into the Church of England, but became president of the society started by Gladstone in an attempt to emulate the Apostles.

Yet in some ways there was a much more powerful influence on the early Apostles than F. D. Maurice, and this came from a non-member. Maurice had, however, pointed out that a spiritual revival was more likely to come through an interest in the development of current literature than through political activity. A potent source for this was, he indicated, none other than Samuel Taylor Coleridge, though some other Apostles looked to Keats, Shelley and Wordsworth.

But Coleridge was a primary source of inspiration for the Society. Members met him, talked with him, and his name would often occur in debates. It should be remembered that Coleridge was not just a poet. He was a journalist who contributed regularly to the *Morning Post*, and he was described by a contemporary as a man with 'the largest and most spacious intellect, the subtlest and most comprehensive, in my judgement, that has yet existed among men.'

Coleridge was a colossus of his time. His theories and interests were well ahead of his epoch and they matched the inquiring minds of the Apostles, especially in relation to the psychological problems of the individual. While today he is probably best known for such poems as *The Ancient Mariner* and *Kubla Khan*, he was a serious student of psychology long before that subject became popular. He had studied the question of subconscious thought and the importance of dreams when Freud and Jung were not even born. He could lay claim to having personally created the words 'psychoanalytic' and 'psychosomatic' which have comparatively recently found their way into English dictionaries.

Coleridge was himself a Cambridge man, which endeared him to the Apostles. He was also a brilliant conversationalist, and, had the Society been in existence in his own time at the University, he would have been a natural choice for membership. As it was, his influence on the Society was such that there was a *coterie* inside the Apostles who called themselves 'the Mystics', who were followers of Coleridge in his ultimate creed that, while imagination was the path to truth, fantasy only led to illusion. As one who had ruined his health by taking laudanum in large doses at one time, Coleridge should have been in a position to prove his theory.

The urge towards mysticism alternated with the quest for new, radical and evangelical approaches to religion and philosophy. It also produced some unusual, even untypical interests among members. One of these was the cult of the Saint Simonians which excited some and angered other Apostles. This was a cult which tried to make a religion out of an all-embracing love. It was launched by one Barthélemy Enfantin in the mid-1820s. Enfantin, a serious-minded Frenchman, was sufficiently earthy and cynical to allow his allegedly high principles to hide his real motive, which was to make free love respectable. He had been strongly influenced by Claude Henri, Comte de Saint-Simon, and, after meeting this aristocratic socialist in 1825, became the founder of Saint-Simonism, and an enthusiastic propagandist of his ideas for social and religious reform.

For Enfantin sex was a religion and religion meant nothing unless it had a sexual connotation. He published a manifesto favouring communism, as he understood it, and advocating a plea for universal sexual promiscuity under the misleading title of 'The Enfranchisement of Women'. Armandine Lucille Dudevant, better known under her pseudonym as 'George Sand', the novelist, very quickly saw through the schemes and hopes of Barthélemy, or *Père* Enfantin, as he now called himself:

'"*Père*" Enfantin is a banker whose currency is love and he pays out in hearts of gold and *billets doux*,' she said, 'but what is the use of such things when the man controlling them has the mentality of a high priest of finance?'

Enfantin, having failed to persuade George Sand to be his female Messiah, set up his Abode of Love in a sombre mansion in which he held court. *Le Nid*, as it was called locally, was described as 'a gigantic harem where every woman was a bride and every bride the property of Enfantin.' Yet, despite the fact that Enfantin was not very successful in establishing his cult in his own country, his gospel in diverse forms spread to Britain, Germany and America. In Germany it flourished under a society called the Ebelians, named after Archdeacon Ebel, while in America it flowered under such titles as the Bible Communists and the New Haven Perfectionists. In Britain it took roots in Denmark Hill, near London, and Wales.

The Apostles even debated the principles of Saint-Simonism. Some of them went to London as observers at the cult's meetings. James Spedding, an Apostle, wrote to a fellow-member, W. H. Thompson, of Trinity, in June, 1832, to say that the Saint-Simonians were active again and holding 'fortnightly meetings in Burton Crescent which . . . leave little doubt of the speedy developement [sic] of the free woman; who has become a Mother since the last accounts, and Mothers they say are not so common among that class. I have half a mind to buy a curly wig and go to the next meeting incog."[9]

Spedding's comments on Mother and Mothers with capital letters are a little obscure, but it suggests a certain amount of mild amusement at the expense of the cult and its activities. This theory is borne out by a report by Spedding that Arthur Buller, another Apostle, had thought of dressing up as a woman to attend a Saint-Simonian meeting 'and offering himself as a candidate for the Motherhood.' Buller, who later became a barrister, then a judge in Calcutta and ultimately a Member of Parliament with a knighthood, was a notorious lecher in this period as well as being a practical joker of an original turn. His lechery in his Cambridge days was of a homosexual nature and it may well have been in this context that Buller thought of attending a Saint-Simonian meeting disguised as a female.

Richard Trevenix Trench, an Apostle who became first Dean of Westminster and then Archbishop of Dublin, was not merely unimpressed by the Saint-Simonians, but regarded them as a dangerous and subversive cult. Writing to another member of the Society, W. B. Donne, in December, 1831, he inquired: 'What think you of the St Simonians? To me the seem the most perfect expression of the Spirit

11

now at work – primogeniture, aristocracy, heredity, all that rested on a spiritual relation will no longer be recognised, must be swept away before the new industrial principle.'[10]

It will be noted that some of these early Apostles were not particularly lucid or felicitous in their prose. Often what they were trying to say was lost in an onanistic torrent of words. They started with a single idea, then either talked or wrote too much about it, confused themselves and lost their ultimate message in prolonged sentences made worse by erratic punctuation. Much the same could be said of the early Apostolic theology, for they even tried to produce something of this kind. It was a mishmash of evangelistic enthusiasm, Coleridgianism and mysticism plus a great deal of self-doubting and questioning.

As far as can be ascertained only one Apostle, George Wrangham, of Magdalene, actually participated in Saint-Simonism in Britain. For a short while he was attached to the Denmark Hill cult, then he joined the Lampeter Brethren, an offshoot of the cult established in Wales by Arthur Augustus Rees and Henry James Prince. It was Prince who, shortly afterwards, founded his Abode of Love at Spaxton in Somerset, where for many years he remained the absolute leader of a small carefully chosen community surrounded by females whom he called his 'spiritual brides'. Prince had been given a curacy at Charlinch in Somerset and it had been in this period that, like so many evangelists, he had become obsessed with and fascinated by sin. This did not endear him to the male parishioners, especially when he talked of a farmer's wife and a milkmaid having come to him 'for conversion and ghostly counsel.' Such evangelical zeal, couched in a mysticism which the simple country folk could not understand, was bound to create dissensions in the parish.

George Wrangham went down to Charlinch and later to the Abode of Love at Spaxton.

'I am in two minds about this experiment,' he wrote to a non-Apostolic friend, Adrian Worship: 'At Charlinch, I do comprehend from my own experience and observations that Prince caused dissension in his domain. Male parishioners forbade their wives to go to his evening meetings, and some of the women so threatened said they would quit their homes if thus prevented from attendance thereupon. Yet, one is compelled to admit, that the ideal of a loving community – *an earthly paradise* such as Prince portrays – is something to ponder on, something to wish for and even something desirable to experience. It may well be that this does show us a new and unexpected route to the regeneration of society we all desire and that what he has in mind is a marriage of minds and not of bodies. Yet bodies must be in harmony with minds, and that is the dilemma. And minds must be in harmony with bodies; therein lies another problem. Yet, what think you of a man who claims that the *Song of Songs* has awakened his mind to delights he had never dreamed to be possible? He has told Léonore Labillière, a disciple of the St-Simonists, that he had become intoxicated with the *Song of Songs*. "Dreaming of trumpets calling him to fleshly delights with the Shulamite girl, no doubt," was her terse and rather unkind comment. Yet, I wonder whether she may not be right. I am drawn to much of St-Simonism, but you will understand my reservations."[11]

# 2

# THE LOTUS-EATERS

'To hear each other's whisper'd speech;
Eating the Lotus day by day,
To watch the crisping ripples on the beach,
And tender curving lines of creamy spray;
To lend our hearts and spirits wholly
To the influence of mild-minded melancholy'
(Alfred, Lord Tennyson)

There is a strong parallel in the pattern of Tennyson's 'Song of the Lotus-Eaters' and the semi-mystical attitudes of the Apostles in the late 1820s and early 1830s. By this time earnestness had given way to a more sophisticated approach to the problems of life, philosophy and religion. In short, the debating society had stirred itself up, and the brew which it concocted had many ingredients.

If George Tomlinson had left very little mark upon the society, others had begun to have a considerable influence. After F. D. Maurice, Edward Romilly, later a Member of Parliament and High Sheriff of Glamorgan, and John Sterling, a most remarkable character whose early promise was snuffed out by his equally early death, both had a part in re-directing the society. Suddenly the Apostles became rather less earnest and constructive, arguing at considerable length without necessarily expecting the answers to lead anywhere. They were, in fact, Lotus-Eaters all, cultivating introspection, loving argument for argument's sake, behaving in an ultra-civilised manner, yet never quite knowing in what direction they were going, or whether such knowledge mattered. Yet they would vigorously have denied such suggestions.

In some respects it is much easier to assess accurately the sages of a thousand years ago than those of a hundred years ago. Had the Cambridge Apostles of the 1830s existed in, say, Homer's time, it would have been relatively simple to put them in perspective. It is not so easy to show how the Society came to change in a mere decade. Those of the 1830s really launched the cult of friendship: this was something they revered above all else. As Lotus-Eaters some of them were devoted to laudanum or opium. They sought out drugs as devotedly as the undergraduates of the 1960s. Intellectual discussions actually provoked and encouraged a resort to drugs. Not among all members, but most positively among the few who wished to shine at all costs. Such discussions may have been the result of much soul-searching, but there were times when this verged on the ridiculous, or something akin to insanity. Indeed, one of them, Thomas Sunderland, died insane. The correspondence of some Apostles of the period testifies to the mental instability of some members of the society.

'I am often near to madness,' wrote 'your Apostolic friend, Brother Francis' in 1832, 'and I can only think that this alarming tendency is due to too much introspection and too little action. Atheism raises its evil head in so many directions and at the most inopportune moments like a monster lying in wait for one. I fight it off, but as soon as I win one battle another confronts me. Perhaps pantheism is the answer, and perhaps through this process I can glorify Shelley and make him as genuine as Wordsworth. Do I mean genuine, or something quite different – authoritative, perhaps?' It is not certain exactly who 'Brother Francis' was, but it seems likely that he was one Francis Garden, who was elected an Apostle in 1830 and later became a clergyman.'[1]

Similarly, Arthur Hallam suffered from recurring fits of depression. He wrote as one Apostle to another, J. W. Blakesley, in April 1830:

'How I am to get through the summer, "the sweet little cherub that sits up aloft" only knows. If I die, I hope to be buried here . . . if my past follies and reckless life have not clipped my wings, I trust soon to – fly over the moon, unless indeed I tumble into it in the shape of a lunatic . . . I have floated along a delicious dream of music and poetry and riding and dancing and greenwood-dinners and ladies' conversation till I have been simply exhaled into Paradise, spiritually speaking . . .'

Of the Apostles of the 1830s Alfred, later, Lord, Tennyson, his beloved friend, Arthur Hallam, Richard Monckton Milnes (later Lord Houghton) and John Sterling were in their respective ways vital influences in the Society. These were years of turmoil ranging from the intense arguments (mainly philosophical) about the old and the new schools of poetry to the political controversies aroused by the Reform Bill, which was eventually passed in 1832. This bill, in addition to granting a sweeping redistribution of Parliamentary seats, also gave the franchise to borough householders paying a ten-pounds rental and in counties to those with a rental of fifty pounds. The uproar which these proposals created had resulted in riots in Cambridge during the Michaelmas term of 1830. Special constables were sworn in and even the Apostles for once prepared for action rather than talk. This much is evident from Apostle James Spedding's account of events at the time:

'Blakesley is Captain of Poets and Metaphysicians – and visions of broken heads and arms, scythes and pitchforks disturbed the purity of our unselfish contemplations and the idealism of our poetical imaginings. But the threatened army did not make the threatened attack . . . our heads are still sound to talk nonsense and metaphysics, very much to my satisfaction and the disappointment of the more adventurous spirits among us.'[2]

Two Apostles, George Venables, later to become a judge, and Henry Lushington composed a poem on the 1830 situation:

'At dawn we heard, that night by six
Nor love nor money purchased sticks.
Quick ranged in numbered bands
We watched each post and passage straight
From Jesus to the towered gate
Where sceptred Edward stands.'[3]

Alfred Tennyson was not very happy at Cambridge and his association with the Apostles in the early years was not particularly successful. He had complained in a letter to his aunt that 'the revelry of the place [Cambridge] is so monotonous, the studies of the university so uninteresting', so it is not surprising that he left without obtaining a degree. He entered into some of the Apostolic debates and it is recorded that he voted 'no' on the question 'Have Shelley's poems an immoral tendency?' His son mentioned that he had a note of his father's referring to an Apostolic meeting which went on until after 2 a.m. Tennyson wrote that 'John Heath volunteered a song, Kemble got into a passion about nothing, and Thompson poured large quantities of salt upon Douglas Heath's head because he talked nonsense.'[4]

Perhaps the problem for Tennyson was that in his own mind he was quite clear about what he thought and felt, and could express these things in a disciplined, commonsense and yet aesthetic manner, and that he found much of the Society's late-night chatter superfluous to his needs. Here was a poet who knew that words made music, whose poems were superb examples of onomatopoeia whether in the quick tempo of bubbling into eddying bays and babbling on pebbles, or in the sensually

16

slow murmurings of the mild-eyed Lotus-Eaters. Thus, when it came his turn to read a paper on the subject of 'Ghosts' to the Society, he suddenly felt that his ideas on the question could not be in harmony with the Apostolic demand for debate. What they required and what he wished to say were incompatible, so he tore up his thesis and as a result immediately put himself in disfavour.

The Society's records show that he was fined five shillings for non-attendance at meetings, and that as a result of further absenteeism he was asked to resign. Yet that was not the last of Tennyson's associations with the Apostles and the story had a happy ending. Members began to realise that Tennyson thought in terms of poetry and that this had inhibited him from prose essays. As the years passed by they became more and more impressed by his poetry. It took many years for the re-admittance of Tennyson to come about, but in 1855 there was a unanimous move to support this. At the annual dinner of the Apostles that year he was restored to membership as an 'Angel'.

By this time the Society thought rather more highly about Tennyson than he did of them. This is not altogether surprising because the letter informing him of his honorary membership, signed by the ultra-serious biblical scholar, F. J. A. Hort, who had become secretary of the Apostles, was pompous in the extreme. Hort said that there had been a tradition that nobody should be re-elected who had not written at least three essays for the society. But in his letter to Tennyson it was not quite clear as to whether this tradition had been discarded, or whether it was not considered valid.

Even after he resigned from the Apostles in 1830, Tennyson exerted considerable influence within their ranks. This was partly because of his friendship with Arthur Hallam, one of the favourites of the Society during his relatively brief life. Hallam was only seventeen when he went to Trinity College and his contemporaries 'saw his charm and felt his strength and bowed before him in conscious and inferiority in everything.'[5] As to whether the Tennyson – Hallam friendship was homosexual is only relevant to the subject of this book in that it coincided with the beginning of a kind of sublimated homosexual cult within the Society.

Referring to this with the utmost delicacy, Frances M. Brookfield, a friend of some of the early Apostles, declared that 'our minds are dazzled by their [the Apostles'] achievements, but our hearts are warmed by their mutual love.'[6]

Arthur Hallam put it somewhat differently when he wrote the lines:

'Oh! there is union, and a tie of blood
With those who speak unto the general mind,
Poets and sages! Their high privilege

17

> Bids them eschew succession's changefulness,
> And, like eternals, equal influence
> Shed on all times and places.'

Hallam wrote an essay on 'Platonic Love' for the Society in 1829, though this was said to have been curiously disguised as an appreciation of Cicero and his friendship for Atticus. He was in some respects very much the brilliant, but mixed-up kid of his generation, flirting with atheism while wishing for a stronger faith, and excusing his latent homosexual tendencies by saying that only through human relationships could one understand the love of God.

When Hallam died only four years after being elected an Apostle, Tennyson produced his poem, *In Memoriam*, in which he not only referred to the Apostles, but to his friendship with Hallan. This lengthy poem was addressed 'In Memoriam A.H.H., *obiit* MDCCCXXXIII':

> 'Forgive what seem'd my sin in me;
> What seem'd my worth since I began;
> For merit lives from man to man,
> And not from man, O Lord, to Thee.
> Forgive my grief for one removed,
> Thy creature, whom I found so fair.
> I trust he lives in Thee, and there
> I find him worthier to be loved.'

In canto 87 of *In Memoriam* Tennyson refers to the Society when he writes of walking past 'the reverend walls in which of old I wore the gown', and noted that . . .

> 'Another name was on the door:
> I linger'd; all within was noise
> Of songs, and clapping hands, and boys
> That crash'd the glass and beat the floor;
> Where once we held debate, a band
> Of youthful friends, on mind and art;
> And labour, and the changing mart,
> And all the framework of the land.'

In that canto Tennyson caught something of the spirit and inspiration of the Apostles in the 1830s when all the members were eager to savour new experiences and explore new horizons. It was in this mood that in May, 1829, Richard Monckton Milnes went up in a balloon with another undergraduate and one of the early aeronauts and wrote to Hallam: 'Your

18

friend in the skies speeds this note to you at an elevation of about one mile and a half from the base earth where you are grovelling.' Tennyson referred to this incident in his poem, *A Dream of Fair Women*.

In similar mood John Sterling wrote enthusiastically from Trinity Hall: 'Commend me to the brethren, who, I trust, are waxing daily in religion and radicalism.' Later he paid this tribute to the Apostles: 'To my education in that Society I feel I owe every power I possess, and the rescuing myself from a ridiculous state of prejudice and prepossessions with which I came armed to Cambridge. From the 'Apostles' I, at least, learned to think as a free man.'[7]

The underlying philosophies of modern poetry were a major preoccupation of the Society both in their debates and in informal gatherings of two or three members. That the Apostles produced a number of poets in this period seems clear from their records. Some of the papers read at debates were actually produced in the form of poems. Two Apostle poets distinguished themselves – Tennyson, who won the Chancellor's Medal with his poem, *Timbuctou*, in 1829, and William Johnson, who secured the same prize by a single vote in 1843 with his poem, *Plato*.

Tennyson, addressed poems to other Apostles apart from Hallam. In 1830 in *Poems, Chiefly Lyrical*, he wrote a Sonnet to JMK (John Mitchell Kemble), which began:

> 'My hope and heart is with thee – thou wilt be
> A latter Luther, and a soldier-priest
> To scare church-harpies from the master's feast . . .'

Kemble was an authority on Anglo-Saxon. His fellow-members in the Society appear to have decided early on that his mission in life was to enter the Church, climb to the top and put the whole ecclesiastical establishment in order. But Kemble changed his mind on this score and eventually became Licenser of Plays instead, a post he held until his death.

Tennyson addressed poems to various Apostles. To 'J.S.' (James Spedding) in 1833 he offered condolences on the death of Spedding's brother. Other poems were to J. W. Blakesley (later Dean of Lincoln), to whom Tennyson referred as 'Clear-headed friend' and in January, 1854, an ode to 'The Rev. F. D. Maurice', who had become godfather to his son, urging:

> 'Come, when no graver cares employ,
> Godfather, come and see your boy:
> Your presence will be sun in winter,
> Making the little one leap for joy.'

One poem by Tennyson in 1833 refers to the St Simeon Stylites. It should be stressed that the St Simeon Stylites had nothing whatsoever to do with the St Simonians or with Charles Simeon, a Cambridge preacher. The St Simeon Stylites were a class of ascetics found in Syria, Egypt and Greece between the fifth and tenth centuries. They were said to take up their abodes on the tops of pillars which were sometimes equipped with a small hut from which they rarely, if ever, descended. The Reverend Charles Simeon was a Fellow of King's, a leader of the Evangelicals and founder of the Church Missionary Society.

During those first few decades, although Cambridge University was still an exclusively male preserve, some Apostles would have liked to introduce female members to the Society. Indeed, serious proposals for the admission of women were made even in the 1830s. But the clergy in Cambridge – and naturally this applied particularly to the early Apostles, most of whom became clergymen – were violently hostile to the presence of women in the University. It was from the Church that the main opposition came when the subject of granting privileges to women arose. 'Those infidel places,' was how some Cambridge clergy referred to women's colleges. Although Girton College, the first for women, was founded in 1869, it was not until 1970 that the Society elected the first female Apostle.

An American who was at Cambridge in the 1940s, C. A. Bristed, described in his work, *Five Years in an English University* (1873), how 'the English upper classes are tolerably moral in their own sphere. Their women are well brought up. Their young men respect ladies; perhaps it would be more correct to say *they are afraid of them.*'

Again, it was the clergy who were firmest in their opposition to preventing female guests attending High Table in colleges, as well as opposing any suggestion for electing women as Fellows of a male college.

When a proposal was made to admit women to degrees in 1887, it was roundly denounced by those in holy orders and so the plan was defeated. 'I am opposed to giving women privileges of this kind. I honestly believe they are better off as they are,' W. W. Skeat told Henry Sidgwick, an Apostle who was a strong advocate for advancing the cause of women at the University. In fact, sixteen years earlier he had written to fellow-Apostle, Oscar Browning, to say: 'I am growing fond of women. I like working with them.'

Some of the hostility of 1887 had resulted from resentment among the clergy five years earlier when a Grace had been passed, allowing Fellows to marry. But in 1834 there were two indications that some Apostles would welcome females as members. Arthur Buller, having taken an interest in the St Simonian movement in London, reported back to Cambridge that:

'the St Simonians' idea of having brides in their Church is one we might equally consider as desirable for the Apostles . . . well, perhaps not quite "brides", but why not have female members as "Sisters" for the Bretheren. I cannot but help recalling that one other famous society initiated such a scheme, none less than the Knights of St Francis of Wycombe in the last century. This could enliven our proceedings.'[8]

The second plea for admitting women was in a more serious vein. Francis Garden, in a letter to Monckton Milnes in November, 1834, discussing the cult of Tennysonianism, as he described it, suggested:

'Miss Mellish ought to be sent to Cambridge and made an Apostle. She is in every way worthy, having laid a glorious foundation of Wordsworthianism, and gradually erected on it a glorious palace of Shelleyanism and Coleridgianism, crowning it with the airy minarets of Tennysonianism.'

Alas, there is no indication as to who Miss Mellish was. No more was heard about introducing women members until the early 1890s when John Ellis McTaggart hinted that the Society might be losing something of real value by not admitting females. Had they been eligible for membership, he urged, 'then Caroline Stephen [a member of the talented Stephen family] would have been worthy of the honour.'[9]

Perhaps this prompted Bertrand Russell to suggest some action in February, 1894. For then he told his wife that he was working on a paper for the Apostles, taking as his theme the admittance of females to the Society. His paper had the somewhat enigmatic title of 'Lööberg or Hedda?', but it posed the question 'Should we like to elect women?' Whether the interposition of the words 'like to' made a marginal difference in the voting is a moot point. Possibly it did. Nine members voted 'yes', while only the homosexual activist, Goldsworthy Lowes Dickinson, cast a 'no'.[10]

Bearing in mind the vote on this occasion, it is remarkable that women were not actually admitted to membership until seventy-six years and two world wars later.

The 1840s saw an influx of talent into the Society with such men as Henry Maine, Edward Stanley, James Fitzjames Stephen and William Harcourt. The first-named was to become Sir Henry Maine, whose works on both civil and international law received great acclaim. In 1847 he was appointed Regius Professor of Civil Law at Cambridge. From 1862-69 he was legal member of the Council of India, after which he became professor of jurisprudence at Oxford.

Edward Stanley, who became the fifteenth Earl of Derby, served as a government minister under both Gladstone and Disraeli, and Sir William Harcourt, after being professor of international law at Cambridge, entered the House of Commons and served as Solicitor-General in Gladstone's first ministry and later as Home Secretary, Chancellor of the Exchequer and leader of the House under Rosebery's administration.

Generally speaking, the Apostles have produced rather more senior civil servants than politicians, but in the 1840s and the 1850s a number of them went into politics. It was about this time that a kind of 'old boys' network' developed through the Society's links with 'Angels' in politics. The latter tended to recruit from the younger Apostles and both Stanley and Harcourt chose their parliamentary private secretaries from this quarter.

Gradually, too, the influence of the Apostles extended to the world of literary reviews, notably the *Westminster Review*, the *Athenaeum* and the *London Literary Chronicle*. John Sterling actually purchased the *Athenaeum*, and through his managements of that paper set up in London a meeting place and dining club for Apostles who were thereby introduced to people in the sphere of literature. His life was one long struggle against ill-health, but he owed his reputation largely to his genius for making friends in many quarters. The late Maynard Keynes is said to have described Sterling's work, *The Sexton's Daughter*, as being 'the best poem of the nineteenth century' – a gross exaggeration by almost any literary standards, but nevertheless an impressive tribute from such a lifelong reader of poetry as Keynes.

But it was mainly in the field of law that Apostles of this era made their mark. Outstanding among these, Sir James Fitzjames Stephen was called to the bar at the Inner Temple in 1854, and later became legal member of the Council of the Viceroy of India and then a judge of the High Court of Justice in India.

An early portrait of Alfred
Tennyson

Art critic Roger Fry

Philosopher G. E. Moore

Maynard Keynes, whose
influence on economic thought
was world-wide

# 3

# INSURRECTION

'The last temptation is the greatest treason:
To do the right deed for the wrong reason'
(T. S. Eliot)

The spirit of insurrection filled the minds of a number of Apostles during their early period. True, it was not insurrection of quite the same nature as that which influenced a number of Apostles in the 1930s, but it was a positive spirit of revolt. This spirit was exemplified by a desire to help the downtrodden and oppressed wherever they might be found.

Even the poets and Lotus-Eaters among the Apostles were affected by this spirit. One of the eager Radicals who took this line was George Stovin Venables, a great friend of Thackeray (whose nose he had broken in a fight at Charterhouse) and who was for many years chief political writer for the *Saturday Review*. There is a hint of the Apostolic feelings of the era in the joint verses of Venables and Henry Lushington (both elected to the Society in the 1830s):

> 'So, all looked gladly for the morn;
> And yet I know we did not scorn
> The Hungry Multitude . . .
>
> 'We loved the past with Tory love,
> Yet more than Radicals we strove
> For coming years of gold.'[1]

There is rather more than a suggestion here of romantic radicalism, and it was eagerly consummated at the first opportunity for action by such Apostles as John Sterling, Arthur Hallam, Tennyson (more because of Hallam than of deep conviction), Trevenix Trench, J. M. Kemble and

W. B. Donne, later Librarian of the London Library and another Licenser of Plays, as their consultant. It all started when the Apostles looked around for deserving causes to support and some of them made friends with Spanish liberal exiles in London, including one of their leaders, General Mina.

'It was the fashion among the Apostles to be Radical, a fashion less political than literary and metaphysical,' Graham Greene has commented. 'When politics were touched upon,' he adds, 'It was in an amused and rather patronizing way. "twas a very pretty little revolution in Saxony,' wrote Hallam in 1830, 'And a respectable one at Brunswick' (the dilettante tone has charm after the sweeping statements).'[2]

Just as in the 1930s a band of Apostles, including Julian Bell, who lost his life in the cause, joined up in Republican forces against Franco's legions, so in the 1830s an earlier group of Apostles linked up with the so-called Spanish liberals. To a large extent, both causes were somewhat lacking in their respective conceptions of democracy and liberalism, and there were other Apostles in both periods who saw this and were opposed to the interventions. During the reign of King Ferdinand VII of Spain the Government of National Defence at Cadiz had adopted a new constitution, but such a designation was hardly accurate. Though Ferdinand, under revolutionary threats, promised to respect this constituton, he reasserted his authority with the help of French bayonets in 1823 and repudiated his pledge. From then on he imposed a rigid despotism upon his people. He persecuted those liberals inside Spain and condemned others to permanent exile.

One of the leaders of the Spanish rebels was General Torrijos, a soldier and diplomat who was also a friend of Sterling's parents. As John Sterling had enormous influence at that time with Apostles past and present, he was instrumental in raising funds for the exiled Spanish liberals to aid their plans for insurrection against Ferdinand. Trench and Kemble journeyed to Gibraltar to join the insurrectionists there, while during the summer of 1830 Hallam and Tennyson travelled to the Pyrenees where they passed on money and coded messages to the revolutionaries. Hallam later complained to his friend, Tennyson, that his father '. . . does not seem to comprehend, that after helping to revolutionise kingdoms, one is still less inclined than before to trouble one's head about scholarships, degree and such gear.'[3]

But for his health failing him about this time, it is probable that Sterling would have gone to his death, for he was deeply committed to this foreign adventure. A ship had been purchased in the Thames and secretly loaded with arms. The plan was for it to be sailed to Deal where General Torrijos and a contingent of Spaniards were to come aboard and then proceed to Spain. But news of this plot reached the Spanish Embassy in London, as a result of which the ambassador interceded with the authorities and river police were dispatched to board the craft. Sterling was on board when police arrived, but managed to escape and go down to Deal to break the news that there was no chance of getting away from the Thames. But, despite the fact that he had been pronounced to be suffering from a tubercular condition, he took Torrijos in an open fishing-boat across the English Channel to St Valery, from whence the Spaniards finally reached Gibraltar by various routes.

But the revolution ended disastrously and all the efforts and fund-raising of the Apostles concerned were in vain. The plotters were consistently betrayed, first in London, then in France and, finally, in Spain. Sterling, who had largely master-minded the Apostles' part in all this, grieved deeply over the outcome for many years afterwards. His own cousin, Boyd, was one of the many who were arrested and executed. 'This horrible fate of such a man and one whom I had known as well as you and I know each other,' he wrote to John Stuart Mill, 'has overpowered me completely. I can think of nothing else and cannot write of it without excessive pain.'⁴

There is an ironic footnote to this story of the Apostles' Spanish escapade. It shows that however devout and idealistic the Apostles may have been, however much on countless occasions they stressed that their only concern was to establish the truth, some of them had an Achilles' heel where veracity was the issue. Frances M. Brookfield, a nineteenth century contemporary of various Apostles, tells this story concerning John Kemble and his part in the Spanish insurrection:

'When Jacky Kemble returned from the Torrijos affair in Spain, to College, he had a story of adventure which had three versions. In the first, say in the stage of friendly confidence, he would say – "I once strayed beyond our lines alone and unarmed and suddenly came upon fifteen Spanish Grenadiers, who were closing round me, when I took to my heels, and though pursued by a few shots, escaped with my life and unharmed." Somewhat later the version began in the same way as the first, but proceeded – "I disarmed them – most of 'em – wounded several – and the rest fled, with the Devil take the hindmost." The third, or three o'clock in the morning version, commenced like the others, but continued – "they fell at my feet to a man and implored mercy." "Well, what did you do Jacky? Did you let them go?" "No, by G—, *I slew them all!*"'⁵

It may come as a surprise that there was, in a strictly technical sense only, a traitor to the British Crown among the ranks of the Apostles long before the positively confirmed case of Anthony Blunt. This statement having been made, it should at once be added that he was a traitor who declared himself as such, and one who was prepared to suffer for his beliefs, a much nobler creature than the infamous Blunt. While Blunt escaped for years with his knighthood intact and the tacit silence of the Establishment, William Smith O'Brien was actually found guilty of treason and sentenced to death.

His story is of special interest as it exemplifies that peculiar Apostolic spirit down the years which led many members to put marriages, careers and even their lives at stake for a cause in which they truly believed. In this respect they were truly Apostolic in every sense of the word, biblical and Cantabrigian.

William Smith O'Brien was a member of an aristocratic Irish family claiming descent from the ancient Earls of Thomond. The second son of Sir Edward O'Brien, baronet, he was born at Dromoland, County Clare, in 1803. Educated at Harrow and Trinity College, Cambridge, his election as an Apostle took place on 27 November, 1824, at the same time as six other new members, an unusual number to be elected all at once. O'Brien's family has been described as 'among the most ancient in Europe . . . old when Greece and Rome were in their infancy', yet, despite a high regard for his ancestry, William learned while at Cambridge how to free himself from family and Establishment influences.

He graduated in 1826 and within two years was elected as a Member of Parliament at Westminster in the Tory interest and a supporter of Sir Robert Peel. But, possessed of a warm and generous spirit, with a deeply-felt compassion for the poor and underprivileged, he soon began campaigning for a new deal for Ireland. He distinguished himself in the House of Commons by making forceful speeches, urging that something positive should be done for the poor of Ireland. Thus, increasingly, he tended to alienate himself from his party.

The Irish had for generations foolishly put their faith in a single crop – potatoes. When that failed, stark famine confronted them. O'Brien maintained, with some considerable logic, that successive British governments should have foreseen the impending disaster in Ireland.

But, as the Reverend P. Fitzgerald accurately described in his portrait of the period:

'People were left to die in their thousands and tens of thousands without any legal enactment for their relief . . . mothers with infants at their breasts were lying dead upon the highways . . . from the

26

immense mortality the dead were cast in heaps into the same pit, unshrouded and coffinless.'[6]

Thus it can perhaps be understood how the young O'Brien reacted to this disregard for human life in such passionate, if quixotic, manner. At this stage he was still committed to the Tory cause, even though strongly criticising his party's lack of compassion. He even fought a duel with a follower of Daniel O'Connell, arguing that the O'Connellites were 'more interested in Roman Catholic emancipation than with the harsh issues of human tragedy.' Yet, though a Protestant himself, O'Brien actually advocated the payment of Roman Catholic clergy by the State. In 1831 he lost his seat in Parliament and shortly afterwards surprisingly returned to Cambridge where he was made President of the Union. But he took no part in Union debates.

In 1835 O'Brien was elected as MP for Limerick, and gradually he moved in the direction of Irish nationalism and independence. The following year he introduced a bill which would have gone a considerable way towards relief of the poor in Ireland, but this measure was subsequently shelved. For a long time he had opposed O'Connell on many matters; now he supported him on some questions. Yet, always impatient for results and frustrated by what he regarded as obstructive tactics by MPs and ministers, in 1846 he overreached himself, being sent to prison for one month in a cellar of the Houses of Parliament for persistently defying the Speaker's orders. Then in 1847 he founded the Irish Confederation. In a speech made in Dublin in March, 1848, O'Brien urged the formation of a National Guard. What were to be the functions of such a Guard he did not say. The implication, however, was clear: the National Guard should coerce the Government, if all else failed.

In the eyes of the Establishment O'Brien committed the fatal error of going to Paris to present a congratulatory address from the Irish Confederation to the newly formed French Republic. He was received by the French romantic poet, Alphonse de Lamartine, who was Foreign Minister in the provisional government, but the latter was sufficiently realistic to make it clear that he did not intend to interfere in 'the internal affairs of the United Kingdom.' 'We shared the same ideals, the same sheer joy in the new poetry,' ruefully declared O'Brien on his return from France, 'but sadly we made no progress on important matters.'.

Later in 1848 he made his last speech in the House of Commons. It was during this memorable and unique declamation that O'Brien not only spoke openly of the need for a 'Republic of Ireland', but, when challenged and told this was treasonable language, rashly replied: 'If that be treason, then I avow treason.' He went on to admit that for the first time he had invited his fellow-countrymen to arm themselves.

Unquestionably O'Brien had allowed himself to be provoked into making statements which could hardly help his cause. But the starting of legal proceedings against him by the Government was an act of sheer folly. By acting in this fashion, the Government in effect removed the pin from the grenade of insurrection. O'Brien was in Wexford when news of the issuing of a warrant for his arrest on a charge of treason reached him; he travelled to Kilkenny, showed himself to the people from St Canice's Cathedral and on Sunday, 23 July, declared at Callan: 'I throw myself on the country as your outlawed leader.'

In that part of Ireland there was no authority who could or would arrest him. The Government had no idea of his whereabouts, with the result that, in default of prompt action by the authorities, people flocked from the neighbouring counties to meet him. Mullinahone was the next rallying point and those who waited for O'Brien remained in the streets without food or shelter for the whole day. When he arrived he was so touched by this spontaneous demonstration that he bought bread to be distributed among the people.

Yet even at this stage he seems to have been in two minds as to his course of action. One day he declared that he did not mean to offer violence to anyone's person or property, the next, at Ballingarry, he spoke of military manoeuvres and exercises for recruits, nominating commissions in the army he was about to raise.

A contemporary poet composed these lines:

> 'Pikes and sticks and whirling fists
> Were all they had to raise,
> But they rang the church bell all the
> Night O'Brien for to praise.'

But the nocturnal ringing of the church bell produced relatively few adherents for O'Brien's army, though at Killenaule he had a more enthusiastic reception and bouquets of flowers were showered upon him. An alarm was raised when the cavalry were reported to be in the vicinity and barricades were hastily thrown across the streets.

The revolt, however, was doomed by the apathy of O'Brien's potential supporters, though this was something which the Government did not realise at the time. This was the '45 Rebellion in miniature, if one substitutes Dublin for Whitehall and the Commons for Derby. In Dublin there were both gloom and panic; the Government seemed terrified that there would be a nation-wide insurrection and all the Irish regiments were sent out of the country to be replaced by English and Scottish contingents.

This over-reaction is laughable when one considers that at Commons, a mining area, O'Brien found himself with only three of his chief adherents and about one hundred colliers. Yet at this moment batteries were being set up outside all large towns and orders were being issued to build Martello towers on the south coast of Ireland in case there should be an invasion from France to assist the rebels.

The O'Brien Insurrection, if it can possibly be so termed, was doomed from the beginning. At Ballingarry, when a posse of armed police clashed with O'Brien's private army, the latter numbered no more than one hundred men with firearms and pikes. Yet at first the police turned away, believing the rebels to be stronger both in numbers and fire-power. Then followed the deplorable farce of Widow Cormick's 'cabbage patch'.

Mrs Cormick was out when police sought shelter in her house and in cowardly fashion barricaded themselves inside with her children as hostages. O'Brien, to his credit, courageously went out to parley with the police and to persuade them to let the children out. The police's reply was a volley of fire. Thus, in ignominious and humiliating conditions for both sides, the revolt ended. Widow Cormick became a somewhat sketchy, but morally very real figure in Irish history; the rebels collapsed and mass arrests were made.

'They hid behind the windows of the Widow,
They fired across the shoulders of her kids.'

Not for many a year was England to be allowed to forget the day when police trampled over Widow Cormick's 'cabbage patch' and skulked in armed fright behind the whimpering children. Revenge came when the rebels were rounded up, to be imprisoned or deported. O'Brien was arrested at the railway station at Thurls and taken to Kilmainham Jail. Later he was found guilty of high treason and savagely sentenced to be hanged, drawn and quartered.

Though there was no publicised movement to lend support to O'Brien, nevertheless his friends, and some Apostles, rallied round him. In Cambridge University there was a feeling that whatever he had said or done, the manner in which O'Brien had been dealt with was out of all proportion to his actual misdeeds.

The Apostles, among whom was the brother of O'Brien, Edward, a barrister who had also been at Trinity, felt they must rally to his cause. Swiftly, discreetly and with a surprisingly cautious attitude for the Apostolic tradition, they launched a campaign in support of O'Brien. This was one occasion upon which the legal talent of the Apostles was to be mobilised in favour of a member. It was agreed that those members of the Society who had entered the legal profession should pool their knowledge and opinions to submit a case for saving O'Brien's life.

Eventually O'Brien's sentence was commuted by a special Act of Parliament to transportation for life. Attempts had been made to persuade O'Brien to make some positive withdrawal of his commitment to treason, but these had not succeeded. He was put aboard a ship at Kingstown which was sailing to Tasmania. On reaching Hobart, the capital of Tasmania, he refused the offer of a ticket-of-leave, which had been accepted by his companions in exile. He was then confined on Maria Island off the mainland. Perhaps he believed he could still stage a come-back and return to Ireland: he made an attempt to escape, but this was unsuccessful and he was removed to Port Arthur.

About this time his health deteriorated and he was given parole in New Norfolk. Friends at home had not forgotten him and from time to time there were submissions to the authorities that he might be dealt with more leniently. In 1854 he was pardoned on the strict understanding that he did not return to the United Kingdom. The same year he went to Europe where, during his travels, he wrote his *Principles of Government, or Meditations in Exile*, a tract which is still relevant today.

Two years later, following more representations from his Apostolic friends, O'Brien was given a full and unconditional pardon and in 1857 he returned to Ireland. Though taking no part in politics, he wrote occasional letters on current topics to *The Nation*, and in 1859 he went to America. In 1863 he visited Poland, and the following year, while staying at Bangor in North Wales, he died. His body was taken over to Ireland where he was buried in the churchyard of Rathronan in County Limerick, his funeral being the subject of fervent nationalist demonstrations. His *Principles of Government*, which had been printed as a pamphlet in Dublin in 1856, was published as a book in the year of his death.

Though much more has been written about the Spanish insurrection, which some Apostles supported, the story of William Smith O'Brien is much more interesting and relevant. It is especially relevant because it exemplifies the passionate idealism and devotion to an ideal despite all the odds which some of the early Apostles possessed.

But William Smith O'Brien had these qualities in excess of most other members. Here was a self-admitted traitor who served a cause which offered no prizes, no temptations, no rewards, but who could nevertheless claim to be a genuine martyr and in his own way a patriot for his own people – in effect the people who served his family and other families like his. He had married in 1832, had two daughters and five sons and was an admirable family man. There was undoubtedly a streak of vanity in his make-up and he was always demanding swift results regardless of the practicality of any of his propositions. But in comparison with Anthony

Blunt and his fellow-conspirators – self-styled idealists who subscribed to every kind of treachery – he was a paragon among men.

# 4

# THE CURSE ON
# HENRY ROBY

'And now art thou cursed from the earth . . . a fugitive
and a vagabond shalt thou be in the earth'
(Genesis, iv, 11-12)

By the end of the 1840s the Society (this was how it was now generally
known, the name *Conversazione* having long since disappeared) had
become the pre-eminent club of its kind in Cambridge and had achieved
something of a mystique of its own. Its members were noted for their
exceptional gifts and revered because of them, even outside the Society.

From having been dominated by earnest Anglican would-be reformers
in its early days, the Society had become increasingly absorbed by
examining doubts, questioning all orthodoxy and developing into a
group which was nonconformist in a secular rather than a religious sense.

Thus it was that members often produced essays which were
confessions of doubts about certain theological premises, or anxieties as
to whether such-and-such an action, habit, book or poem was immoral.
Young manhood in this period – at least in the educated classes – seemed
to suffer from retarded growth both emotionally and mentally. Adolescence was being extended not only into the early twenties, but in some
cases until the early forties.

It was in 1840, in manoeuvres leading up to the election of a University
High Steward, that it became evident that some of the doubters were
trying to succeed by subterfuge. There is an oblique reference to this in
D.A. Winstanley's *Early Victorian Cambridge*, when he states that this
election 'was the signal for active operations to begin, and committees
were set up in London and Cambridge.' The campaign manager in
Cambridge was Joseph Blakesley, a Fellow of Trinity and himself an
Apostle and Whig. It was from this time onwards that the Society began
to become much more secretive.

Between the late 1840s and the end of the 1850s a remarkable diversity of talent and opinion flowered among the new Apostles. There was Oscar Browning, later to be described by the perceptive if acerbic E. F. Benson as a genius 'flawed by abysmal fatuity'. In some respects Oscar Browning was typical of many Englishmen of his class and generation who never quite grew up. He was not the only Apostle to possess this flaw, but he remained something of a clown all his life.

Two other notable Apostles of this period were George Otto Trevelyan and James Clerk Maxwell. Trevelyan was the first of three key members of the Society of this same name between the 1850s and the 1930s. He lived to see two of his three sons elected. As Sir George Trevelyan he became Chief Secretary for Ireland in May, 1882, a few days after the murder of Lord Frederick Cavendish in Phoenix Park, but he resigned this post two years later with prematurely whitened hair. He had entered the House of Commons in 1865 and retained his seat until 1897. Other offices he held were those of Lord of the Admiralty and Chancellor of the Duchy of Lancaster, with a seat in the Cabinet. His principal achievements in politics were the abolition of purchase in the Army and the enfranchisement of the agricultural labourer.

Until the 1850s membership of the Society had generally gone to men interested in the arts and philosophy, rather more of the latter than the former. James Clerk Maxwell was almost the first scientist to be elected. For many years the view persisted that one only elected a scientist if, in the words of the late Sir John Sheppard, 'he was a very nice scientist.' But this Scottish physicist made a great impression on the younger Apostles and helped them to take a new look at philosophy.

Maxwell had distinguished himself by delivering a paper entitled 'Ovals' to the Edinburgh Royal Society when he was barely fifteen. He graduated as a Second Wrangler in 1854 and won the Adams Prize in 1857 for a thesis on 'An Investigation of Saturn's Rings'. In 1871 he became a professor of physics at Cambridge and soon made a name for himself as a pioneer in the connecting of the phenomena of electricity and magnetism.

Leslie Stephen, a son of Sir James Fitzjames Stephen, has referred to Clerk Maxwell as 'in my day its [the Apostles'] most famous member. He was a fascinating object to me; propounding quaint paradoxes in a broad Scottish accent; capable of writing humorous lampoons upon the dons, and turning his knowledge of dynamics to account by contriving new varieties of 'headers' into the Cam.'[1]

An Apostle of a different kind was F. W. Farrar, best known for that priggishly and sickly sentimental novel of public school life, *Eric, or Little by Little*, in which a boy is practically damned for eternity for writing on a wall that one of the masters was 'a surly devil'. Farrar had been educated at King William's College, Isle of Man, and the novel *Eric* is said to have been based on his own schooldays. Elected an Apostle in 1852 and made a Fellow in 1856, Farrar's novel, *Julian Home*, depicted something of his own life at Cambridge. He was appointed headmaster of Marlborough before eventually becoming Dean of Canterbury. His florid but eloquent preaching gained him many admirers, but he still seems an untypical Apostle even for those early years. Perhaps there is a clue to the reasons for his election in the fact that in later life he wrote *Eternal Hope*, which attacked the doctrine of eternal punishments. Was this an antidote to *Eric*?

Another member elected in this era was Henry Montagu Butler, who eventually became Master of Trinity after having been headmaster of Harrow. He had a passion for publishing his discourses, and his works included *Sermons Preached in the Chapel of Harrow School, Belief in Christ and Other Sermons*, and *University and Other Sermons*. It was the golden age of the sermon, a word which today is debilitated into that of a homily. Yet the man who seems to have exercised an unusual degree of control over the Society at this time was Fenton John Anthony Hort, elected in 1851. He was somewhat doubtful about joining the Apostles when it was first mentioned to him – a doubt which subsequently he found to be wholly reprehensible in a later member. Hort was the self-appointed guardian of Apostolic principles, the devoted watch-dog of the Society, but he was regarded with awe as one of the outstanding undergraduates of his time.

His fear was that the Society had been accepting too many frivolous, or at least insufficiently serious members, and he only accepted membership upon being assured by Frederick Maurice, then a professor of moral philosophy at the University, that this was something worthwhile. Hort's doubts perhaps revealed more than anything else the wide differences in outlook of Apostles of this period. They were doubts as to whether the selection of members was conducted with decorum and sagacity.

Just as Henry Butler doted on his sermons, so Hort devoted his life to a critical study of the New Testament, editing with his friend, Westcott, a new edition of it translated from the Greek. Hort was elected Hulsean Professor of Divinity at Cambridge in 1887. He quickly established himself as a key member of the Society and became its secretary in 1855. A diligent student of the Society's records, it was partly at his instigation that Tennyson was made an honorary member the following year.

There was not much secrecy about the Society and its activities in the period up to about 1850. Charles Astor Bristed, the American who was at Cambridge at this time, though not an Apostle, has declared that the Society 'did not make any parade of mystery, or aim at notoriety by any device to attract attention; they did not have special chambers for meeting, with skeletons in the corner, and assemble in them with the secrecy of conspirators . . . It is known that they met to read essays and hold discussions, with occasional interludes of supper. I have more than once seen the compositions which were prepared for these meetings: the authors did not seem to think that either the interests or dignity of their club suffered materially from letting an outsider so far behind the scenes.'[2]

From all this and other sources it can be fairly deduced that at this time, though the Society was a closed one, it was not especially secretive. Some members were discreet, others indiscreet about what they thought could or could not be divulged. Nor were the record books regarded entirely as secret, even in Hort's time. In a letter he wrote to a non-member, John Ellerton, in 1851, Hort said that 'the record book of proceedings is very amusing; think of Maurice voting that virtue in woman proceeds more from fear than modesty! It is a good sign that there is always a large number of neutral votes. Some of . . . [there are a number of illegible words here] are ludicrous enough, e.g. on the question whether we ought to follow the text of Scripture or the discoveries of science as to the formation of the earth . . .'[3]

Some Apostles of the 1850s have even cast doubts as to whether or not there was an oath of secrecy demanded of members in this period. Another American, William Everett, elected to the Society in 1862, seemed to think there was no such oath, but, as he was writing in 1907, his memory may have been playing him tricks. 'For several years after its institution the Society maintained no particular secrecy,' he wrote, adding 'it is a tradition that the various elections and rejections made it extremely unpopular.'[4]

Evidence from another source suggests that Everett may well have been correct. In 1844 Richard Monckton Milnes, yet another of the Apostolic poets, published a volume of his works with the dedication:

'To members of the Conversazione Society, established and still continued in the University of Cambridge . . . in grateful remembrance of knowledge communicated, affection interchanged and intelligence expanded.'

Henry Sidgwick, Knightsbridge Professor of Philosophy, elected to the Apostles in 1856, stated that 'Absolute candour was the only duty that the tradition of the Society enforced . . . The greatest subjects were continually treated, but gravity of treatment . . . was not imposed, though sincerity was.'[5]

It would seem, however, that it was Hort who did much to change all this and that his influence in the Society was formidable. Hort may have had a sense of humour of a kind, but he was easily outraged for no apparent reason. Nevertheless, what Hort propounded became in effect Society law, and indeed the Hort influence still remains at Cambridge today, as the existence of the Hort Theological Society testifies. Its purpose is to encourage the study of theology and religious studies throughout the university.

In 1855 an incident occurred which for some extraordinary reason seems to have aroused the wrath of the Apostles and of Hort in particular. Henry John Roby, the son of a Tamworth solicitor, who had been educated at Bridgnorth Grammar School, from which he won a scholarship to St. John's College, was elected to the Society in February of that year. Shortly afterwards, having been asked to attend meetings in the usual way, he resigned from the Society with the excuse that he really did not have the time for such things. Roby's own account of this affair is as follows:

'Hort and, I believe, Pomeroy [R. H. Pomeroy] (who was struck with an essay I wrote in May, 1855, for the Society on a passage in Plato [it is not clear which society this was]) got me elected into the Society of "Apostles" at Trinity, where I met H. M. Butler, Maxwell, Elphinstone. The rule was that the host for the evening read an essay, which was then discussed, or in default gave a supper. The members were irregular in their attendance. I remember no discussion worth a straw. I had much work at that time and found the meetings dull and after a bit, perhaps a year, resigned my membership. Such a course was said to have been unprecedented and I received, instead of an acknowledgement of my resignation, a fulmination in the shape of a resolution of dismissal, drawn up, I believe, in form by Hort.'[6]

Now both before that date and afterwards quite a few Apostles have for one reason or another resigned for reasons not normally accepted as adequate under the Society's rules. This happened in the case of Tennyson, though chiefly because he tore up his essay and declined to deliver it. Though his resignation was accepted, he was received back into the Society years later with acclamation. There was no reproof. In 1913 Bertrand Russell, writing to Goldsworthy Lowes Dickinson, mentioned that 'My friend Wittgenstein was elected to the Society, but thought it was a waste of time, so he imitated henry john roby and was cursed.'[7] Yet the records of the Society show that whatever may have transpired in 1913, Wittgenstein, who was elected in November, 1912, was not recorded as having resigned until January, 1929, seventeen years later. Nor is there any record of his having been 'cursed', so possibly Russell was joking.

36

Russell, in explaining the case of Roby, stated in his autobiography that 'Henry John Roby was elected a member of the Society, but wrote to say that he was far too busy to attend the meetings, and was therefore ritualistically cursed and his name was spelt without capitals from then on. Ever after that when a new member was elected the curse was solemnly read out.'[8]

Why was Roby's resignation considered to be such a special case? One suggestion is that his resignation was an insult to the other members, but this explanation does not ring true, especially as Roby himself seems to have indicated that attendance by other members was 'irregular'. Whatever the facts may be, the incident reflects no credit on Hort. For it was Hort who was the principal instigator of the ritualistic cursing of Roby and it was this sanctimonious theologian who devised the actual curse and its wording.

Roby was at this time a person of some consequence and standing in the University. A Senior Classic in 1853, he was no mere undergraduate, but had been given a Fellowship of his college in 1854. From that date until 1861 he was a lecturer and tutor. Possibly he had made himself unpopular with some of his attacks on the system of isolation under which each college was supposed to do all that was necessary for the education of its members without any outside aid, regardless of how modest were its funds. He had dared to criticise and attack such richly endowed colleges as King's and Trinity for ignoring the 'plight', as he called it, of smaller and poorer colleges. This undoubtedly made him enemies. In 1858 he published '*Remarks on College Reform*', which included some of these criticisms.

Yet why should Roby be unpopular with fellow Apostles because of this attitude when some of them, possibly even a majority, were in favour of drastic reform of the University statutes? The Cambridge University Act of 1856 allowed each college to undertake, subject to the approval of the Commissioners, the reform of its own statutes. Roby, in his published criticsm, which was full of caustic wit and practical wisdom, made it clear that he was in favour of an elected governing body as opposed to the rule of succession by seniority.

It was from the time of the expulsion of Roby following his resignation that an air of mystery began to envelop the Society, and so it has remained ever since. What Bertrand Russell cited as a post-Roby tradition has been maintained until modern times, and this has been borne out by various members, dead and living. The so-called ceremony of the curse on Roby has been kept up with the election of each new member. The curse has been read to him, and he has been bound to secrecy. Yet some of those Apostles who have taken this oath have nonetheless mentioned it in their memoirs. Others insist that the secrecy is absolute and that all records are inaccessible to any curious outsider. In his book, *Cambridge between the Wars*, T. E. B. Howarth, wrote: 'More exclusive than the Heretics [a Cambridge society of the 1920s] – though only just – and probably a great deal less lively (and certainly less heterosexual) were the Apostles . . . Fortunately, its proceedings were so secret that it is not possible, even were it desirable, to chronicle every least heart-throb and *éclaircissement*, as is now the vogue among the residuary legatees of the Bloomsbury epic.'[9]

Michael Straight, who was enrolled a member of the Society in 1936, tells of his first meeting in Maynard Keynes' room at King's:

'I held up my right hand and repeated a fearful oath, praying that my soul would writhe in unendurable pain for the rest of eternity if I so much as breathed a word about the Society to anyone who was not a member. It seemed a bit harsh, but Sheppard, who carried a cushion with him wherever he went, patted me with his free hand and told me not to be alarmed.

"'You see," he explained, "our oath was written at a time when it was thought to be most unlikely that a member of the society would speak to anyone who was not Apostolic." I asked Sheppard how he would define the term *Apostolic*. He beamed at me in his childish way. "One must be *very* brilliant and extremely nice!" he said.'[10]

The Sheppard referred to was, of course, Sir John Tressider Sheppard, of King's, one of the chief talent-spotters for new Apostles in the era between the two world wars. When Michael Straight inquired whether any member of the Society had ever been found lacking in those qualities, Sheppard told him that 'there was a horrid man long ago . . . who was thought to be Apostolic and who was indeed elected . . . He then said that his only interest was in being elected, and that he could not afford to waste his time by attending our meetings.'

As Sheppard was not elected to the Society until 1902, he could only have had this story about Roby second-hand, or, more likely third- or fourth-hand. Had Roby, by his refusal to attend meetings, pricked the pomposity of some Apostles? Had nobody before questioned whether some of their discussions might be a waste of time – for some, if not for all? An outrageous thought, perhaps, bearing in mind how seriously the Society took both papers and discussions. One story, probably untrue, though by no means untypical of Roby, is that he shocked the Society by proposing to read a paper asking the question 'Are our Saturday night meetings a waste of time', with the supplementary question 'Are we doing enough to improve the academic status of the university?'

Roby was not exactly an adolescent shooting star who burned himself out early in life. In 1861 he married and, as in those days marriage automatically put an end to any Fellowship, he accepted the second mastership at the College of God's Gift at Dulwich, known today as Dulwich College. This was at the time that the new Alleyn's College at Dulwich was being planned, with Charles Barry as its architect, and Roby was able to see one of the lesser public schools developing along the lines he envisaged. While at Dulwich he showed his dissatisfaction with the Latin Grammar of King Edward VI, then still in use at schools, by writing an *Elementary Latin Grammar*, which became a best-seller. In 1872 he produced what was perhaps his chief achievement in this field, an enlarged grammar of the *Latin Language from Plautus to Suetonius*.

When Lord Palmerston appointed a Commission to do for the lesser grammar and public schools what had already been done for 'the seven great public schools', as he put it, Roby was appointed secretary. It is true that Roby could be an awkward character if thwarted in plans in which he passionately believed, and he had numerous rows with the Schools Commissioners, mainly after he had himself been made a Commissioner. 'Hand in hand with Dr (later Archbishop) Frederick Temple,' wrote Roby's biographer, 'he took a leading part in inquiries and legislation affecting over eight hundred schools for boys and girls, most of them in an appalling state. The reforms were largely due to him.'[12]

Sometimes, in trying to give an honest answer to awkward questions, he gave a wrong impression. In 1872 he was said to have sealed the doom of himself and of the Commission by an answer to a single question on religious instruction. Roby was pressed to say that there was the possibility that teachers could make this instruction Nonconformist or nothing and that, if they became Mahommedans, they could teach the Koran. 'Yes,' replied Roby caustically, 'if they became Mahommedans, they probably would.' This was erroneously interpreted as meaning that Roby wanted to banish religion from the schools curriculum.

In 1886 he was made an honorary Fellow of his old college, St. John's. In later life he indulged in a variety of pursuits ranging from a professorship of jurisprudence at London University, working as a sewing cotton manufacturer, helping to found Manchester Grammar School for Girls, finally to becoming Liberal MP for Eccles from 1890-95, at which latter date he lost his seat.

In his *Reminiscences of My Life*, privately printed for his family only, Roby mentions that in 1877 he received a letter from a Mr L. L. Roby, of Topeka, Kansas, requesting information about the Robys in England. 'He said he had found 1,800 Robys in America and hoped with my help to bring the number up to 2,500.' Roby inspected many rolls and registers for his American correspondent.

Henry Roby went to retire at Grasmere in the Lake District, where he was well known as a generous host. Here he celebrated his eightieth birthday by climbing to the top of Scafell, England's highest peak. He died in January, 1915.

Such a career, such commitments to the cause of education, were undoubtedly in the Apostolic spirit of that age, so why was not Roby, like Tennyson, readmitted to the Society? Possibly he would have declined to be readmitted, as he does not seem to have had much of an opinion of the Society. Yet, at the very least, why was the curse not removed long ago? Surely, after his death, this was the most logical, let alone the most charitable duty, especially as the Apostles had long since declared against the appalling doctrine of eternal punishment.

It is all the more puzzling when one considers that Roby, like many of the Apostles, had been an ardent campaigner for the laicisation of the University and the abolition of religious tests for undergraduates and graduates. Indeed, Hugh Sykes Davies, himself an Apostle, elected in the 1930s, has stated that in the 1850s and 1860s this campaign was the Society's 'main business.'[13]

It was about this time when there was a spirit abroad in the ranks of the Apostles that the society should be much more secretive in its activities, or 'go underground', as one member suggested. There seemed to be a desire to preserve the élitism of the Apostles at all costs, and, in doing so, to turn themselves into a kind of academic closed shop.

Thus privacy developed into secrecy, and the latter became a sacred cult. This in turn caused some Brothers to inquire whether this was a new development, or whether there had always been a tradition of absolute secrecy, a few being concerned as to whether ultra-secrecy was necessary, a majority apparently eager to show that total concealment was in the original rules. Thus, in 1863, this very question was raised by Apostle John Jermyn Cowell (elected 1859) in a letter to Lord Houghton (formerly Richard Monckton Milnes):

'I was anxious to know whether in your time in Cambridge the Society was kept a secret, or whether the brothers openly talked of it. According to all traditions in my time, it was considered that the Society ought to be talked about by its members and that much of its utility depended upon its being kept to a great extent secret. This seemed to me so obvious that I had always supposed it was the rule from the earliest times of the Society; until about two years ago some brothers started a new practice and told all about the Society to their friends and acquaintances at Cambridge . . . The innovators maintain that they are only reverting to the primitive system which prevailed till

twelve years ago. Would you tell me whether:
"1st.  publicity or secrecy was the rule?
"2nd.  the rule varied, and, if so
"3rd.  when? and with what results?
"4th.  whether publicity or secrecy was the rule during the years
      preceding 1847 and 1848 when the Society was nearly coming
      to an end.'"[12]

Cowell at the same time sent a 'Remonstrance' to the Society on this question of secrecy, urging that it should be forbidden to show Apostolic books to non-members and that members should be instructed not to talk about the Society outside its own closed doors.

It is hard to understand quite what Cowell meant about the Society 'nearly coming to an end' in 1847-48, because there is no evidence of this. It is true that four Apostles resigned and became 'Angels' in 1847, but in that same year there were three new members, and three more joined the following year.

Cowell's real concern may well have been that the activities of some Apostles were drawing too much attention to the Society. William Smith O'Brien's *Principles of Government* had already been published as a pamphlet when Cowell chose to question the need for absolute secrecy in the Society. One young Apostle, John Burwell Payne, elected in 1863, commented that 'Past indiscretions by members of the Society have caused some members to wish to keep our thoughts underground. May they be defeated.'[14]

The following year an Apostle actually published an account of the Society in *Macmillan's Magazine*. He was William Dougal Christie, elected in 1836, who had retired from the diplomatic service the previous year after serving as Consul-General in Brazil and the Argentine. For a brief period Christie had been MP for Weymouth in the 1840s. His article, however, was mainly about certain members he singled out as worthy of attention and revealed nothing of special interest.

There was, however, another and much more significant and important reason for the sudden passion for secrecy in this period. Some members wanted to use the Society as a spearhead group to undermine the Church of England's domination of University life, and especially to remove the statutory obligations of the Thirty-Nine Articles. This was not so much an anti-Church movement as a liberalising one, bent on destroying an unfair (one could almost say an ecclesiastical-authoritarian) control of matters which should have been outside the Church's legitimate sphere of influence. The upper hierarchy of the Church of England at that time showed its worst aspect in its attempt to maintain a ridiculous and illiberal control at both Oxford and Cambridge, and this showed itself in a refusal to allow Fellows to marry and still retain their Fellowships; antagonism to women students and insistence on the acceptance of all its rules by Nonconformists, atheists and members of any other religion. It was in fact the Church Fascist, if ever there was one. To uphold this state of affairs the Church was prepared to strike hard at anyone who refused to toe the ecclesiastical line.

Leslie Stephen has shown how his own life at Cambridge was 'cut short by my inability, unfortunate or otherwise, to come to terms with the Thirty-Nine Articles. I was not indeed cast out by the orthodox indignation of my colleagues. At Cambridge there was no bigotry . . . But I had to resign my tutorship which involved specifically clerical functions . . . I am often tempted to regret that I did not swallow my scruples.'[15]

Hence the other reason for secrecy in the Society was to prevent victimisation by the Church. One of the leaders of the undercover move against the 'Ultras' of the Church of England was John Daniel Williams, elected in 1849, and who became an 'Angel' in 1854.

Hugh Sykes Davies, poet and Fellow of St. John's, who became an Apostle in the 1930s, stated that 'The secrecy is something that makes people suspicious, but there are sound reasons for it. In the last century the Apostles were foremost in working for the University's liberation from the Church and the secrecy was intended to protect them from victimisation.'[16]

Had Leslie Stephen been an Apostle, it is just possible that he might somehow have been rescued from the fate which befell him.

# 5

# THE WISH TO LEARN

'The essential value of the Society is a Belief that we *can* learn, and a determination that we *will* learn, from people of the most opposite opinions'

(Henry Sidgwick)

From the late 1850s throughout the 1860s this view stated by Henry Sidgwick was the creed of the Apostles, though it was often expressed in rather more ambivalent terms. Sidgwick was unquestionably one of the most vital figures not only in the Apostles, but in Cambridge during this period and for long afterwards. It would be true to say that as a directing force in the Society he followed in the footsteps of Frederick Maurice and John Sterling.

Sidgwick was important in that he did not merely dwell in the world of conventional philosophy which had hitherto been the concern of the Apostles. In some ways he was the forerunner of what today are known as the experimental philosophers. He was the ultimate doubter, so much so that he doubted those who had positive doubts just as much as those who had absolute beliefs. The son of an Anglican clergyman of Skipton, Yorkshire, he spent his whole life trying to fit all his diverse ideas into a philosophy which would satisfy his commonsense. It cannot be said that he succeeded, because, while his mind rejected any faith, his heart yearned for one. He became a disciple of John Stuart Mill's utilitarianism, and thus Mill took the place of Coleridge as the Apostles' chief inspiration from outside the Society.

The Apostles had moved from that never satisfactory creed of Tory evangelism to liberal Christianity, which implied some doubts on some subjects, and thus on to a prolonged period of trying to resolve doubts while being dedicated to a quest for truth. This may all sound somewhat boring and pompous to anyone living in the latter part of the twentieth century, yet it would be totally unfair to present the Apostles in this light. Sir Walter Alexander Raleigh, a contemporary member, commented that

43

Sidgwick's role was that of 'a referee in the duel fought between Faith and Doubt.'

Originally Sidgwick had been reluctant to join the Society when he was approached, thinking it would interfere with his work. But once he had joined, he had no doubts whatsoever. He described the Apostolic spirit as 'the pursuit of truth with absolute devotion and unreserve by a group of intimate friends, who were perfectly frank with each other and indulged in any amount of humorous sarcasm and playful banter, and yet each respects the other.'[1]

He may have irritated the agnostics by seeing both sides of the question of faith and doubt, but his major work, *Methods of Ethics*, published in 1874, won him a considerable reputation outside the university just as much as in it. In 1883 he was elected professor of moral philosophy, a post he held until his death. Nobody could have taken more care in precisely defining what he thought and in making sure that he wrote exactly what he meant. But behind and beyond all this was Sidgwick's feeling that sometimes intuition was more important than logic. It was this feeling which led him towards a study of what today we call the paranormal.

Certainly Sidgwick, even though this was not his intention, paved the way to the Apostles becoming a society of total doubters, if not atheists. In 1869 he resigned his Fellowship because he decided he could no longer subscribe to the Thirty-Nine Articles of the Church of England. Despite his insistence on the need for logic and careful argument in coming to decisions, he became an increasingly confused thinker, largely because he always wished he could believe in some new creed. Perhaps this was best exemplified in one of Sidgwick's own phrases, which has an oddly familiar ring today – 'neo-Christianity'. One has only to listen to the unconvincing pronouncements of some modern bishops to know exactly what he had in mind. But, to be charitable, Sidgwick was probably a better Christian than any of them and certainly a more honest one.

Sidgwick himself thought that the Apostles 'absorbed and dominated' him, but Leonard Woolf made the point that this was 'not quite the end of the story . . . every now and again an Apostle has dominated and left an impression . . . upon the Society. Sidgwick himself was one of these . . . refertilising and revivifying its spirit and traditions.'[2]

This was undoubtedly an epoch in which the Apostles came to regard themselves as the intellectual counterpart of Nelson's 'Band of Brothers'. In the beginning this was simply a question of a strengthening of friendships, and a mutual agreement that any divergence of opinions should never be allowed to change those friendships. But gradually towards the end of the century, this was changed again, or, as Professor

Skidelsky has put it: 'Bound together in secrecy and friendship . . . this stretched into later life. The love of truth and communion with friends replaced the service of God as the inspirer of conduct.'[3]

That this friendship was so highly regarded is perhaps best shown by the poet William Cory Johnson's account of his being visited by an Apostle when he was teaching at Eton: 'We went through several hard subjects in the old Cambridge way, in the method of minute comparison of opinions without argument which I believe to be peculiar to the small intellectual aristocracy of Cambridge. So those three days have lifted me more than six weeks of mere reading.'[4]

Just what had the Apostles debated on their Saturday evenings since the Society was founded? Early on the subjects for debate were undoubtedly somewhat earnest and dull. In the first three years of the Society's existence these questions were thrashed out: (1) 'Are the Gospels presented honestly in their interpretation by the clergy of today?'; (2) 'Is the Bible used as an instrument for keeping the poor quiet?'; (3) 'What is the future task of evangelism?'

Except for the second question, these are subjects which might well be set for any PSA ('Pleasant Sunday Afternoon') gathering of the masses, though it is doubtful whether their minds would be stirred to say anything memorable.

Gradually, however, there was a distinct switch away from religion, as poetry and the Coleridge school gained ground. Questions posed for debate in the early 1830s included: 'Is an intelligible first cause deducible from the phenomena of the universe?', to which, it is recorded, that Tennyson voted 'no'.

'Is there any rule of moral action beyond general expediency?' This time Tennyson voted 'yes'.

Gradually, the questions posed became less pompous and rather more sophisticated and even humorous. Sometimes they were, however, almost fatuous – e.g. 'Should things be real?' It is recorded that the vote on this was inconclusive.

'Are all mankind descended from one stock?' Four members voted 'yes', two abstained, and three said 'no'.

'Is the practice of fornication justifiable on principle or expediency?' One voted 'yes', the rest said 'no'.

'Has the application of the system of "The Division of Labour" since the beginning of the reign of George III been beneficial to the country?' This was rejected with a unanimous 'no'.

'Is the Greek drama founded upon true principles of art?' Seven voted 'yes', one said 'no' and there was one abstention. It will be noted that although tradition has it that there were always at least twelve Apostles, not always were twelve present at meetings.

45

'Is there an intelligence outside this world of ours which provides us with intuition and a unique source of information?' There is no indication as to how members voted on this subject.

This last question is the type of query which Sidgwick himself would have been most likely to raise, and it is surely some indication of how he managed, if only for a brief period, to interest the Apostles in the paranormal. In this respect Sidgwick was in advance of his time, though he does not seem to have created any permanent interest in the paraphysical and paranormal within the Society. But he and F. W. H. Myers, another Trinity man, were founders of the Society for Psychical Research, while Professor C. D. Broad and Professor Wilson Knight were also members of this society.

Among other prominent members of the Society in the sixties and seventies of the last century were Charles Henry Tawney, George James Howard, ninth Earl of Carlisle, the Honourable Charles Lyttelton (later the eighth Viscount Cobham), the Honourable Alfred Lyttelton (who not only played for England at both cricket and football, but was Secretary of State for the Colonies), Sir Frederick Pollock, Robin Mayor and the Balfour brothers, Francis and Gerald.

These were vintage years for the Apostles, with an increasing number achieving success in the world outside Cambridge. Pollock was called to the Bar in 1871 and then appointed professor of jurisprudence at University College, London, also finding time to produce a life of Spinoza. Mayor, a Fellow of King's, entered the Education Department in 1896 and had a distinguished career as a civil servant, eventually becoming chairman of the Committee on Co-operation between the Universities and Training Colleges. His daughter, Teresa, eventually married another Apostle and became Lady Rothschild.

Family links in the society were fairly frequent. Apart from the Trevelyans, the Lytteltons, the Balfours, in later years there were the Luces (father and son) and the Llewellyn Davies family, the brothers Crompton and Theodore and Crompton's son, Richard (later Lord Llewellyn-Davies).

Although a number of Apostles have become Cabinet Ministers, however, it is not certain that any of them reached Ten Downing Street. But, while there is no confirmation of this and indeed many rebuttals, some assert that Arthur James Balfour, later Earl Balfour and the creator of the Balfour Declaration on Palestine, was a member of the Society. Professor Peter Allen, of the University of Toronto, who has made an intensive study of the Apostles of earlier years, at one time stated that 'A. J. Balfour, W. K. Clifford and F. W. Maitland' were members in 'the 'sixties and 'seventies'. But while A. J. Balfour's name appears on one list of early members, it is omitted on two others, which leaves room for considerable doubt. As a result of this discovery Professor Allen now takes the view that A. J. Balfour was never an Apostle. Two Balfours are clearly listed – Gerald William (A. J.'s brother and the second Earl Balfour, elected in 1872) and Francis Maitland Balfour (elected in 1875), while A. J.'s sister, Eleanor, actually married an Apostle, none less than Henry Sidgwick.

However, though there now seems to be little prospect of proving it, further research suggests that A. J. Balfour may well have been a member, albeit as briefly as Henry Roby. Educated at Eton and Trinity, of which college he was made an honorary Fellow in 1902, Arthur Balfour was, of course, a leading light in that other small and élite society called the Souls, which numbered among its members men and women from the highest ranks of society and one other future Prime Minister, Henry Asquith. Two Apostles were also members of the Souls – Harry Cust and Alfred Lyttelton. The late Guy Burgess, himself an Apostle in the 1930s and unfortunately now best known for his defection to the Soviet Union with Donald Maclean in 1951, has stated that 'Arthur Balfour was selected as a member for the Society, but owing to very special circumstances was allowed to withdraw from it.' This statement was made to the late Hugh Sykes Davies, and, as Burgess was at one time friendly with members of the Balfour family when researching what he called 'a final volume' to Lady Gwendolen Cecil's biography of the great Lord Salisbury, this may well be the answer to the mystery of A. J.'s membership.

By the time that Sidgwick, along with the eccentric F. W. H. Myers, W. F. (later Sir William) Barrett and an enthusiastic young student, Edmund Gurney, had founded the Society for Psychical Research in 1882, he was by then an 'Angel' and no longer the dominant figure in the Apostles. His interest in psychic phenomena only attracted a very few of the younger Apostles. When one of them proposed the question 'Can we communicate with the departed?' as a subject for debate, he was almost unanimously rejected. Alfred Whitehead, an Apostle who later left England to become a professor of philosophy at Harvard, is said to have caustically commented on this proposal that 'such matters are best left to Myers, or his paramour, Eusapia Palladino.'

Antagonism to Myers rather than disloyalty to Sidgwick would seem to be one reason why discussions on psychic matters were avoided by the Society. Myers was not very popular in some circles at Cambridge, and the Apostolic grapevine did not miss much gossip about outsiders. Members of the Society had learned that Myers was reputed to have stolen the work of another Cambridge man and claimed the product as his own. But, apart from such tittle-tattle, Myers was suspected of all manner of sexual quirks and it was alleged that he looked upon psychical research as giving him opportunities for voyeurism. However, this was probably an unjust accusation for a man who, until he became absorbed by his studies of spiritualism and mesmerism, was best known as a poet and essayist. Whether he actually knew Eusapia Palladino is irrelevant; she had acquired a reputation as a medium, but was also notorious for introducing eroticism into séances. Myers was sufficiently odd in his behaviour, nonetheless, to insist on accompanying young Edmund Gurney and his bride on their honeymoon to Switzerland, even against the most vehement protests from the bride.[5]

Dr Whitehead came from a family of clergymen and his chief influence in the Society was as a spotter of talent and a recruiter of new members. He started out in life as a mathematician and then became a philosopher, finding himself more at home in that field than in religion. It was in establishing a logical relationship between philosophy and science that he made his name. His *Principles of Natural Knowledge*, based on lectures he gave at Trinity, was outstanding in this context, and it was followed up by *The Concept of Nature*, published in 1921. He retained his Fellowship at Trinity for life, despite his departure to America where he was highly regarded. Though many of his own writings were occasionally spoiled by the obscurity of his language, he was at his best as a teacher and, especially in the USA, won some lifelong friends among his students. It has been said that he sometimes employed obscurity of diction as a deliberate ploy to make his students think.

Perhaps his great achievement at Harvard was to give it something not only of the atmosphere of Cambridge, but of the Apostles as well. He also fought hard to give more freedom to junior Fellows in America, especially those with the American Ph.D., so that they could operate outside the university. This led to the creation of the Society of Fellows, of which Whitehead was the planner and the founder.

No doubt Whitehead was influenced in his campaign for American junior Fellows by the efficacy of the British Universities Test Act of 1871, which enabled many promising graduates to make careers for themselves in Oxford and Cambridge which would previously have been barred to them. This Act made it possible for Dissenters to take the MA degree and also to hold a college Fellowship, or any other university post which had previously been barred to them.

It was the wives, often more than their husbands, who played such a prominent part in the Society for Psychical Research. Sidgwick's wife, Eleanor, who was eventually Principal of Newnham, so dominated some meetings of the SPR that, according to the medium Harry Price, 'Sir William Barrett once wrote to me that he was "treated like a child" at the Council meetings, and that Mrs Sidgwick always gets her own way.'[6]

Another Apostle, Arthur Verrall, married Margaret de Gaudrion

Merrifield, of Newnham. She soon became an enthusiastic supporter of the SPR and drew her husband and her daughter into the field of psychic research. These two women helped to stimulate an Apostolic interest in the work of the SPR, and, although this subject never became of vital importance to the Society, it was for a time fashionable. Verrall had been indefatigable in building up the Apostles at a time when they were suddenly short of members. He also believed he owed everything to the Society: 'the best thing that ever happened to me in my life' was how he described it.

Those Apostles who took an interest in the SPR, however, mainly stressed that this lay in study of the parapsychological rather than the psychic. Not that this change of words made much difference, for what they chiefly sought in such researches was a substitute for the kind of beliefs they had lost. They were the eternal doubters feverishly seeking a substitute for religion. It is certain that most of them, however philosophically-minded they might be, missed the whole point of psychic research, which, if it means anything at all, is to do with science, not religion.

One scathing critic of psychic research, unnamed, alas, presented a paper to the Apostles on 'Is parapsychology another word for hebephrenia?' Or, to put it in simpler language, 'Is parapsychology an attempt to make adolescent insanity respectable?'

Meanwhile Sidgwick had not helped the cause in which he believed by establishing contacts with the notorious Madame Blavatsky, who in her time appeared as a remarkably sincere medium to some and an outrageous fraud to others. E. M. Forster has recorded that Lowes Dickinson, another Apostle, attended meetings of the SPR for a time and studied esoteric Buddhism. But it would seem that Dickinson soon lost interest.

It is interesting to record that Whitehead, who had dismissed the idea of a debate on the question of communicating with the departed, later allowed for some such possibility in a vague kind of way. In expressing what he called his 'vitalist philosophy' he put forward the view that life permeated the universe in much the same way as water filled a sponge. But Whitehead himself had a strange character. Perhaps his occasional waspish remarks did not commend him to his fellow Apostles, as hardly any of them, except Bertrand Russell in a later age, had anything to say about him. Russell, who owed his nomination to the Society to Whitehead, was hardly complimentary about his mentor: 'Whitehead . . . like many people possessed of great self-control . . . suffered from impulses which were scarcely sane. Before he met Mrs Whitehead he had made up his mind to join the Catholic Church, and was only turned aside at the last minute by falling in love with her. He was obsessed by fear of lack of money, and he did not meet this fear in a reasonable way, but by spending recklessly in the hope of persuading himself that he could afford to do so.'[7]

This last criticism may well have applied in the earlier part of his life, but the story of his career in the United States does not suggest such serious aberrations. It may well be that some of the bile in Russell's criticisms of Whitehead was due in part to the fact that whereas Russell was a pacifist in World War I, Whitehead was a firm supporter of the Allies and disapproved of his fellow-Apostle's attitude.

One other philosophically-minded member of the Society took some serious interest in the paraphysical. This was John McTaggart (1886), who, along with Roger Fry, came to Cambridge from Clifton, where both of them had been very unhappy. In the case of McTaggart, because of a slight curvature of the spine, games at his public school had been sheer torture for him. He had been brutally treated and kicked for being unable to take any adequate part in rugger and only belatedly was he excused games altogether. Here was an example of that 'muscular Christianity', which the hockey-playing Winnington-Ingram lauded when Bishop of London, and which to many others like McTaggart must have disillusioned them about organised religion. McTaggart, partly due to the influence of his mother, had been an agnostic since the age of six, and this showed itself in a peculiar way when he embarked on his philosophical reflections as, for example, in his *Studies in Hegelian Dialectic* (1896). While a lecturer at Trinity, he set out to rationalise his own somewhat conflicting philosophical ideas. While disbelieving in God, he fervently believed in the immortality of the soul. This in turn led him to express a belief in reincarnation, but he did not receive much encouragement from fellow members, nor from the SPR. It is curious that this latter society paid little attention to such theories. Myers, for example, accepted the doctrine of reincarnation, but stressed the arguments against it.

There was keen interest in the work being done at continental universities, especially in philosophy, and notably in Germany. Some studies had been made of the various forms of anarchism as a viable philosophical or political creed. Josiah Warren, the American who held that 'every man should be his own government, his own law and his own church', and the French economist, Proudhon, were sometimes cited in debates, but the man who captured the imagination of some Apostles was Prince Peter Kropotkin. In the early 1880s there was an attempt to bring the Prince to Cambridge, a move strongly supported by some Apostles with whom he had talked. Kropotkin was at that time weighing up his chances of finding support for his socialist-anarchist theories in Victorian England. Corpus Christi College actually offered him a Fellowship.

In July, 1881, the Anarchists were able to arrange an International Revolutionary Congress in London at which the Prince himself was present. But even those Apostles who supported Kropotkin soon found that they were themselves not ready to embark on quite so violent and provocative a programme as he suggested, which was 'to attain . . . the annihilation of all rulers, ministers of State, nobility, the clergy, the most prominent capitalists and other exploiters, any means are permissible, and therefore great attention should be given specially to the study of chemistry and the preparation of explosives, as being the most important weapons.'[8]

But the response to this proposal was at best lukewarm, and Kropotkin ruefully commented that 'My wife and I felt so lonely in England, and our efforts to awaken a socialist movement in the country seemed so hopeless, that in the autumn of 1882 we decided to remove to France . . . If only Cambridge had been the capital of England and if those scholars there claiming to be the New Apostles had been in active politics, the sad saga might have been very different.'

The criteria required for joining the Apostles varied to some extent with each succeeding group, and this resulted in some surprising decisions against enlisting certain prominent and even obvious candidates. For example, though Fitzjames (later Sir Fitzjames) Stephen was an Apostle, his distinguished brother, Leslie, was rejected. 'He [Leslie] was ambitious to be invited to join the Apostles,' wrote Lord Annan, 'but no invitation came . . . the Apostles passed him over. Intimate friendship came hard to one who was as shy as he was.'[9]

On the other hand James Kenneth Stephen, the second son of Fitzjames, was elected to the Society in 1879. A cousin of Virginia Woolf and Vanessa Bell, this member of the Stephen family is perhaps best remembered for two small volumes of verse and parody, *Lapsus Calami* and *Quo Musa Tendis*, published in 1891, a year before he died in a mental home. Brilliant, witty, but eccentric and given to lengthy periods of depression in later life, J. K. Stephen was appointed as tutor to the Duke of Clarence, the eldest son of the Prince of Wales (later King Edward VII), in 1884 to prepare him for entrance to Trinity. In 1885 Stephen was made a Fellow of his college and he became a close companion of the Duke and extremely devoted to him.

Like his royal pupil, Stephen has been named as a major suspect for the identity of Jack the Ripper, the uncaught killer of various women in the East End of London between 1887 and 1891.[10] While not in any way supporting this proposition, it must be admitted that Stephen was a much likelier suspect than the Duke of Clarence, and indeed the case against the royal prince has long since been totally demolished. Suspicion was first directed towards the Duke by a surgeon, Mr Thomas Stowell, in

November, 1970, who declared that he had seen the private papers of Sir William Gull, a medical consultant to Queen Victoria. These referred to a man named as 'S' who seemed to answer to the description of the Duke in Stowell's mind, presumably because he knew Sir William Gull was consulted by royalty. Perhaps the papers referred to a 'distinguished family' and titles. Unfortunately Stowell's own papers about this affair were destroyed by his son after his death.

Michael Harrison, who has studied the Stephen theory of the Ripper in great detail, believes that some ten murders can be ascribed to him rather than the six or eight normally attributed to the Ripper. This view is based on a number of arguments, firstly that Stephen kept chambers in Lincoln's Inn and was within easy reach of the East End of London; secondly, that there were no obvious alibis for dates when he might have committed the murders; thirdly, the similarity of his handwriting (even allowing for disguising it) with that of Jack the Ripper in the various verses he composed and sent to the police and others; fourthly and finaly, an analysis of some of Stephen's verse.

Whatever caused Stephen's mental instability is not absolutely clear, but he became a patient of Sir Wiliam Gull, a specialist in paraplegia, diseases of the spinal cord and abscesses of the brain, following an accidental blow to the head in 1886. While at Cambridge, he wrote a number of verses which revealed an obsessive hatred of women, including one called 'Kaphoozelum' about the 'ten little whores of Jerusalem' (all the Ripper's victims were prostitutes). Quentin Bell, in his official biography of Virginia Woolf, refers to J. K. Stephen as 'the author of light ingenious verses which, in their day, took the town by storm' and adds that 'one day he [Stephen] rushed upstairs to Virginia's nursery, drew a blade from a sword stick and plunged it into the bread . . . but the most difficult and painful thing about his insanity was that it led him to desire Stella Duckworth, Virginia's elder half-sister, and violently pursue her.'[11]

Stephen resigned from the Society and became an 'Angel' in 1882, but in his Apostolic period he produced some remarkably strange verses that do cast doubts on his mental stability. They were not all in the light-hearted bawdy style of 'Kaphoozelum', as will be seen from the following two quotations from verses he had published in *Granta* and *The Cambridge Review* in 1891:

> 'If all the harm that women have done
> Were put in a bundle and rolled into one,
> Earth would not hold it,
> The sky could not enfold it,
> It could not be lighted nor warmed by the sun;

Such masses of evil
Would puzzle the devil
And keep him in fuel while Time's wheels run.'[12]

That is ominous enough in its tirade against women, but even worse was this truly vicious poem called *In the Backs*:

'As I was strolling in the Backs,
I met a woman whom I did not like.
I did not like the way the woman walked:
Loose-hipped, big-boned, disjointed, angular . . .
. . . I do not want to see that girl again:
I did not like her: and I should not mind
If she were done away with, killed, or ploughed.'[13]

There were other verses in much the same vein, composed before the alleged accident to Stephen's head. While they are no proof that he was the Ripper, they do strongly suggest an extremely sick state of mind, and, perhaps even worse, how Apostolic influence managed to get such evil drivel published in university magazines.

Lord Annan has recorded that 'the standard of Cambridge scholarship in Stephen's time [he was referring to Leslie's and Fitzjames's time] was low by that of the greatest European universities.'[14] In a large measure this was reflected in the debates of the Apostles, for however brilliant may have been the minds of some of those taking part, the choice of subjects often bordered on the puerile, the trivial or the farcical. One fatuous question posed was 'Is any event necessary?' and it is said that three replied 'yes' and three voted 'no'. The philosopher, G. E. Moore (elected 1894) ended his argument by saying that work was not virtuous, but 'only necessary', an observation for which a philosophic mind was hardly required. Another of Moore's papers asked 'Can we turn Monday mornings into Saturday evenings?', apparently wondering whether it was possible to allow the Apostolic spirit and enjoyment to be conjured up outside those Saturday night meetings. A majority seemed to think this wasn't possible.

An apt, if somewhat severe, summing up of the Cambridge Apostles in the latter part of the century would be that its members in their over-eagerness to learn, not only became muddled, but that they failed to become positive pioneers. They were groping all the time. All manner of philosophical books and papers were written, though not all of them were published, yet few of them set out anything that was radically new, or that had not been expressed, albeit in a different form, by other philosophers in other countries.

They were doubters almost to a man. Doubt in academic life just as much as in politics can sometimes prevent tragedies. But it can also produce lack of commitment, lack of confidence, incoherence and indecision. Periodically, especially in Britain, this fatal flaw dominates in academic circles and wreaks great harm in the process. In many instances it develops into a mindless clamour for consensus politics, something which may work in an ideal and highly civilised society, but which more often, as in Britain today, swiftly turns into a meaningless phrase, pregnant with humbug.

It was in the 1870s and 1880s that the beginnings of this half-doubting, half-consensus-minded rot began, even though it was not until several decades later that it spread into politics. Slowly, from those days onwards the doubters increased their grip in public life. It was a kind of 'wet rot' which eroded the Establishment, the professions, the nation and the empire, gradually leading to the loss of the will to govern.

That the presence of this rot was not detected much earlier on was due to the fact that the vast majority of the population were spared all this. They still had hardly any doubts, and this was the way in which they brought up their children. They believed passionately in God, Sovereign and Empire and the feasibility of the 'greatest good for the greatest number.' Two reigns later they showed that they were prepared to die in hundreds of thousands for their convictions. It was only when the doubting academics were able to convey their misgivings to a wider public that the old enthusiasms and passionate beliefs began to wither among the masses.

The early Apostles had not suffered from doubt in its extreme form; they were always ready to question and to argue, but not to fill themselves with self-stultifying doubts which paralysed their minds and produced philosophies which won Fellowships but did nothing to improve the quality of life, or to benefit the nation.

Nor should it be thought that this was largely a question of religious doubts. It went far beyond that. It became doubt for the sake of doubt in far too many instances. Perhaps the farcical side of these doubters is best depicted by Bertrand Russell's account of a conversation in the Fellows' Garden at Trinity between Myers and Marian Evans (George Eliot, the novelist). Russell recorded: 'George Eliot told F. W. H. Myers that there is no God, and yet we must be good; and Myers decided that there is a God, and yet we need not be good.'[15]

George Rylands, enthusiast of the theatre

Donald Lucas, classical scholar

Alexander Penrose

Sir John Sheppard, talent-spotter of the Apostles

A group of members of the 1930's: left to right: Richard Llewellyn-Davies, Hugh Sykes Davies, Alister Watson, Anthony Blunt, Julian Bell and Andrew Cohen

# 6

# THE HIGHER SODOMY

'Even the womanisers pretend to be sods, lest they shouldn't be thought respectable'

(Duncan Grant)

From the 1830s onwards there had always been distinct undercurrents of homosexuality in the Society, though, as has already been pointed out, these were for the most part sublimated and platonic rather than physical. But from the turn of the century the sublimated turned into the consummated and homosexuality became almost a creed.

Indeed, another factor in the clamour for secrecy in the late 1850s may well have been a feeling among a number of members that they were in danger of exposing the freedom of their thoughts on sexual matters to a wider public. By this time the aggressive homosexuality of William Johnson had become a byword outside the Society, and some felt that this called for a closing of the ranks.

Johnson, who had come to King's from Eton, became a Fellow in 1845, and for more than a quarter of a century functioned at the same time as both a Fellow at King's and a master at Eton. From these vantage points he was one of the first Apostles to encourage the recruitment of homosexual favourites. While his oustanding work was the translation of the epitaph to Heraclitus by his friend, Callimachus, Johnson will best be remembered as the author of the *Eton Boating Song*. This was composed one night when he could not sleep, apparently a recurring problem in his life, for he wrote that whenever he could not get to sleep . . . 'I do a song with a tune in my head, or perhaps two.'

In 1872, following a homosexual scandal and threats of blackmail, Johnson resigned his academic posts and changed his name to William Cory. The scandal involved a former pupil of his, the Earl of Rosebery, then an up-and-coming Liberal MP.

Perhaps he summed up his personal problems when he wrote:

'You say there is no substance here,
One great reality above;
Back from the void I shrink in fear,
And child-like hide myself in love:
Show me what angels feel. Till then
I cling, a mere weak man, to men.'[1]

It would be wrong to suggest that the Society has always been dominated by homosexual influences and preferences. It is true that in certain lengthy periods of its history it has been infiltrated by homosexuals and to some extent manipulated by them. This showed itself in William (Johnson) Cory's time, and in the latter part of the nineteenth century and again through the first thirty years of the twentieth century. This, admittedly, represents a very long period of homosexual influence, but it must be stressed that not all Apostles allowed themselves to be subjected to this.

The homosexual phase in Apostolic life bloomed in the latter part of the last century, reached hot-house proportions in the early part of this century, becoming blatantly and even ostentatiously aggressive under those two predacious pederasts, Giles Lytton Strachey and John Maynard Keynes. It wilted briefly after World War I, but became prevalent again in the late 1920s and the early 1930s. As it has been a recurring theme in the past history of the Society there is a risk that its constant repetition in recalling various incidents or anecdotes may not merely become monotonous, but unjust to the very many heterosexual members down the ages. For this reason alone it is proposed briefly to depart from the strictly chronological order by including all the homosexual overtones and undertones in this single chapter and thereafter to close the door on the subject.

Oscar Browning was among the high priests of this sexual cult. He was neither sublimated, nor particularly discreet. Like William Johnson, he was not only a master at Eton, but through his Eton and King's connections helped to recruit future Apostles. Johnson had in fact been Browning's tutor at Eton, and Browning, like Johnson, was dismissed from Eton because, according to his headmaster, he took 'too personal an interest in the boys' – a typical Victorian understatement. Not only did Browning pursue the theme of a homosexual closed society inside the Apostles, but under the guise of taking a paternal interest in the working classes, he often invited sailors and labourers off the streets into his room at King's. The origin of the phrase 'Hello, Sailor' is said to have derived from Browning. In naval phraseology the lower deck's name for a homosexual as a 'Brown Hatter' was originally a 'Browning Hatter'.

It was as an exponent of the training of teachers that Browning made his mark and, to a lesser extent, with such works as *Modern England, Modern France* and *History of Europe 1814-43*. His dismissal from Eton did not deter him from seeking a parliamentary career, but in this he was not successful. As a Liberal he contested seats in Norwood, East Worcestershire and West Derby, but failed on each occasion.

Raymond Asquith wrote to his father in June, 1900, with a caustic comment on this strange man who had a habit of bursting into fits of giggles:

'I went over to Cambridge to speak at their Union. It is a detestable place to speak in, and the Cambridge orators are as repulsive a crew as I have ever seen: not one of them speaks English – I don't mean the idiom, but the dialect: they all have the manner and accent of Welsh missionaries . . . I sat next to Oscar Browning, who is their treasurer . . . and was quite unbearable.'[2]

Such a comment was, however, not only rather unfair, but indulging in hyperbole to compare the speakers at Cambridge to Welsh missionaries. But then both Oxford and Cambridge had this juvenile hate for one another, and, for potential intellectuals, they showed it in childish ways. The Apostles, for example, always wrote oxford without the courtesy of capitals, thus implying the same kind of disregard as was used towards poor Roby. 'Cursed, idiotic oxford' was one frequently quoted opinion which became almost a slogan. It was in this period that the saying originated that 'an Oxford man goes about as though he owned the world, while a Cambridge man gives the impression that he doesn't care a damn who does own it.' What, of course, the Cambridge man meant, though he would not admit it, was that while Oxford men gave the impression of what Raymond Asquith's father called 'effortless superiority,' those of Cambridge felt they could afford to ignore such outward show because they *knew* they had inherited the earth. This was certainly an Apostolic viewpoint.

Yet there were some among the Apostles who could have the good grace to be self-critical occasionally. Charles Merivale, who later became Dean of Ely, and was elected to the Society in 1832, could look back on its activities in later years with some reservations:

'Our common bond has been a common intellectual taste, common studies, common literary aspirations, and we have all felt, I suppose, the support of mutual regard and perhaps mutual flattery. We soon grew . . . into immense self-conceit. We began to think we had a

mission to enlighten the world upon things intellectual and spiritual
. . . We lived in constant intercourse with one another, day by day,
met over our wine or our tobacco.'[3]

It was in such intercourse in the rooms of individual members of the
Society that homosexuality flourished in that period. Yet at the same time
it was something much more than that: it was the formation of intense
and passionate relationships which in many cases lasted for a lifetime and
induced a special kind of loyalty. On the other hand, as David Newsome
in his work on A. C. Benson, the essayist and critic, has made clear,
when writing of the 'flavour and life-style of late Victorian Cambridge
. . . much will be said hereafter of the *mores* of an earlier age with regard
to romantic friendship within exclusively male communities, a phenom-
enon so normal and respected throughout the period covered . . . that
the greatest care must be taken to avoid slick and dismissive judgements
. . . In the nineteenth century the normality of both men and women
forming highly emotional relationships with those of their own sex, of the
same age or sometimes older or younger . . . was neither questioned as
necessarily unwholesome, nor felt to inhibit the same relationship with
the opposite sex leading to perfectly happy marriage.'[4]

The freedom of discussion concerning homosexual tendencies and
theories in an age when homosexuality was regarded as one of the worst
crimes and was punished so severely may seem surprising. It was in this
period that Oscar Wilde received a savage sentence of two years' hard
labour for such offences, and his wife immediately changed her name and
those of her two sons by deed poll. Goldsworthy Lowes Dickinson, who
was elected to the Society in 1885, gives an explanation for this. He
suggests that, despite the perils if one was caught in a homosexual act,
conditions then were more favourable for homosexual relationships of a
permanent kind because 'society does not condemn or suspect the
common practice of men living together.'[5]

Thus whereas in one sense society today is more tolerant of
homosexuals, the aggressive, self-advertising homosexuality which has
developed out of that tolerance has actually made the practice of men (or
women) living together a target for ridicule, malice and unjustified
suspicions in many cases. Even the bachelor or spinster living on his or
her own is sometimes unjustly suspected of being a deviationist.

Lowes Dickinson was a shy man who came to Cambridge via
Charterhouse. According to this own confessions he did not realise that
he had homosexual tendencies until he reached university, though he was
aware of being aroused by the sight of certain shoes and boots from an
adolescent age.[6]

Possibly, for the reasons set out above, Dickinson found in becoming a member of the Apostles he had entered some kind of sanctuary which would protect him for life. The Society, he stated, 'formed for many years a very important part of my life, though not so much at my first election as in the year or two following, when McTaggart, the philosopher, Roger Fry and Wedd (afterwards classical teacher at King's) were the active members. We met, as still the society meets, on Saturday nights. A paper was read and we spoke in turn, drawing lots for the order . . . The soul of the thing, as I felt it, is incommunicable. When young men are growing in mind and soul, when speculation is a passion, when discussion is made profound by love, there happens something incredible to any but those who might breathe the magic air.'[7]

Here, in this essentially sincere and valid personal impression of the Apostles, Dickinson, perhaps more than any of them, captures something of the magic which the Society has distilled over the years. Possibly that magic was at its peak in the era of *fin de siècle*. He creates the image of young men lifted up to the clouds by the sheer delight of swapping ideas and discussing things they had never before dared to envisage. To be one of a chosen few was rather like being admitted to the court of Camelot. But one begins to understand Dickinson's viewpoint more easily when realising that it was in this very period that he developed a passionate enthusiasm for Shelley, not so much for his poetry as for the ideas which lay behind it. His other great enthusiasm was for all things Greek and especially for Plato. This emerges in his considered opinion much later on in life that he could see at last 'how mistaken was my own early view, finding expression in Plato and appealing to me there, that the love for men is of a higher kind than that for women. It may be, but it seldom seems so.'[8]

Nonetheless, the theory that the love of man for man was greater than that of man for woman became an Apostolic tradition. It was summed up in one of the later Apostolic secret phrases of this period – 'the Higher Sodomy'. Note the capital letters. This was said to reflect the view that women were inferior to men both in mind and body, and that this put a homosexual relationship on a much higher plane.

Not surprisingly sex as a major subject and homosexuality as a subsidiary subject were among the themes chosen for discussion from time to time. Some of these produced outstanding essays which were talked about for years after they had been delivered. One such was the cryptically entitled 'Violets or orange blossom?', a paper by John McTaggart, which set out a plea for homosexual love.

McTaggart was a homosexual during his early days at Cambridge, but eventually married a girl from New Zealand. It is noteworthy that, in announcing his engagement to her, he informed fellow Apostles that this made no difference to his viewpoint which was still supportive of homosexual love. Paul Levy writes that this McTaggart paper eventually 'disappeared from the Ark (where the Society's records were kept) and was lost.'[9]

It was not the only paper of its kind to disappear. Yet another, attributed to Nathaniel Wedd, was said to have been phrased 'Is it right to doubt the Virgin birth?' Certainly the question sounds very much in line with Wedd's own views. He was described by Lionel Trilling as 'a cynical, aggressive, Mephistophelian character who affected red ties and blasphemy.'[10]

Wedd was highly critical of the Christian religion, telling his friend Frederick Bulmer in a letter of 13 September, 1898, how he despised 'the High Church Doctrines about the Presence and all the bloody, swinish bunkum that the prize idiots of the two universities use to cloak their erotic tendencies.'

Homosexuality was paradoxically related both to fervent Christian believers and to atheists. In the case of the former quite a few of the clergy and those preparing to enter the Church entertained a hypocritical and sophistical theory that in some esoteric way all was well if one's sexual adventures were confined to the same sex and not to females. Some practising Christians among the earlier Apostles had subscribed to this theory, one which has been sustained and upheld by some Church of England clergy (bishops among them) well into the 1980s. But, more importantly, homosexuality was also a revolt against the Church and its teachings, a protest against that most dubious and controversial of all Christian doctrines that people are born sinful.

This led to just as many debates on religious issues as on sexual problems. Thus 'Goldie' Dickinson delivered a paper on 'Shall we elect God?' – meaning, of course, should He be elected to the Apostles. This was based on an imaginary description of the Society holding a meeting in heaven, considering this very question. The debate was interrupted by God suddenly making an appearance and answering the Apostles' objections to his becoming a member. Despite cries of 'God out! God out!', he claimed that He was the true founder of the Society.

'Is self abuse bad as an end?' was one of the few badly phrased subjects for debate. It is recorded that the majority voted 'no', but that two Apostles, G. E. Moore and G. H. Hardy, said 'yes'.

Moore, the author of *Principia Ethica* and whose philosophic cult had such an influence over more than fifty years, was always prominent in these debates, bringing his sceptical mind to bear on a variety of topics, among them: 'Is it a duty to hate?' In debating this theme Moore attacked some of the muddled concepts of Christianity as it was sometimes taught. With admirable logic he pointed out the inconsistencies of the doctrine that one must love all men, enemies included.

'Should God hate the devil?' was another provocative paper.

'Achilles or Patroclus?' This was a title chosen by Moore in producing a paper on love and friendship, and, clearly, in selecting this he was extending his theme to include the 'Higher Sodomy'. Moore himself held conventional views on sexual behaviour, but his experiences in such activities were extremely limited at this time. Indeed, he told close friends that until he came to Cambridge he had no idea that sodomy was ever practised in modern times. His relative innocence showed in his speech, and one Apostle insisted that the real title for the debate was 'Must copulation be lustful?'

On occasions these debates turned into somewhat morbid and astonishingly childish confessions of sexual experiences, frequently on masturbation and deviations. If sexual matters were taboo for conversation in society generally in these late Victorian days, the Apostles seem to have been not merely totally uninhabited, but obsessed with such themes. One paper on the subject of profanity and indecency asked 'Is the reader or the writer obscene?' Yet another posed the question 'Should man marry man?'

G. E. Moore was a major influence in the Society at this period, and that influence lasted for very many years. Yet while some of his pupils and admirers have praised him for his commonsense, others have suggested that his philosophy offered little towards tackling the problems of everyday life, or politics. 'By far the most valuable things which we know or can imagine are certain states of consciousness which may be roughly described as the pleasures of human intercourse and the enjoyments of personal objects,' wrote Moore. Perhaps Paul Johnson has summed him up best by declaring that Moore's philosophy proclaimed the way not merely for a society of mutual admirers, but for the formation of 'programmatic freemasonry, a mafia almost.'[11]

Moore was the son of a doctor and descended from a Quaker family on his mother's side. Having been passionately devoted to religion when he was a boy, he eventually gave up his faith and insisted that 'we should spread scepticism until at last everyone knows we can know absolutely nothing.' And the substitute for all this? It amounted to nothing much more than 'the perfect love of friendship'.

It is understandable that the Honourable Roden Noel (elected 1857) wrote a year before his death in 1894 that he had once heard the Apostles 'mentioned with bated breath as the Society for the Propagation of Atheism' on account of there having been 'twelve students who belonged to it' who 'were at one epoch all Freethinkers.'[12]

Lowes Dickinson's links with the Apostles were continued long after he 'took wings'. In his unpublished manuscripts a scrap of paper, dated February, 1931, was attached to a typescript, stating: 'This was written some time after the war and read to the Society. It took about two hours. The general verdict, if I remember right, was "what a fuss about nothing.""[13]

Sir Dennis Proctor (elected 1927), who handled the unpublished papers of Dickinson, said that this particular paper was 'apparently another work on the theme of homosexuality in the form of a dialogue between 'Vivian' and 'Audobon', the names which Dickinson had given to the characters cast in the roles of himself and Ferdinand Schiller in *A Modern Symposium*, in which the former reveals to the latter his feelings of passionate love.' 'I do not think it would have much appeal to a modern reader,' commented Sir Dennis.[14]

Ferdinand Schiller was one of three highly successful brothers whose father had a business in India. Dickinson enjoyed a passionate affair with him. However, more often than not Dickinson found himself sexually frustrated because most of the men he fell in love with were heterosexual.

The homosexual theme, as well as the actual practices, gained impetus in Apostolic circles in the early part of the twentieth century. It was then that Duncan Grant, later one of the Bloomsbury set, made his quip that homosexuality had become so fashionable and prevalent that 'even the womanisers pretend to be sods, lest they shouldn't be thought respectable.' In 1911 Beatrice Webb, in a letter referring to Bertrand Russell, wrote to Lady Courtney that she was sorry that 'Bertie went to Cambridge – there is a pernicious set presided over by Lowes Dickinson, which makes a sort of ideal of anarchic ways in sexual questions – we have for a long time been aware of its bad influence on our young Fabians.'[15]

Yet the arch-apostle of aggressive homosexuality in the Society was not so much Dickinson, or other of his homosexual contemporaries such as Eddie Marsh (later Sir Edward Marsh, Churchill's private secretary) and Roden Noel, Wedd and McTaggart, but Giles Lytton Strachey, the man who revolutionised the art of biography. Bertrand Russell, who became a member in 1892, said 'after my time the Society changed in one respect. There was a long drawn-out battle between George Trevelyan and Lytton Strachey, in which Strachey was on the whole victorious. Since his time homosexual relations among members were for a time common, but in my day they were unknown.'[16]

This is a massive understatement. In fact, in Russell's day probably a majority of the Apostles were homosexual, and it is hard to see how Russell could possibly not know about this, even though he himself was heterosexual.

Lytton Strachey took a great interest in the history of the Society and, as much because he delighted in gossip as anything else, he took advantage of his position as secretary to the Apostles to delve into papers in the

'Ark'. Strachey loved to make lists of those among past members who were secret and practising and who were non-practising homosexuals.

One cannot help regretting that the spirit of satire – the one vital factor in eighteenth century Britain which kept a curb on all intellectual pretension and nonsense – was lacking in the 1890s. The Apostolic antics and postures invited the creation of the equivalent for the period of today's *Private Eye*. Alas, it did not come about. For here in abundance were the kind of people who in this day and age among the enlightened would be dismissed as intellectual poseurs, or, as Noel Coward more eloquently put it in his 'Green Carnation' number in *Bitter-Sweet*:

> 'Haughty boys, naughty boys, every pore
> Bursting with self-inflation,
> We feel we're rather Graecian
> As our manners indicate,
> Our sense of moral values isn't strong.
> For ultimate completion
> We shall really have to wait
> Until the Day of Judgment comes along.'

'What is the highest expression of an unique friendship?' was one of the more pretentious papers delivered in this period. For some reason it was decided that this particular paper should be deleted from the records. The name of the originator of the question is also witheld.

Strachey himself, however, had a keen sense of satire and this prevented him from committing some of the follies which his views actually encouraged members to indulge in. Here was a carefully controlled homosexual, a cunningly concealed Machiavellian director of operations, a skilled hand at getting his own way, an effortless dictator. His manner was languid and anything but dictatorial, he exuded sweet reasonableness, yet he controlled the Society as nobody before or since has managed to control it, sensing his secretaryship as perhaps his only chance in life of being able to exercise power. Strachey used that power not merely to select, but also to reject certain embryonic members. Paul Johnson puts it this way: 'From the Apostles he [Strachey] grasped the principle of group power: the ability not merely to exclude, but to be seen to exclude. Within his magic circle exclusiveness became a kind of mutual life-support system.'[17]

Homosexuality probably reached its peak in the Society when Strachey and Maynard Keynes formed a remarkable partnership in conducting its affairs. Here were two minds both devoted to achieving power and influence in their respective ways. Keynes himself was the chief protagonist of the homosexual cult, obsessed with the subject to an abnormal degree for one with such a good intellect and wide interests. So obsessed, in fact, that when, years later, he married the Russian ballet dancer, Lydia Lopokova, the news was received with outraged horror among some of his friends. Some of them never forgave him; others maliciously speculated as to what was the real reason for the marriage. It slowly dawned on them that this was all part of Keynes's power game.

'The Apostles repudiated entirely customary conventions and traditional widsom,' declared a smug and at the same time delighted Keynes. 'We were in the strict sense of the term Immoralists.'[18]

Keynes was an ideal partner for Strachey. The two men were devoted to the same sexual cult and had the same contempt for conventional thought. But there was a difference between the two men. In Strachey's case this was more a question of perversity for its own sake than any carefully thought out philosophy. Keynes was reacting positively against the Puritan ethic: he hated Puritanism in any form and not least in the form it had long taken at Cambridge. Both men, however, regarded homosexuality as the supreme state of existence, 'passing Christian understanding' and being superior to heterosexual relationships.[19]

Keynes's hatred of Puritanism is important in the light of his economic theories. He was to become the man who has gone down in history as the most outstanding economist and architect of social progress of the past seventy years, though some would dispute such an assessment. But it was his hostility to the puritan ethic which stimulated and lay behind his economic theories – spend to create work, spend one's way out of depression, stimulate growth. It was also his hatred of Puritanism which caused him in early life to devote rather more time to pursuing homosexual conquests than to economics. More positively, his papers to the Society were in the main nothing whatsoever to do with economics. One such paper, often cited, was on the subject of 'Beauty'. Keynes's much admired theories on how best life can be improved by pouring out so-called Government money – i.e. the money taken from the people in taxes – were marked by an abysmal ignorance of what life for the masses was like and how much they survive in the long run solely by their own efforts and not by the benevolence of any government. Cambridge may have acquired over the ages too great a respect for the puritan ethic, but it must be remembered that a degree of Puritanism has usually been beneficial to Britain, whereas an over-reaction against it has often been disastrous. Puritanism is horrible in its excesses (e.g. a British form of communism inspired by Puritanism would probably be the most revolting interpretation of communism), but it is always dangerous to over-react to it.

Keynes and Strachey between them largely took over the vetting of 'embryos' when it came to selecting new members for the Society. This marked a distinct change from earlier procedure when the general rule was that selection must be carried out only through unanimous agreement. In the early 1900s what Strachey and Keynes urged was what was eventually accepted, despite some opposition. It came to be the custom to choose members for their good looks even more than for their brains. There was, however, still some snobbery: if the prospective new members were good-looking *and* came from 'good families' so much the better.

Arthur Hobhouse (later Sir Arthur Lee Hobhouse), who was not particularly distinguished in his university career, was chosen by Strachey and Keynes because he 'looks pink and delightful as embryos should'. Hobhouse was immediately selected as Keynes' next homosexual conquest, and he signed his letters to him as 'Your constant true love, JMK.'[20]

By the period between 1905 and 1910 homosexuality in the Apostles' circles had become blatant even in public. Patrick Wilkinson, Fellow of King's College, in *A Century of King's*, has written that a visitor to the college in 1908 was surprised at 'the openness of the display of affection between [male] couples.' Others noticed that James Strachey and George Mallory stroked one another's faces in public, while Gerald Shove and Francis Birrell ostentatiously revealed their mutual devotion. On another occasion James Strachey was discovered serenading Rupert Brooke. All these except Mallory and Birrell were members of the Society.

'We can't be content with telling the truth – we must tell the whole truth, and the whole truth is the Devil,' wrote Lytton Strachey to Maynard Keynes. 'It's madness of us to dream of making dowagers understand that feelings are good, when we say in the same breath that the best ones are sodomitical.'[21]

This marked the apex of the homosexual cult among the Apostles. It was never again to be quite so blatant, even though laws were eventually relaxed and public opinion changed. The tide began to turn when homosexuality actually caused rifts within the Society, something which was brought to a head when Wittgenstein was nominated. Ludwig Wittgenstein was a member of a wealthy Austrian industrialist family who had come to Cambridge via Manchester University. The complication arose because, though homosexual himself, Wittgenstein loathed the idea of making homosexuality a cult and absolutely rejected the doctrine of the 'Higher Sodomy'. This was one major reason for Wittgenstein rejecting the Apostles in the early years of his career. Another was his hatred for another continental member of the society who was also homosexual, and who had coveted one of Wittgenstein's favourites.

As war approached the homosexual cult declined, and after the First World War it merely flickered intermittently. It is true that because of the flamboyance and outrageousness of the few members who were homosexuals in the 1920s and 1930s, this influence tended to be exaggerated by some commentators outside the Society. But the old-fashioned mannerisms of a homosexual kind prevalent among some of the 'Angel' dons was on occasions firmly rebuked. Sir John Sheppard once referred to a fellow Apostle who was still an undergraduate as 'my very own precious boy', and received the monumental rebuke 'I am not a boy, I am not precious and I am in no way whatsoever yours or anyone else's boy.' Such a response from an undergraduate Apostle to an 'Angel' would have been unthinkable in Strachey's time when to be called anyone's 'dear boy' was regarded as the highest compliment.

It took a long time for Sir John Sheppard to come to terms with the fact that the 'Higher Sodomy' was not widely popular. In 1920 John Webster's seventeenth century play, *The White Devil*, was produced at Cambridge under Sheppard's direction. He was so delighted that the Newnham College authorities had banned female students from acting in the Webster play so that all female parts could be taken by young men that he gave a party to celebrate this.

Yet homosexuality continued among some membes to have a kind of élitist appeal, even though after World War I this was rather more discreetly propagated. It is true that a highly popular song of the period was parodied in rightist circles as 'Pacifism, socialism, white slavery and buggery, wearing their old school ties', but the cult itself kept a relatively low profile. George Steiner, one of the most perceptive observers of the period, states that

'What is not in doubt is the general fact of the strongly homosexual character of the élite in which the young Blunt [later Professor Anthony Blunt] flourished at Trinity and King's Colleges in Cambridge – and, most especially, of the Apostles, the celebrated semi-secret society of intellectual and aesthetic souls which played so distinctive a role in the English philosophical and literary life from the time of Tennyson to that of Strachey and Bertrand Russell. Neither sociology, nor cultural history, neither political theory nor psychology has even begun to handle authoritatively the vast theme of the part played by homosexuality in western culture since the late nineteenth century . . . There is hardly a branch of literature, of music, of the plastic arts, of philosophy, drama, film, fashion and the furnishings of daily urban life in which homosexuality has not been crucially involved.'[22]

On the other hand it should be stressed that the portrait of the Apostles of the 1930s as 'a centre of homosexuality' is inaccurate. There was nothing remotely like the flamboyant homosexuality of the Strachey –

Keynes era. Whatever there was of this nature was relatively discreet in Apostolic circles. Indeed, discretion on all counts was an essential dictum of the Apostles at that time. Indiscretion was frowned upon as a lack of internal discipline. Guy Burgess, who occasionally bragged of his homosexual conquests, was perhaps the one outrageous exception. But even he could be astonishingly discreet on occasions; indeed it was this very talent for discretion at the right moment which enabled him to have so many close friends in high circles in more than one country. As to Anthony Blunt, he was extremely prudent in conducting his peccadilloes. He is said to have been furious when some fellow students once put the tailor's dummy of a young boy in his bed.

It was not so much among the Apostles, but at King's where homosexuality was notorious in this distant period, and the editor of the University magazine, *Granta*, was actually sent down for referring to it. Unquestionably, Sir John Sheppard's mannerisms gave rise to much of this notoriety: his affected phraseology encouraged many jokes at his expense. Thus it was that the homosexual fraternity in the university continued to have a remarkable influence for a minority group. Even among the Apostles, though muted, their influence was often predominant in the selection of new members, even of heterosexual members. It all made for the creation of cosy and exclusive little coteries within the Society. The homosexuals may not always have had their own way and heterosexuals may have predominated outwardly but their scheming and solidarity with one another and not least their almost inborn cunning (partly due to a feeling of being liable to some kind of persecution) have all been extremely effective. This has extended to influences in other fields – in politics, diplomacy, the Civil Service, literature, the arts generally and, more surprisingly, into the sphere of the intelligence services.

There was one occasion, after the Apostles' London annual dinner in 1937, when homosexuality did emerge as a binding force in the Society. On that occasion discretion was cast to the winds, and, after a dinner at which the wine flowed freely, some members moved on to a party at Eddie Marsh's home and all ended in a drunken orgy. It was the occasion of one of the rare rows between Blunt and Burgess, in which the latter was easily the victor. Marsh looked on with mild amusement: it was probably Eddie's swan-song.

It is not the purpose of this history of the Society to enter into the pros and cons of the 'Higher Sodomy', or even less of its more rarified aspects. That inflated doctrine has, one hopes, thankfully ended. Commonsense, changed public attitudes, new legislation have had some effect in dispelling nonsense and in making esoteric homosexuality redundant. So it is merely a question now, in reviewing the past, of letting facts and what members have said on this subject speak for themselves. But what such facts convey down the years is that the homosexual faction within the Apostles has at various stages worked in a mafia-like manner.

A sexual mafia can be a very dangerous influence – whether homosexual or heterosexual – if allowed to operate as a recruiting body, whether in the Civil Service or any of the other services of the nation. But of the two, as history has shown over two thousand or more years, a homosexual mafia is by far the most dangerous. And, as history also shows in recent times, relaxation of the laws against homosexuality does not necessarily make the difference which altruistic law-makers sometimes believe to be the case.

In Apostolic circles one would hope (and so it would seem) legal changes have been sensibly and quietly accepted. But in many circles, it is not always the case. Their motto would appear to be: homosexuality between consenting adults is legal, so let us publicise our liaisons.

# 7

# GOD AND THE DEVIL

'In the beginning was matter, and matter begat the devil,
and the devil begat God'
(G. E. Moore in a paper read to the Apostles)

The Edwardian age is generally seen today as one in which all classes managed to enjoy themselves in the belief that the British Empire would last forever. The upper classes took this view with complacency, while the poorer members of the community optimistically hoped that some of the imperial prosperity would eventually rub off on them. This latter view was encouraged by the Liberals' huge majority at the general election of 1906.

As far as the educated classes were concerned, Bertrand Russell expressed this complacency rather differently. He said that he noticed a great change in the Apostles from the generation ten years junior to his son. 'We are still Victorian,' he remarked, but, referring to the Keynes and Strachey generation, they 'aimed rather at a life of retirement among fine shades and nice feelings, and conceived of the good as consisting in the passionate mutual admiration of a clique of the élite.'[1]

This new development within the Apostles was not at all what G. E. Moore, their leading philosopher at the turn of the century, intended. While Moore still has his advocates today, it is not always easy to define accurately all he meant and what he intended. '. . . No one, who has asked himself the question, has ever doubted that personal affection and the appreciation of what is beautiful in Art and Nature are good in themselves,' wrote Moore. To that one might reply, in the words of the late Professor Joad: 'it all depends upon what you mean by beautiful and good.'

True, Strachey and Keynes distorted much of what Moore meant, and later generations may be forgiven if they find it not always easy to understand Moore. One can see how his statement just quoted could be twisted into something quite different by Strachey and Keynes. Then again, there is the quotation from Moore at the beginning of this chapter. Having made his assertions about matter, the devil and God, Moore proceeded to add that then there was the death, first of God, then of the devil, and matter was left as it was in the beginning. Almost any modern scholar might be forgiven for saying that Moore was turning the blatantly obvious into something meaningless. It was that early Edwardian failing of the Apostles trying to be clever for the sake of being clever and often when there was nothing to be clever about. They thought they were the equal of the German philosophers, yet none of them were in the same class.

One of the chief problems of Moore, like those of so many Englishmen of his generation and of subsequent generations up to the First World War was his prolonged adolescence: for too long he remained a boy with a man's mind, a very dangerous combination. On the other hand Moore escaped from the obsession with doubts which affected Sidgwick, and developed a utilitarian philosophy which, provided one picked out the practical items from the muddled ones, offered a practical mode of life for a complacent generation. Just how complacent that generation was, even at the top, can be judged from its unprotesting tolerance of such horrors as the holocaust of the Somme.

Bertrand Russell has paid his own tribute to the Apostles: 'The greatest happiness of my time at Cambridge was connected with a body whom its members knew as 'The Society', but which outsiders, if they knew of it, called 'The Apostles'. This was a small discussion society, containing one or two people from each year on the average, which met every Saturday night . . . It is by way of being secret in order that those who are being considered for election may be unaware of the fact. It was owing to the existence of The Society [note that Russell always puts The Society in capital letters] that I so soon got to know the people best worth knowing, for Whitehead was a member and told the younger members to investigate Sanger [Charles Percy Sanger, elected 1892] and me on account of our scholarship papers . . . It was a principle in discussion that there were to be no taboos, no limitations, nothing considered shocking, no barriers to absolute freedom of speculation. We discussed all manner of things, no doubt with a certain immaturity, but with a detachment and interest scarcely possible in later life.'[2]

In Russell's time the Society meetings lasted until about one o'clock in the morning, and after that members would pair off and pace up and down the cloisters of Neville's Court, carrying on discussions for one, two and sometimes more hours. Russell does make the point in his memoirs that prior to being elected in the middle of his second year, he had not previously known such a society existed. Thus it would seem that

70

the Society was more secretive in the late 1890s and early 1900s than it had been in its earlier years.

This increasing tendency towards secrecy – later to be broken by the very people who sought to perpetuate it at this time – was largely dictated by the Society's wish not only to be exclusive, but to protect itself against some of those who were anxious to be members. Michael Holroyd, the author of the biography of Lytton Strachey, makes the point that the Apostles 'would behave in peculiar ways to achieve this end.'[3]

To be brilliant and sparkling in debate usually counted for more than choice of subject. The latter occasionally descended to dreary levels such as McTaggart's paper on 'Does youth approve of age?', Strachey's 'Ought the Father to grow a beard?' and the literary critic, Desmond MacCarthy, wanting to know 'Is this an awkward age?' – a somewhat awkwardly phrased question. It may well be asked whether secrecy and exclusivity did not lead to juvenility and the kind of questions which no serious public debating society would entertain. On the other hand what evidence there is suggests that dullness of topic often led to witty speeches.

It would be unjust to John Ellis McTaggart not to make reference to his part in a debate on socialism at the Cambridge Union in November, 1889. This was a debate in which he and H. M. Hyndman took part. McTaggart was highly praised for his precision and the incisiveness of his sentences. Some of these would well apply today. How, under a socialist ideal, he asked, could a central government, which muddles even the little it has to do at present, control such vast affairs, including business? 'And could an emotional democracy attain the hardness of head required in a man of business?'

Another Apostle of this era was Edward Morgan Forster, the novelist, who entered King's in 1897. Forster was a protégé of Lowes Dickinson, then a Fellow of King's, and of Oscar Browning and Nathaniel Wedd. It was the last-named who instilled into Forster his passion for Greece and Greek philosophy. Forster's Greece, declared Lionel Trilling, was that of 'Myth and mystery, of open skies and athleticism, of love and democracy.'[4]

Like Lowes Dickinson, Forster found Cambridge a paradise after life in his public school, which type of education he thereafter constantly derided. This system, he said, sent boys out into the world 'with well developed bodies and undeveloped hearts.' It was one of those theories which was partly true, but which became obsessive when expressed in his novels. But for Cambridge University he had nothing but praise: 'everything was done with ease . . . boys . . . received education, often for the first time in their lives.' This feeling of there being some kind of a Utopian existence at Cambridge and the intense and passionate friendships he acquired there later caused Forster to make that controversial statement that 'If I had to choose between betraying my country and betraying my friend, I hope I should have the guts to betray my country.'[5]

It was unfortunate for the reputation of the Society, perhaps, that this phrase was taken out of context at the time of the unmasking of Sir Anthony Blunt and other Apostolic agents of the Soviet cause, and quoted in the media as evidence of the Society having had a subversive influence. It has never been the subversive or anti-patriotic cell which some people, citing Forster, have sought to portray. Nevertheless, it was evidence of how the homosexual mafia can operate and how from the earliest times it has tended to be a crypto-protection society in that the bond of friendship has been used to cover up all manner of questionable activities and sometimes even to protect members from being prosecuted. This was truer in the 1880s and 1890s than in more recent years.

Roger Fry, the painter and art critic, was also at King's, and elected an Apostle in 1887. Fry was one of these Apostles who, like Lowes Dickinson and Forster and later G. E. Moore, was to have an effect on the Society over a period of several decades. He was, of course, a main link with the Bloomsbury Group, and eventually he became Slade Professor of Fine Art in Cambridge from 1933 until his death. But in the 1890s Roger Fry was a pungent critic who posed all manner of tricky questions for the Society, one of which was his essay on the subject of 'Must a picture be intelligible?' Not unnaturally, in the light of this last query, in his regard for modern painting he crossed swords with George Moore, the Irish novelist and critic whose work, *Modern Painting* (1893), had condemned the mode of construction of such painting in Britain and had attacked the Royal Academy and other institutions. Fry wildly asserted that Moore was 'conservative, retrospective, anti-democratic; he distrusts revolutions in art; he distrusts new schools with new scientific systems.'[6]

'New scientific systems'? What did Fry mean? Here was the art critic using language in a careless, nearly meaningless manner – almost, one might say, in an unApostolic way. For whatever may have been the demerits of George Moore's opinions, few in this or any other century could deny the merits, loving care and the patient revision bestowed by him on his prose. George Moore was one of the very few authors who would actually pay considerable sums of money for revising his own work at proof stage.

One can perhaps justifiably not dwell too much on the Bloomsbury-ites: they were much more insular than they themselves believed, forming an almost incestuous literary circle in the sense that they fed upon one another's ideas and made an indigestible meal of them. But

Forster and Fry were among the mildest of anti-Establishment Apostles of their day. A much more bigoted member was Godfrey Harold Hardy (elected 1898), of Trinity. His influence extended to generations of Cambridge students from the earliest 1900s to the post-World War I period. Hardy was so blatantly anti-Establishment and unorthodox that few took him for anything but a mathematical genius who found relaxation in buffoonery. A fanatical atheist, he refused to go into any college chapel even on formal business. He regarded God as 'his personal enemy', wrote Lord Snow.[7]

Hardy described himself as 'the fifth best mathematician in the world'. The son of the bursar and art master at Cranleigh School, he went from Winchester to Trinity with an open scholarship. He was an infant prodigy at mathematics, allegedly being able to write down numbers up to millions at the age of two. Maths and cricket were his twin passions in life, and he used cricketing similes when discussing mathematics, or marking papers. In the 1920s he would refer to an undergraduate being 'in the Hobbs class', while in the 1930s he introduced a new phrase, 'the Bradman class' and he would call an unblemished, accurate paper 'a maiden over'. Equally he would apply mathematical tests to cricketing theories and in assessing not only the strengths and weaknesses of players, but how long it would take, say, to get the 250 runs needed for victory. On two occasions Hardy attempted suicide by taking an overdose of drugs, the first time following the death of a close male friend. Fits of depression dogged him all his life.

Quarrels with various prominent figures in Cambridge led to his leaving for New College, Oxford, where his left-wing influence was very marked. In his rooms at Oxford he flaunted a photograph of Lenin on his mantelpiece.

A very different and much more serious character was Edward Howard Marsh, who went up to Trinity from Westminster School. Here was a sympathetic, eminently adaptable classics scholar who was to become that *rara avis* of British civil servants – a bohemian and a patron of the arts, and possibly the most influential Apostle in the outside world for a period of more than fifty years.

There was, however, nothing of the 'way out' Edwardian about Marsh. He was the Society's navigator: when the going was heated and controversial, Eddie Marsh could usually be relied upon for sound and dispassionate advice. With equal facility he could dampen down acrimonious exchanges, smooth over personal difficulties and yet in some instances actually promote the claims of the 'way-out' younger members. Gradually, he was regarded as the fount of all wisdom when all else failed. 'See what Eddie thinks about it' became a well known piece of advice. Bertrand Russell has said of him that 'he had been a close friend of mine when we were undergraduates, but afterwards he became a civil servant, an admirer of Winston Churchill and then a High Tory.'[8]

This was not altogether an accurate description of this intricately well balanced character. If Edward Marsh ever regarded himself as a High Tory, which is extremely unlikely (originally, of course, Churchill was a Liberal Cabinet Minister), it would be in an aesthetic rather than a political sense. He always enjoyed listening to the other person's point of view. This was as true of him as a patron of the arts as in the field of politics. He was a painstaking and fastidious critic, yet he sometimes found it very hard to condemn outright an appallingly bad play. While he loved to praise and encourage young artists, poets and sculptors, he disliked being harsh. At Cambridge he had a close friendship with G. E. Moore, while later he endeared himself to Maurice Baring, through whom he was brought to the notice of Sir Edmund Gosse. Eddie Marsh was the pioneer of the production of Ibsen's works on the British stage.

There is a curious euphemism concerning Marsh in his biography in the DNB: 'As a result of mumps and German measles in early adolescence Marsh was destined never to marry.' The truth is that all his life Marsh, while having many women friends who adored him, including Asquith's daughter, Violet (later Lady Violet Bonham-Carter), his real attachments were to male friends. Quite often, if not always, such attachments were platonic and disinterested.

In the Civil Service Marsh's rise to eminence was swift and sure. He served Joseph Chamberlain and Alfred Lyttelton before becoming Winston Churchill's private secretary in 1908, and for the next quarter of a century he was always working for Churchill whenever the latter was in office – in the Colonial Office, the Board of Trade, Home Office, the Admiralty and the Treasury. It was both an irony and a personal tragedy that he was not to share in Churchill's greatest triumph, for he retired in 1937 before his old master became Prime Minister. Each man regarded the other with the utmost respect and admiration and each was totally loyal to the other. For Marsh, Churchill was 'indisputably the greatest figure in English history, with the possible exception of Alfred the Great', and for Churchill Eddie was 'a loss to the nation . . . a master of literature and scholarship and a deeply instructed champion of the arts.'[9]

Eddie Marsh was even present with Churchill at the Siege of Sidney Street in London's East End. When Churchill joined the Army in World War I, Marsh served Asquith, and after Asquith's fall he was unemployed until Churchill was back in office, and then he worked under him at the Treasury from 1924-29, afterwards serving the Labour Minister, J. H. Thomas, at the Dominions Office until he retired in 1937.

In many respects Marsh was a much more influential Apostle than

Moore, Strachey or Keynes. This was most evident in a practical way, whether in politics or the arts. His very considerable influence extended from politics to the Armed Forces, from Whitehall to Cambridge, where he not only maintained the closest links, but sought out new talent for both the professions and the arts. He was a close friend of Rupert Brooke, another Apostle, whose literary executor he became. The patronage of Eddie Marsh in almost any branch of the arts was sufficient to guarantee success to many from Maugham to Dylan Thomas. He was a trustee of the Tate Gallery and an avid collector of pictures, a governor of the Old Vic and an adviser to the Institute of Contemporary Arts.

An agnostic in religious matters, a conservative with a very small 'c' in politics, an astute diplomat in the corridors of power, Marsh, with his upturned eyebrows and monocle, has been described as 'a bohemian gourmet in a clean collar'. He was always anxious to advance the cause of young Apostles, not only early in the century, but as late as the 1930s when he had retired. There were occasions when such favouritism was apt to be ill-advised – encouragement for Anthony Blunt and friendship for Guy Burgess. To the latter he gave an introduction to Churchill, something which Burgess was later to exploit on many occasions. Marsh was the friend of Robert Ross and Somerset Maugham and his fastidious and often highbrow tastes in literature and painting did not prevent him from enthusing about the sentimental musical shows of his devoted friend, Ivor Novello.

But Marsh was, without question, a thorough professional both in the Civil Service, diplomacy and the arts. He knew how to get things done. He managed to escape very early on from the cult of the Apostles at the turn of the century when they began to take themselves ridiculously seriously. Often, but not always, Marsh would save them from the nonsense they contemplated. He was certainly critical in a mild and detached way of how they referred to themselves as 'The World of Reality', while all else was mere 'Appearance'. This was probably a quirk of the metaphysicians among them who insisted that space and time were totally unreal. An example of this was contained in a letter from Crompton Llewellyn Davies to Bertrand Russell, congratulating him on becoming a member, and confounding 'those absurd humbugs Space and Time, which have the impudence to pretend that they are now separating us.'[10]

Not all members made such a success of their lives as Eddie Marsh, who was unique in that his achievements, however considerable, were behind the scenes. There was Desmond MacCarthy, handsome, brilliant, charming and remarkably talented, but, despite great things being expected of him, disappointed both his friends and himself. This was an era in which many men made their reputations effortlessly and almost solely in the role of literary critic and reviewer of books, and MacCarthy proved to be one of these.

Yet he was always expected to become an author of distinction. His friends founded a Novel Club and a Memoir Club with the sole purpose of persuading MacCarthy to write a book. Alas, his life became too disorganised and full of personal problems for him to accept this seemingly easy challenge. The essay was still highly prized at this time not only in literature, but in journalism, too. It was the easy way to make a living. MacCarthy himself commented that 'Idleness and fecklessness have spoilt me for myself and others.' Yet he lived to receive a knighthood and a Cambridge doctorate just before his death in 1952.

But if he could not write books, MacCarthy could put his genius into his conversation, a talent which predominated with so many members of the Society. When it came to writing books he was almost totally undisciplined, unable to concentrate on any given theme and useless in developing any idea beyond, say, a short essay or review. He certainly helped other Apostles to have good reviews, but perhaps the most surprising thing is that, despite his failure as a writer, he was honoured by a knighthood. The story is that his 'K' was backed by pleas from three Apostles, one of whom was in the Treasury at the time.

Though membership of the Society was open to the whole university, in the early 1900s the Apostles were predominantly from King's and Trinity. Just how secret the Society was supposed to be may be judged from Lytton Strachey's letter to his mother, telling her of his election.

This was marked 'Private and Confidential' and it stated: 'This is to say – before I am committed to oaths of secrecy – that I am now a Brother of the Society of Apostles. How I dare write the words I don't know.'[11]

Strachey's father was a general who had served in India for more than a quarter of a century, but the prime influence in his early life was his mother, not only his greatest confidante, but herself somewhat of a rebel. Born Marie Silvestre, she was a free-thinking French schoolmistress who had been a supporter of the Women's Progressive Movement.

Strachey and John Tressider Sheppard were elected at the same time, October, 1902. Their entry marked quite a distinctive change in the Society, imperceptible perhaps at first, but very soon Strachey was to become the leader in succession to G. E. Moore. There was gradually a more sophisticated, yet light-hearted atmosphere at meetings. They became more outrageous in choice of subjects for debate, and more frolicsome in demeanour. Cushions would be hurled playfully across the meeting room, sometimes there would be such games as blind man's buff and ring-a-ring-of-roses around the speaker. On one occasion a game of charades was introduced after a debate. Another time Charles Percy Sanger, who had been Second Wrangler, delivered an essay on copulation: he later became a barrister. Meanwhile Strachey, always anxious to shock, posed the question in a debate in 1902: 'Christ or Caliban?', arguing that Caliban had more to offer because he stood for freedom from all restraints.

Religion, imperialism and immortality were all the targets for virulent opposition by various speakers, though Strachey was usually the principal opponent of anything or any ideal upheld by Victorian society.

One of Lytton Strachey's closest allies in the Society was Leonard Woolf, who later married Virginia Stephen. Strachey and Woolf formed an inner circle of Apostles who often met separately from Society meetings. Desmond MacCarthy, Roger Fry and Sheppard were members of the group which later included such people as Keynes, Harry Norton and James Strachey. Marsh was never the member of any one group, though accessible to all. This inner circle was later to be enlarged and to develop into what was known as the Bloomsbury Group, about which so much has been written that further comment here is unnecessary except to make the point that for a time the group was dominated by Apostles, or 'Angels'.

Virginia Woolf seems to have been privy to at least some of the Society's secrets and she described the Apostles as 'the society of equals enjoying each other's foibles' and added that 'politics and philosophy were their chief interests.'[12] One detected a note of regret, possibly even of wistful criticism, in Virginia's implied suggestion that the society neglected the arts, and especially music and painting.

Indeed, Virginia Woolf was possibly the most perceptive of the Society's critics at this time. She was thoroughly aware of the Edwardian 'way-outness', though she put this in much greater detail. The Apostles were, she said, 'lacking in physical splendour . . . They were clever and unworldly, but arrogant, prickly and withdrawn. They were men who tended to be devoid of female company.' It was an apt and accurate portrait.

# 8

# THE KEYNESIAN INFLUENCE

'The Society, except me, thought it was probably their duty to join the Salvation Army or collect statistics about West Ham, and that we all lead selfish lives'
(Maynard Keynes, October 1907)[1]

After Lytton Strachey probably the dominant influence in the Society for many years was John Maynard Keynes. A product of Eton, where he displayed a great contempt for his examiners even though they regarded him highly, he brought to Cambridge a high degree of arrogance and assertion of personal superiority over his contemporaries. Surprisingly, this told in his favour rather than against him. Just as the mindless, sadistic public school bully held sway among the hearties, so did the intellectual bully (which was what Keynes was) dominate when he came to King's.

To be fair, perhaps the Society needed a shake-up. Certainly it was time that economic theories were given rather more consideration than philosophic theses. If Victorianism had been rejected, there was still the question of Edwardian complacency. Yet there is little real evidence that any positive or serious attention was given either to economic matters, or to the threat of a war between the imperialists and the would-be imperialists, something which was clearly on the horizon in the early 1900s, but which politicians and intellectuals seemed to prefer to ignore.

In short, the Apostles continued to function according to their own time-scale, and as David Williams, an astute observer, has pointed out, 'experiencing the grand, ordinary moments of human existence – like marriage and the begetting of children – a lot later than is common among less rarefied folk.'[2] David Williams in his review of G. E. Moore's biography goes on to say 'headline phrases like "The Agadir Incident", or the "Drang nach Osten" seemed to pass him by. Moore was a bit of grit in the oyster-shell, requiring protective pearl-stuff to be spun between itself and the rubs of the world.'

Keynes, however, like Strachey, was well aware that current issues needed to be debated rather more frequently than had been the tradition previously, and in this he was supported by the two Trevelyans (Robert Calversley and George Macaulay). Keynes became secretary of the Society only two years after his election in 1903, when there was only one undergraduate member, Hobhouse, and he decided right away to recruit new talent. The 'Angels' had probably held sway for too long, and some of them had latterly given more time to the Bloomsbury Group and the Midnight Society than to the Apostles.

Newcomers in the undergraduate ranks at this time included James Strachey (Lytton's younger brother), Henry Norton, Gerald Shove, Cecil Francis Taylor and Rupert Brooke. Yet such issues as Free Trade versus Protection and even votes for women aroused more interest in the Society than the storm clouds gathering all over Europe, or the need for an imperialist nation to get its economic priorities right. Bertrand Russell even stood unsuccessfully as a candidate supporting the suffragettes in a Parliamentary by-election in Wimbledon.

There was now much more careful scrutiny of subjects submitted for discussions. These were vetted with rather more seriousness than had been the case in previous decades. No longer was it easy to persuade members to listen to such topics as 'Why we like Nature', which, almost unbelievably, was one which Edward Marsh had produced as a paper.

An Apostolic contempt for non-members still existed. Many who deserved to be admitted were banned. Professor Arthur Pigou, of King's, an economist who in many ways rivalled Keynes, never became an Apostle, partly because Keynes wished to keep the Apostolic fishpond free from other economists as far as possible. Scientists were also disfavoured: Jeans, Eddington and many later scientists were not members. The Society seemed quite satisfied to assert its influence purely in the literary scene. Thus the Apostles were regular contributors to the book review pages of many papers and magazines. Leonard Woolf controlled the literary pages of *The Nation*, Desmond MacCarthy did much the same with the *New Statesman* while Strachey's uncle was at the helm of *The Spectator*.

Keynes was secretary of the Apostles during his fourth year at King's, at a time when the Society was reduced to one undergraduate member and desperately needed recruits. This situation was to recur over and over again in the Society's history, but was somehow always put right. The thrill and the feeling of authoritative influence which the election of new Apostles gave to Keynes was something which strangely outweighed even his own ambitions for a career. To secure the man he wanted, to manipulate the selection of new members, all this was to Keynes something he cherished almost as a sport.

A new interest for the Apostles was psycho-analysis, and this was largely stimulated by James Beaumont Strachey (elected 1906), who, having done badly in his examinations at Cambridge, went to Vienna to be psycho-analysed by Sigmund Freud. From then on not only did his career change for the better, but he became a vigorous disciple of psycho-analysis. Later he made a name for himself as a musicologist.

Lytton Strachey and Woolf cross-examined Keynes before he was admitted to the Apostles. There were various carefully conjured up parties before he was actually approved. Sheppard was his 'father' or sponsor in the end. But once he was admitted Keynes soon became the dominant figure. It is true that his friendship with Lytton Strachey began to disintegrate when both men were competing for the affections of a Trinity undergraduate, Arthur Lee Hobhouse, but even as late as 1920 Strachey was addressing letters to Keynes as 'Dearest Maynard'.

Keynes himself was a somewhat indeterminate Liberal – indeterminate in the sense that if his policies made any sense at all, they required the kind of controls and *dirigisme* of which most traditional Liberals have been suspicious. But he did not get things entirely his own way, either on the Liberal front, or that of the young Socialists. Politics increasingly influenced the Society's membership and this was revealed in many ways. Though Keynes was anti-Fabian, Fabianism became a vital topic in Apostolic circles. A Fabian Society had been formed at the University: Hugh Dalton (later to become Chancellor of the Exchequer in the Attlee government of 1945-50) was one of its earliest presidents, and in 1909 he was succeeded by Rupert Brooke. Fabianism had, somewhat preten-tiously, been chosen as a name because of Quintus Fabius Maximus, who had asserted that 'lengthy consideration and careful debating' was vital for progress towards an ideal state. Or, as Cole and Postgate opined, 'it envisaged socialism as a heap of reforms to be built by the droppings of a host of successive swallows who would in the end make a socialist summer.'[3] Quintus Fabius was probably wiser than Cole or Postgate, just as George Bernard Shaw was nearer to getting things right than either Sidney Webb or Annie Besant, two other prominent Fabians.

But apart from the Fabians, Apostolic influence was extended to various political causes. Chief of these were anti-protectionist and anti-imperialist lobbies, of both of which G. M. Trevelyan's *Independent Review* was one of the principal supporters. This journal had a majority of Apostles on its editorial committee.

Rupert Brooke was one of the most popular of the Apostles of his day, probably only to be compared with Hallam at the time of Tennyson's membership. He had rooms in the Fellows' Building of King's and was instrumental in founding the Marlowe Society, an undergraduates' dramatic club. Brooke had written a thesis on Marlowe, of whom he was

80

a great admirer, and this undoubtedly explains his choice of title for the club. It was perhaps only incidental that the club was named after another homosexual. As an actor, Brooke was best known for his performance as Dr Faustus. Meanwhile Lytton Strachey lived in attic rooms on the King's staircase called 'Muttonhole Corner.'

It is some indication of the ultra-secrecy of Apostolic selections at this time that Strachey, when conducting the vetting of Brooke as an 'embryo', used code words both for Brooke and his vetters – 'Sarawak' for Brooke and 'Bobbie Longman' for those called upon to assess him. 'Poor "Sarawak"' was put to a very severe test and he didn't come up to the mark,' said Strachey. 'The catechism floored him.'[4]

Nonetheless, Brooke was duly elected, possibly because his preliminary assessors were not members of the Society. So it would seem that in vetting embryos sometimes the evidence of outsiders was given weight, if not total credence. Certainly the two people identified under the single code name of 'Bobbie Longman' were not Apostles.

Brooke, who came to King's with a scholarship from Rugby, was a somewhat mixed-up character, part-socialist, part-romantic, an explorer of sorts, heterosexual, yet always attracting the attentions of homosexuals. Even Keynes was reported as showing little enthusiasm for the election of Brooke to the Society. Yet, despite all this, he was very soon an outstandingly successful member. He often gave the impression of having a strong anti-semitic trait in his character, possibly encouraged by Hilaire Belloc, whom he introduced to members of the Society. At the same time he was a vigorous opponent of intolerance and persecution whenever it was to be found. In one speech to the Society he denounced the 'unholy collaboration of barbarism and Christianity', claiming that this combination, whenever it had been allowed to get out of hand, had done untold harm to all the arts.

Once, in a letter to his friend, Eddie Marsh, Brooke mentioned that he had been 'canoeing into Cambridge to address the Apostles on the subject of "Intolerance"'. He took the view that a degree of intolerance was justifiable, even essential, because 'only to love generates sloppiness, just as only to despise acidulates.'[5]

Brooke and Marsh kept in close touch long after both men had left Cambridge. They each returned to Cambridge for meetings of the Society, as their correspondence shows. Marsh made a habit of coming up from London each Saturday night for Apostolic meetings.

Both Brooke and Gerald Shove were briefly secretaries of the Society, and it was about this time that the two foreigners of some distinction were elected – Ludwig Wittgenstein and Ferenc Istvan Denés Gyula Békássy. They were elected in the same year, 1912, with results which certainly cast a shadow on the Apostolic ideal of friendship superseding all else.

Wittgenstein, the son of a Viennese millionaire industrialist, came to Cambridge to study mathematics after a brief spell at Manchester University, and Keynes was one of the first to urge his election to the Society, despite considerable opposition. It will be recalled that in the early days of the Apostles unanimity in selection of a member was the rule. In the case of Wittgenstein this clearly did not apply, and it was only Keynes's persistence which succeeded in gaining the acceptance of the Austrian. During this early part of the twentieth century Keynes more than once practically bulldozed all opposition when he wanted a certain student made a member.

Thus Keynes had his way with Wittgenstein, and Marsh, who was present at the Austrian's initiation, wrote to Brooke, saying: 'Maynard says W [Wittgenstein] is an ultra-metaphysician – his passion is to push Russell's logic to its ultimate refinements.'[6]

The shadow cast over Apostolic relationships following Wittgenstein's election was almost entirely due to the presence of Békássy in the society. Ferenc Békássy was a member of an aristocratic Hungarian family, and he came to Cambridge after being educated at Bedales. Békássy was at King's, whereas Wittgenstein was at Trinity. Each had a mutual dislike of the other, and Austro-Hungarian differences, despite the then common empire, had much to do with it. But in the case of Wittgenstein these differences amounted to a paranoid detestation. Jealousy would seem to be the chief element in these differences.

Wittgenstein offered to resign from the Society in an effort to avoid creating further difficulties. So, after one meeting, he handed in his notice. In the end there was a curious compromise: Strachey persuaded Wittgenstein to withdraw his resignation and he remained a member while not attending meetings. But Békássy was far from being the sole reason for Wittgenstein's wish to resign. Francis Bliss, another King's man, had also been elected an Apostle on the same day as Wittgenstein, and, according to Russell, the two men hated one another. Brotherly love really was coming apart at the seams.

Wittgenstein returned to Austria when war broke out and served in the Army. He did not revisit Cambridge until 1929, when once again he joined the Society – this time as an honorary member and a Fellow of Trinity. Then his influence was considerable. Békássy was less fortunate: he also returned home to fight in the Austro-Hungarian Army and was killed in 1915. His great friend, Bliss, fighting on the other side in the Artists' Rifles, lost his life a year later.

Partly through the Apostles, partly through the Bloomsbury Group, pacifism as a cult gradually became more marked than radicalism in the ranks of the Society, Keynes himself was somewhat ambivalent in his views on the subject. But among his Apostolic friends Lytton and James

Strachey, Gerald Shove and Henry Norton were all pacifists. On the other hand Keynes was contemptuous of 'the most Apostolic of the socialists' who became 'hot and dishonest' as soon as anyone criticised their opinions or questioned them. 'It's more difficult to understand than the Christian's attitude – the beastly emotions he [a Socialist] gets out of his belief.'[7]

Keynes was ever ready to pour a douche of cold logic on what he regarded as the politics of fanaticism and emotion. In this respect, and in counteracting the worse aspects of Puritanism, his influence was salutary. Indeed, at a later date it probably acted as a useful deterrent to many undergraduates of a later generation, including some Apostles, from their turning to communism. For this reason it is once again helpful to ignore the strict rules of chronology and to track the Keynesian influence to the 1920s and 1930s. Michael Straight, the American Apostle of the 1930s, has testified that in this period Cambridge was 'dominated by the overpowering intellect of John Maynard Keynes', who attributed communism to 'a recrudescence of the strain of Puritanism in our blood, the zest to adopt a painful solution because of its painfulness.' At this time Keynes created the Political Economy Club, of which both professors, graduate students and some undergraduates were members. He used this club forcefully to oppose Marxist economics.

British Puritanism has always been a frightful, frightening and alarming creed. It is true that some Puritans have managed to avoid the extremism of their doctrines and, in doing so, to contribute something of value to the nation and humanity. Some Quaker families have been prominent among the exceptions. Perhaps Milton is still the shining example, but then Milton could also write a masque about 'pert fairies and dapper elves', a happy picture to which few dyed-in-the-wool Puritans could subscribe. Any form of communism emerging out of British Puritanism would probable be far worse than any other communist system in the world with the sole exception of Russia and East Germany. There Keynes was remarkably perceptive: British Puritanism oozes with hate rather than love.

'Keynes was arrogant. He did shout one down if he felt he could get away with it,' says Professor F. A. von Hayek, the monetarist economist. 'On the other hand he very much admired anyone who stood up to him and challenged his views. He was a formidable figure.'[8]

Keynes became an 'Angel' in 1910 after having delivered to the Society some twenty papers in seven years. His interests were much more diverse than those of most economists and he would enthusiastically debate issues both serious and frivolous which had not the remotest bearing on economics. For a while he took an interest in psychic research and he was more devoted to the arts in the broadest sense than most Apostles.

It was Keynes's interest in the Society for Psychical Research which prompted Rupert Brooke to attend some of its meetings. This resulted in Brooke composing a sonnet which, as he admitted, was 'suggested by some of the proceedings of the Society for Psychical Research'. The sonnet, called *Psychical Research* – an odd title for a poem in Edwardian times – developed the theme of spirits set free by death to

> 'Learn all we lacked before; hear, know and say
> What this tumultuous body now denies;
> And feel, who have laid our groping hands away;
> And see, no longer blinded by our eyes.'

Yet serious, frivolous, or malicious as the Apostles could be from mood to mood, sometimes they tumbled down when at their most rhetorical. At a dinner of the Society in June, 1913, when G. E. Moore presided, James Strachey so lost himself in what was described as 'a poisonous attack' on the Society that he broke down and had to be revived with brandy.[9]

If Virginia Woolf was doubtful whether the Apostles devoted enough attention to the arts, she must have been unmindful of the influence of Eddie Marsh. Admittedly, Marsh's influence came after he left Cambridge and when he was in the Civil Service, but it was just as effective in the sphere of the arts as a whole as Keynes's influence in the field of economics. From about 1910 until at least 1940 Marsh's influence in the artistic world was astonishingly important and effective. He was both a supporter of young artists and a friendly critic. Probably no British literary critic of the present century has been more constructive than Eddie Marsh, often bending over backwards to be more helpful than critical.

Marsh's apartment in Gray's Inn was always open to visiting Apostles to doss down for the night either on beds, or his sofas. From Rupert Brooke in the pre-World War I days to Dylan Thomas in World War II, Marsh was a vital influence. Similarly, Maynard Keynes's backing for British ballet was equally significant. Beverley Nichols, writing shortly before World War II, stressed that the two things in which Britain had then become dominant were in ballet and the production of fighter aircaft. Much of the former was due to Keynes's support and his shrewd advice on financial investment.

Eddie Marsh more than anyone else praised and actively supported Brooke's poetry. 'You have brought back into English poetry,' he wrote, 'the rapturous, beautiful grotesque of the seventeenth century.' At the same time he added his protest against these lines in *Libido*:

> 'Your mouth so lying was most heaven in view
> And your remembered breath most agony.'

'There are some things too disgusting to write about, especially in one's own language,' replied Marsh.[10]

But these were the days of Edwardian revolt against Victorian restrictions, not least in the sphere of morals and family relationships. Once, addressing the Apostles on the subject of 'Decency or Indecency', Brooke declared: 'Parents would die if they knew what we were really like.'

Maynard Keynes worked in the Treasury in World War I and because of this he drew a disapproving note from Lytton Strachey, who wrote to him in February, 1916, saying: 'Dear Maynard, why are you still at the Treasury, Yours, Lytton.'

In June, 1916, Bertrand Russell was prosecuted for a pamphlet which he had written entitled 'Two Years' Hard Labour for refusing to disobey the dictates of conscience', dealing with the case of a schoolmaster named Everett who, on being drafted by the decision of a conscientious objectors' tribunal into a non-combatant unit, maintained that his conscience forbade him to participate in any military activity, and was sentenced to two years' hard labour. Russell was fined £100, which he refused to pay, and his possessions in his room at Trinity were distrained upon and offered for public sale. It is interesting to note that for the first book offered for sale a bid sufficient to cover the monies due was made, so the sale terminated abruptly.

In December, 1917, Keynes himself wrote to Duncan Grant, saying 'I work for a government I despise for ends I think criminal.' By this time Keynes had worked up a hatred for Lloyd George which never diminished, despite the fact that in the early 1930s Lloyd George embarked happily on propagating Keynesian economic theories. It was a curious riddle which was never resolved. On the one hand was the Wizard of Wales, when in opposition in the 1930s, setting out a Keynesian case that in times of depression and unemployment vast sums of governmental money must be spent on public works, while Keynes referred to Lloyd George as 'this extraordinary figure of our times, this syren, this goat-footed bard, this half-human visitor to our time from the hag-ridden magic and enchanted woods of Celtic antiquity. One catches in his company that flavour of final purposelessness, inner irresponsibility, existence outside or away from our Saxon good and evil, mixed with cunning, remorselessness, love of power, that lend fascinating enchantment and tenor to the fair-seeming magicians of North European folk-lore.'[11]

This was not a wholly inaccurate picture, though hyperbolic and allowing Keynes's zest for sparkle to obscure its purpose. Lloyd George baffled Keynes, perhaps because he had succeeded in becoming an international figure despite his lack of academic education. It was almost a love-hate attitude of quite remarkable ambivalence. 'A *femme fatale*' was yet another of Keynes's descriptions of Lloyd George, yet he conceded that of all leading statesmen at the Versailles Conference Lloyd George was 'intellectually the subtlest'. The economic consequences of the Versailles Treaty were what really angered Keynes. Without doubt the Treaty was economically unsound, but the Great Post-War Myth, fathered by Keynes and twisted and transformed by every pontificating do-gooder and Francophobe – that the policies of the Nazi Party were forced upon Germany by a long series of betrayals by the Allied Powers – was never a true picture.

Keynes and Lloyd George never truly linked up, despite the fact that the latter paid tribute to the former's economic policies. Devious, deceitful, unorthodox and erratic as Lloyd George undoubtedly was, he had an astonishingly quick mind and could absorb new ideas easily. Admittedly, he made extravagant claims that if the Liberals were returned to power, he would reduce the number of unemployed by as much as fifty per cent. But, apart from Lloyd George, nobody in the party knew how it was proposed to do this. It would have meant finding work for 700,000 at a time when unemployment was still increasing. The truth is that the kind of Keynesian plan which Lloyd George had proposed could only have been achieved by drastic controls and a socialist economy. Keynes himself must have known that even his policies could not work as speedily or easily as all that. *Can Lloyd George Do It?* was the title of a book by Maynard Keynes and H. D. Henderson which aimed to give the public the economic facts of life. *Can Maynard Keynes Do It?* might have been a better title. The idea of creating employment by increasing public works has always been somewhat of a fallacy except in very special circumstances – immediately after a major war, for example. The Lloyd Georgian – Keynesian theme was that since 1921 a sum of £500 millions had been paid out in unemployment relief: this was enough money to build a million houses. Lloyd George's conjuring trick was that £100 millions a year would bring 500,000 men into employment. Nobody asked what would happen to the house-builders once the building programme was ended. Nobody asked how this could increase real productivity. Nor is there much evidence that the economists proposing these things had even asked themselves such questions.

The Keynesian programme on which Lloyd George went to the polls in 1929 was a technocrat's blueprint without the positive co-ordination of state and private enterprise measures for putting it into action. Without a massive nationalisation programme, which it did not include, it is hard to see how it could ever have been satisfactorily implemented. Keynes himself was not always consistent in this era. He opposed Britain returning to the Gold Standard, yet argued against devaluation; while sometimes urging an agreed policy of reducing some incomes, he dismissed any suggestion in cuts in wages; finally, Keynes, the Free Trader, for a brief period argued in favour of some tariffs.

This, however, is not to denigrate the main thesis of Keynesianism. It was partly on these very theories that, a few years later, President Roosevelt successfully enabled the United States to recover from the slump. Conservatives asserted that Roosevelt was merely copying Mussolini, whereas, surprisingly enough, some Democrats alleged that his economic plans were 'half-baked socialism' and 'communism'. Keynes wrote a brilliant article proving that the New Deal was neither of these things. 'Mr Roosevelt', wrote Keynes, 'has made himself the trustee for those in every country who seek to mend the evils of our condition by reasoned experiment within the framework of the existing system.'[12]

Therein lies the secret of how to make Keynesianism work: 'reasoned experiment', adding, perhaps, one other essential – timing. Keynes has pointed the way, and, in some respects he still does. But there have always been enormous risks in Keynesianism, risks which make a period of stern monetarism almost inevitable. Some of its disciples have wrought more harm than good and the reaction has been towards a stricter interpretation of monetarism. J. K. Galbraith enthused about the 'affluent society', yet his economic theses in the light of world-wide inflation hardly seem apt today. In his revised fourth edition of *The Affluent Society* there is the curious observation that one result of increasing affluence which he had not anticipated was that the under-privileged had lost the political power they once had, and had become rather easy to ignore.

# 9

# AFTER ARMAGEDDON

'Faith to my mind is a stiffening process, a sort of mental starch, which ought to be applied as sparingly as possible. I dislike the stuff . . . My temple stands not upon Mount Moriah, but in the Elysian Field where even the immoral are admitted'

(E. M. Forster)[1]

Apostolic influence in World War I was minimal. The Society was split between those who joined the Forces and fought for their country (and some of whom died in this cause, like Bliss and Brooke), and those who persisted in extolling pacifism as a creed. However, as the activities of the Society more or less dwindled throughout the war, only the pacifist clique who stayed at home exercised much influence.

During the war some Apostles supported the No Conscription Movement, and Lytton Strachey joined the National Council Against Conscription. However, despite this, he did not stand on his pacifist principles, but sought and obtained exemption from war service by producing literally scores of doctors' certificates and details of all his alleged medical symptoms. What one might call an unconscientious objector.

Wittgenstein kept in touch with some of the Apostles even though he chose to fight on the side of the Germanic Central Powers. He wrote to Bertrand Russell from Monte Cassino, having been taken prisoner by the Italians, saying he had attempted to write a book while in the Austrian Army. This was eventually published under the title of *Tractatus Logico-Philosophicus*.

Deaths of members in World War I took their toll of the Society and tended to suspend its activities just as an unexpected death in peace-time had temporarily numbed the Apostles. In 1905 Theodore Llewellyn Davies had drowned while swimming on holiday at his home in Lancashire. As Theodore's brother, Crompton, was also a member of the Society, this caused great gloom in the Society's ranks where Theodore had been highly popular. This period of mourning and inaction lasted for almost a year, and very much the same occurred during World War I as news of casualties filtered through. Eddie Marsh used to say that reading the lists of war dead each day in the morning newspapers made him feel quite sick for several hours.

While the pacifist members of the society – Lytton and James Strachey, Dickinson, Hardy, Norton, Sanger, Sydney-Turner, Bertrand Russell, Woolf and Keynes – were against the war in varying degrees (Keynes managing to be anti-war while actually working for the Treasury), the older generation of Apostles and some of the younger ones had been totally committed to backing the Allied cause. Apart from Rupert Brooke and Bliss, Henry Jackson, McTaggart, James Ward, Whitehead and Frank Lucas were all for prosecuting the war until victory was achieved. Frank Lawrence Lucas (elected 1914), more generally known as 'Peter', had won the Porson Prize for Greek iambics while at Trinity. He joined the Royal West Kent Regiment and was badly wounded and gassed. That he was a gallant officer is beyond question. The *Official History of the War* refers to 'a daring and resourceful reconnaissance by Lieutenant F. L. Lucas'. He was eventually transferred to the Intelligence Corps. Then in 1920 he returned to Cambridge and became a Fellow of King's.

For a time Lucas was secretary of the Society, to which he contributed no fewer than nineteen papers and, with Maurice Oswald Marshall, the pianist, comprised the only two new members the Society had from 1914 until the end of the war. In 1922 he published *Seneca and Elizabethan Tragedy*, which won him considerable acclaim and he was for a while closely linked with the Bloomsbury Group. T. E. Lawrence praised his work as a poet, calling him 'a mental athlete'. A traditionalist in the sphere of literature, he was an opponent of the Leavis brothers in their own loud-mouthed but short-lived literary revolution. Lucas was a forthright character, and in World War II he worked in the Cypher School at Bletchley Park. Yet perhaps he will best be remembered for his work, *The Decline and Fall of the Romantic Ideal*.

Maurice Marshall, who came from Rugby, became a professional pianist after having done some teaching and travelling in the USA in the early 'twenties. He was also articled to a solicitor for a time.

Yet another of the Apostles who joined the Services and made a considerable contribution to victory in World War I was Ralph Lewis Wedgwood (elected as far back as 1893). A son of the well-known Potteries family, after leaving Trinity he entered the service of the North Eastern Railway at the age of twenty-two. In the war he served in the Royal Engineers, first as deputy director of railway transport in France, and eventually being promoted to director of the docks in that country with the rank of brigadier-general. Wedgwood had been a formidable contributor to Apostolic debates on philosophical questions and had even shown himself in favour of the admission of women members. After the war, when the amalgamation of private railway companies became a necessity, he rose to be head of the LNER company and was a pioneer of Britain's first stream-lined train. He was knighted in 1924 and lived to see his daughter, Dame Veronica Wedgwood, become a distinguished historian.

F. L. ('Peter') Lucas was an ardent spotter of new talent for the Society, and this particularly revealed itself when he nominated his first pupil at King's, George ('Dadie') Rylands as a promising 'embryo'. Rylands was duly elected a member in February, 1922, and he became one of the outstanding supporters of the Thespian arts in the Society. An Old Etonian as well as a King's man, he embraced all aspects of life at King's in turn as Fellow, lecturer in English literature, Dean and Bursar. He was also chairman of the directors and trustees of the Arts Theatre at Cambridge, as well as being a Governor of the Old Vic and a member of the Council of RADA. In later life he was a remarkably astute judge of acting talents and helped to advance the careers of a number of leading actors, Sir Michael Redgrave among them, while his studies of Shakespeare won him much acclaim.

It took some time for the Society to recover when war ended. Three members were elected in 1919, Alexander Penrose, Lancelot Charles Rolleston and James Hamilton Doggart, who left King's to become a distinguished ophthalmic surgeon and the author of numerous papers on diseases of the eye. He was also a member of the Anglo-American Physiological Expedition to the Andes in 1921. Penrose was the eldest brother of Lionel Penrose, the psychologist, and Roland Penrose, artist and art critic. Rolleston later became an assistant master at Sherborne and Marlborough; he died in 1939.

Meanwhile there were two other vital influences in the Society in this difficult period. One was Sir Frederick Pollock (elected as long ago as 1865), who was regarded as the most senior of the 'Angels' and still presided at their annual dinner at the Ivy Restaurant in London. The other was undoubtedly Frank Plumpton Ramsey, elected in 1921, a mathematical scholar and Senior Wrangler, the son of Arthur Stanley Ramsey, former President of Magdalene College, Cambridge, and a brother of Michael Ramsey, later Archbishop of Canterbury. Frank Ramsey did a great deal in helping to revive the Society after World War I and delivered some ten papers in all at Saturday night discussions.

Educated at Winchester, Ramsey won a scholarship to Trinity. His interests lay on the border line between mathematics and logic, following in the footsteps of work done both by Whitehead and Wittgenstein. Nobody among the younger members could equal him for power and quality of mind. A shrewd critic of philosophical ingenuousness, he once told the Apostles that 'the chief danger to our philosophy, apart from laziness and woolliness, is 'scholasticism', the essence of which is treating what is vague as if it were precise and trying to fit it into an exact category.'

Maynard Keynes paid tribute to 'his spontaneous gurgling laugh, the simplicity of his feelings and reactions . . . his modesty and the amazing easy efficiency of the intellectual machine which ground away behind his wide temples and broad smiling face.'[2]

While Ramsey was broadly sympathetic to Russell, his pragmatism angered Wittgenstein. This became obvious in Apostolic debates when Ramsey stressed the need for human logic rather than formal logic. In one debate he argued that, while philosophy must be regarded as useful, 'we should bear in mind the proposition that it is nonsense, and not pretend, as Wittgenstein does, that it is important nonsense.'

In the context of Frank Ramsey's remarks it is perhaps worth noting Professor F. A. von Hayek's views on Wittgenstein's philosophy:

'I have known him longer than any one person still living and was sixty years ago very much impressed by his first book. But his later work meant little to me and I have never quite understood the enormous admiration he has gained in Cambridge. Crudely expressed, he always seemed to me the maddest member of a highly gifted but somewhat neurotic family, always on the verge of actual madness and not to be taken too seriously. These may be my limitations, but I just did not find it worthwhile to spend too much time on them – they certainly do not fit into my system of thought.'[3]

Nonetheless, in fairness both to Wittgenstein and Ramsey, it should be noted that Ramsey himself translated Wittgenstein's *Tractatus Logico-Philosophicus*.

Ramsey died at the early age of twenty-six on 19 January, 1930, following an operation. This tragic event robbed the Apostles of a most salutary influence. Only six years previously he had been Allen University Scholar and made a Fellow of King's. In a very short time he had 'revived the Society, acting as a tremendous stimulus on his contemporaries and starting up a new vintage Apostolic era.'[4]

New members in this period were full of promise, but in the long run somewhat unambitious. Yet nearly all of them made their mark in life in some way or other. There was Professor W. J. H. Sprott, the psychologist and author of *Philosophy of Commonsense*; Richard Bevan Braithwaite who eventually became Knightsbridge Professor of Moral Philosophy at Cambridge; George Derwent Thompson, a secretary of the

91

Society and later professor of Greek at the University of Birmingham; Frederick Harmer and Arthur Watkins.

The emphasis in the 1920s was still on philosophical discourse, but this was conducted in a much more professional manner than in earlier decades. It was much less easy for members to get away with brilliantly phrased controversial statements. Psychology and experimental philosophy were added ingredients which did much to stimulate imaginative debates. The Moore and Wittgenstein schools respectively did not have things quite as much all their way as some writers have indicated.

Certainly from about 1919 to the end of the 'twenties philosophy and psychology were regarded as of more importance than politics. There was a feeling, especially among those who had returned from the war, that the politicians had failed the world and had little new to offer. No dictator had as yet arisen to change that outlook, and Bertrand Russell had dampened down any enthusiasm for the Soviet experiment.

Russell was honest with himself in these days immediately after the First World War. 'I saw that all I had done had been totally useless, except to myself. I had not saved a single life, or shortened the war by a minute. I had not succeeded in doing anything to diminish the bitterness caused by the Treaty of Versailles.'[5]

His wife, the former Girton girl, Dora Black, may have written impulsively to Ogden, President of the Heretics Club, that she wished 'we could all be Bolsheviks quick and have done with it,'[6] but her husband took a very different view. 'Russia made me feel little was to be hoped from revolt against existing governments in the way of an increase in kindness in the world.'[7]

Russell, in fact, gave the Apostles a number of warnings on the Soviet Union as a result of his visit there in 1920 along with Mrs (later Lady) Snowden, Clifford Allen and Ben Turner. 'While I was in that country I was permanently conscious of cruelty, poverty, suspicion, persecution and hostility around me. It was one long nightmare,' he told the Society in one debate. The fact that his wife was enthusiastically pro-Soviet in no way altered his opinion. 'Our conversations were continually spied upon. In the middle of the night one would hear shots and know that idealists were being killed in prison . . . With every day I spent in Russia my horror increased.'[8]

For a while Russell's views on Russia generally prevailed inside the Society. Psychology was the magic word at this time, though sociology was regarded with some contempt. Frank Ramsey gave an example of this when he spoke in one debate, arguing that 'this horrible hybrid word, that is neither Greek nor Latin, could become some kind of alternative religion, if we are not very careful.' Prophetic words! His comment may have seemed a light-hearted joke at the time, but not altogether inapt in view of some unhumorous aspects of sociology in the 1960s and 1970s. In the light of certain social consequences when some of its teaching was put into practice, Ramsey's words make even more sense today than they did in the 1920s.

'More than one debate ended up in the 'twenties with arguments as to the value or otherwise of IQ tests,' a Society member of that period told the author. 'Some implicitly believed in such tests, others argued that in the long run they were futile. I recall that it was once pointed out that, whereas in the United States a negro girl with a very modest education had achieved the astonishing IQ of 200, said at the time to have been the highest ever recorded, the late Professor Paul Dirac, who eventually became Lucasian Professor of Mathematics, had an IQ of under 10!'

Scientists were at this time still not particularly popular in Apostolic circles and were much more likely to be found in the ranks of the Heretics Club, where J. B. S. Haldane reigned supreme. However, G. H. Hardy, always an exception on so many occaions, took up the cause of those scientists at Cambridge who were clamouring for the setting up of a professional organisation. Eventually this led to Hardy himself becoming president of the National Union of Scientific Workers, though this was after he left Trinity for Oxford.

Hardy had been deeply impressed by a statement made in April, 1920, by Professor Frederick Soddy, of Oxford, who declared that 'if the world is to be made safe for democracy, scientific men must at all costs make themselves masters in their own house without delay.'[9]

There had been some criticism of the government exploitation of scientists during the war. Sir Frederick Gowland Hopkins, of Trinity, arranged some preliminary meetings to discuss both the criticisms and the idea of founding some kind of professional organisation. There was a great deal of hostility among some Cambridge scientists to the War Office's chemical warfare research work.

The *Scientific Worker*, the official organ of the National Union of Scientific Workers, revealed early on the marked political bias of that newly created union. It was the first scientists' trade union anywhere in the world and was registered as such in 1918. Many scientists kept aloof from it because of its far-leftward looking views. The Cambridge University branch of the union was particularly concerned about chemical warfare and giving aid to the Bolsheviks. It also made some savage attacks on the War Office, strongly backed by Hardy. More importantly, Hardy, with the support of one young Apostle, urged that the union should seek cooperation with the USSR, if not yet in the political field, at least in an exchange of information. The *Scientific Worker* stated that 'the attention of members is directed to the letter from the British Committee for Aiding Men of Letters and Science in

Russia . . .' and even suggested that members might wish to send some gifts.

The idea of a 'Think Tank' first came from the NUSW. It was strongly supported by Hardy, who even suggested that the union might form the nucleus of a 'Think Tank' to aid the USSR in its problems of mechanisation and industrialisation. Records of the union imply that there was connivance in a secret communist membership before 1924. The evidence for this lies in the union's archives which show that 'a communist nucleus' was set up in 1923 by Arthur Serner, the members of which included Maurice Dobb, of Pembroke (a Heretic, not an Apostle), Clemens Palme Dutt and A. L. Bacharach. There is also an interesting surviving document on 'Notes on Organisation and Objects' prepared by Arthur Serner in 1923.'[10]

As a result of these manoeuvres the communist cell in the NUSW was put in touch with Meyer Trilisser, the energetic and capable head of the Foreign Department of the Cheka, known as the INO. One of Trilisser's aims was to develop a network of industrial and scientific espionage in the Western world. He had direct encouragement from Lenin to achieve this. Lenin referred to the British development of radio-telephony and radio-telegraphy, saying 'if we could get this invention, communication by radio-telephone and radio-telegraphy would achieve great importance in the military field.' It was Trilisser who paved the way for Peter Kapitza, then a penniless scholar at the Leningrad Polytechnic, to be given an industrial research scholarship which enabled him to go to Cambridge to study in 1921. The knowledge this young man was to acquire was eventually going to be worth hundreds of millions in any currency in the world by 1945.

Some of the moderates in the NUSW began to fight against the communist infiltrators. For a short time Dame Helen Gwynne Vaughan was president, there being no objection from the communists who regarded the presidency as a sinecure and were only too glad to have her as a responsible 'front' to their own covert operations. But Dame Helen soon realised what was afoot and she resigned in 1924 because she was hostile to the trade union concept of the organisation.

Funds dwindled and finances were very low when Hardy came to the rescue and took on the presidency. His brief period of office (1924-26) was marked by a rearguard action to maintain trade union status. It was the only public office he was ever persuaded to hold and it was yet another example of a non-scientist acquiring office in this always bizarre collection of botanists, economists, mathematicians and pseudo-scientists of left-wing persuasion. There were, of course, a number of genuine scientists in the membership. But lack of funds settled the issue and eventually the NUSW was de-registered as a trade union and Hardy gave up office. The union changed its name to that of the Association of Scientific Workers.

Alexander Penrose was one of a family who distinguished themselves in diverse fields. A prominent figure at King's in the early 1920s, he seems, like a few other Apostles, to have faded out of the academic scene soon afterwards. His younger brothers were Lionel Sharples Penrose (also an Apostle, who was at St John's) and Roland Algernon Penrose (later Sir Roland, who was at Queen's, distinguished as a painter and art critic, and in the forefront of the surrealist movement).

The Penroses were all educated at Leighton Park School, near Reading, an establishment which can claim quite a few Apostles among its old boys. Lionel Sharples Penrose was among the keenest of the debaters on psychological themes in the Society. He later specialised in psychiatric research and became Galton Professor of Eugenics at University College, London, and director of the Kennedy-Galton Centre, at Harperbury Hospital, St Albans. During the war he had served with the Friends' Ambulance Unit in 1918. He gained a first class degree in moral sciences at Cambridge and did a year's study in the psychological department of Vienna University before entering St Thomas's Hospital for clinical studies.

A contemporary of Lionel Penrose says: 'He was probably one of the most stimulating of the Apostles in the early 1920s and he showed us something of the by-paths of psychology and new ways of studying the subject. He had a great sense of humour and a variety of talents ranging from expertise at chess to painting and keeping children amused with an astonishing number of home-made toys and puzzles. He was a member of a Quaker family and therefore had a rooted objection to war in any form. In 1952, when the war in Korea threatened to develop into a global conflict, he founded the Medical Association for the Prevention of War. He took the view that war was like a disease and should be tackled as such, though I think subsequent events made him change his mind.'

His works included a lengthy thesis, *On the Objective Study of Crowd Behaviour*, *The Influence of Heredity on Disease* and *Outline of Human Genetics*. One of his sideline hobbies was the Shakespearian Authorship Society, to which he gave lectures. It amused him to submit the name of Edward de Vere, seventeenth Earl of Oxford, as a likely author of the Shakespearian works, though he did not dogmatize on this.

It was in 1922 that E. M. Forster published *A Passage to India*, widely acclaimed as a literary masterpiece by some, but marred by the author's prejudiced view of the principles of the British Raj which caused him to create his British characters more as caricatures than anything else. Some Britons, returning to India by sea, threw their copies of the book overboard in sheer disgust. It was by no means the best of Forster's work: the late Dame Rebecca West summed it up as a book which was 'very funny because it's all about people making a fuss about nothing, which isn't really enough.'[11]

This was probably a decade when there was too much talk about literature and when the talk began to obscure the realities. Minds became muddled, literary critics used their skill as a toreador would use his cloak to play with a bull – to indulge in self-advertising cleverness. Novels were sometimes used to purvey spleen and hatred, prejudice and cant. Dr. A. L. Rowse described how at this time the record of the British in India was 'undermined and defamed all the way from the impeachment of the great Warren Hastings to the Cambridge Liberal, E. M. Forster, with his absurdly overrated *A Passage to India*, hipped up into being a classic by American liberals like Professor Lionel Trilling.'[12]

Forster was, of course, a strong force in the Society over a very long period, and, from time to time, members used to gather for meetings in his room. He and his fellow-Apostle, Goldsworthy Lowes Dickinson, were continually using the Society to launch attacks on British foreign policy over the past hundred years. In 1924 Dickinson published his work, *The International Anarchy: 1904-14*, which sought to distort all the facts regarding the origins of World War I, arguing that Britain was as much to blame for this as Germany and the Central Powers. Yet, as Winston Churchill was forever pointing out, if ever there was a majority for peace in any Cabinet, it was in that of the pre-war Liberal Government of 1912-14, of which he was a member. Not content with distorting the facts on the origins of the war, Dickinson proceeded to assert that because there had been an evil and vindictive peace settlement, Britain was morally to blame for everything that happened afterwards. Keynes only supported this latter thesis on economic grounds, but never in the same irresponsible way.

By the mid-1920s the Society had regained something of its pre-war distinction and the membership was flourishing. It was greatly aided by a few of the elder 'Angels', but some of the younger members were rapidly making reputations for themselves. Frederick Harmer (later Sir Frederick Evelyn Harmer), who was elected in January, 1925, and for a time was secretary to the Society, distinguished himself in mathematics and economics and eventually entered the Treasury. He served in Washington in the crucial Anglo-American talks in the latter part of 1945. Afterwards he became chairman of the Committee of European Shipowners (his recreation was sailing), vice-chairman of the governors of the London School of Economics and a director of the National Westminster Bank.

Another Apostle of this era was Arthur Ronald Dare Watkins, an Etonian classics scholar, who was a housemaster at Harrow from 1948-58 and the author of *Moonlight at the Globe* and *On Producing Shakespeare*.

This was a strange, in many ways indeterminate period of intellectual curiosity about a wide range of subjects from Keynesian economics and the merits of pacifism as a political creed to what has been called 'Cambridge English', a phrase which at that time meant different things to different people, though today it is more closely identified with the criticisms and tantrums of F. R. Leavis. It must be remembered that 'Cambridge English' really began with Quiller-Couch and Mansfield Forbes in their respective ways, and that the Bloomsbury Circle and Freud were strong influences still in the early 1920s.

Among the Apostles the Bloomsbury Circle still had its links, while G. E. Moore was the creator of what was sometimes called 'the new ethical mood'. This was rather a meaningless phrase taken out of context, which it often was. What Moore really meant was that Victorian ethics were no longer appropriate, something which had been thrashed out long before World War I. But Moore pursued his theme regardless, and, not unnaturally, reflections on the appalling waste of life and talent on the battlefields of Europe helped to stimulate such feelings.

Rejection of things Victorian became a passionate pursuit with some. 'Mid-Victorian' became a contemporary phrase of abuse; Charles Dickens was denounced by more people than Leavis, yet few criticised him quite so unfairly. Leavis laid down his criticism as though it was the dogma and creed of a literary commune, not that of an individual. His view was that to write badly was to be a bad person. But his opinion of what constituted bad writing was, to say the least, very much open to question.

'In the Society only a few of us took such views with any real seriousness. We were apt to discuss them to score humorous debating points,' said the aforementioned anonymous Apostle of this decade. 'It wasn't all that often such things came up, but I do recollect one debate when the subject was posed "what is a bad writer?" There was no agreement on the matter, and I just forget how the question was put. But I remember that the best and most constructive arguments were that the bad writer is, first, the undisciplined writer, and, secondly, the writer who does not allow enough time, or take enough care, to write exactly what he means.'

Which seems to be one good example of sound Apostolic common-sense and escape from rarefied extravaganzas, or fantasies.

On the other hand it was recognised, even if in more elegant terms than Leavis ever managed, that sometimes it is necessary to attack inflated reputations in politics, religion and literature, if one is to obtain a balanced picture. This must always apply to biography, as Strachey rightly showed, and as latterly professor Skidelsky has shown in the case of Maynard Keynes. Not least should it apply to F. R. Leavis. Clearly, the trouble with Leavis was that he had a persecution mania.

There was, however, no denying that, despite his unattractiveness as a personality, Leavis was a stimulating teacher for many undergraduates. On the other hand he lost a lot of sympathy by his attacks on Quiller-Couch and all his works. 'Q', though on the way out, enthused his students by developing the theme of literature not only as being uplifting, but something providing thrills and adventures.

Lytton Strachey was, however, still very much the model for the up-and-coming generation, and the late Cyril Connolly, himself an Oxford man, said of *Eminent Victorians* that it was 'the work of a great anarchist, a revolutionary text-book on bourgeois society written in the language through which the bourgeois ear could be lulled and beguiled – the Mandarin style.' At a London dinner of the Apostles in this era Strachey was asked to propose a toast to 'Eminent Victorians'. There is no firm record of what he said, but one gathers that when asked to define an eminent Victorian, he replied that this would be 'the sort of person whose life would be likely to be written by Lytton Strachey.'

No one can deny that Forster made valuable contributions to the literature of the period, despite the aforesaid criticisms. If he harped on the theme of the undeveloped heart, it was a plea for its expression in life as well as in literature. On the subject of the British tendency of stifling emotions and curbing splendid enthusiasms he was on much firmer ground than on the subject of India, a country he had only briefly visited. The truth was that Indians rather resented Forster for patronising them, while they had an admiration for the imperialist Rudyard Kipling. In the 1920s Kipling was still a dirty name in some academic circles. Yet Radakrishnan, when President of India, went on record of saying that Kipling's *Kim* was the one book of all those produced in the West which came closest to the Indian heart and mind.

Occasionally, gossip and Apostolic discussions leaked from outside Trinity and King's. One question posed was 'Is sociology more important than socialism?' From all reports sociology won. 'I am not surprised,' commented Arthur Benson, the Master of Magdalene, 'as most Apostles seem to come from King's and for more than twenty years King's has regarded sociology as rather like the Ark of the Covenant.' It is interesting to note that at an earlier date, 1910, Benson had written, 'I do think that King's is a very *rude* place, like a great, clever, ill-bred, doctrinaire booby – and considering its huge endowments, it does very little for anything or anybody. It produces people genuinely interested in sociology, but not genuinely interested in other people, and this sort of scientific philanthropy is a stinking product, especially when it is done to parade one's own liberalism rather than to help.'[13]

Much has been made of the alleged influence of G. E. Moore on the Apostles in the immediate post-World War I period. This is not the opinion of all members at that time. Quite remarkably, according to the anonymous member quoted in this chapter, 'sceptics took a much deeper peep into the past. For many of us the essays of Henry Sidgwick were regarded as rather more important reading than anything of Moore.'

This was perhaps the last decade in which Keynes' influence was to be uppermost. After that new members of the Society were to be more concerned with ideologies than economics. In the miners' strike of the 1920s, the bishops of the Church of England, as in the strike of 1984-85, encouraged its prolongation by persuading them Jesus Christ was on their side. That plea worked rather better in the 1920s than it did in modern times, probably because it was put over more elegantly and aptly. The Bishop of Manchester, later Archbishop of York and Canterbury, actually suggested to the miners' leaders that the whole of Christendom was behind them. Keynes backed the bishops.

# 10

# INVESTIGATIVE MARXISM

'Lenin, would you were living at this hour:
England has need of you, of the cold voice
That spoke beyond Time's passions, that expelled
All the half treasons of the mind in doubt'
(Charles Madge, Magdalene College, 1933)

Arthur Koestler has written of this period between 1928 and 1935 as one in which 'the Comintern carried on a white-slave traffic whose victims were young idealists flirting with violence.' While this may have been true of some of the later wave of students in this period, most of the early left-wingers arrived at the communist or Marxist stage by their own individual processes, though probably prodded on by certain of their tutors. Equally, it should be stated that many of them opted out of the Marxist ideology at various stages, a very few in the confusion of the Spanish Civil War, many more when Soviet Russia signed a pact with Nazi Germany, and the few remaining when they realised how obdurate and suspicious the Soviet Union remained after World War II.

This is a diversion from the main theme of this book, but, though only a minority of the Apostles were Marxists, it is important to trace how this ideology percolated the university. This occurred at all levels and with both sexes. Two of the earliest female communists at Cambridge were Joyce Wallace Whyte, who eventually married Sir Cuthbert Ackroyd, who later became Lord Mayor of London, and Kathleen Raine, who arrived at Girton as a science exhibitioner. Kathleen Raine was greatly influenced by Malcolm Lowry and William Empson, the chief contributors to the University magazine, *Experiment*, and Hugh Sykes Davies. Eventually she married Charles Madge who parodied John Milton in composing the lines recorded at the beginning of this chapter.

In Apostolic circles, however, the main event in 1929 was the return of the ultimate philosophical puzzle merchant, Ludwig Wittgenstein. The Society marked his coming back into university life by a supper party given by Keynes at which the Austrian was made an honorary member –

i.e. an 'Angel'. Wittgenstein had given away all the money he had inherited to his brothers and sisters and, before he returned to Cambridge, had been working as a teacher at a village school in Austria. Though on opposite sides during the war, he had come to have a great admiration for the Russians as a people.

But if Wittgenstein had been eccentric in his behaviour in the pre-war days, he was even more so in the late 1920s. He practically never finished any sentence he began, he went into sudden rages and was regarded as a crank by many of his contemporaries among the dons, while even the university authorities had the gravest doubts about him. He was a great friend of the Italian Marxist professor, Sraffa, with whom he used to take afternoon bicycle rides.

Yet, despite all this, Wittgenstein's reputation at Cambridge remained high and he continued to have considerable influence with some Apostles. The deliberate, almost masochistic austerity of his personal life did not seem to be a drawback. 'Luckily, he was not with us much of the time,' says one contemporary member of the Society.

'To listen to Wittgenstein too often was like being dragged back into the Middle Ages. One almost felt that he had been God's representative on earth and that it was Wittgenstein who had been on the Cross, not Jesus Christ. On the other hand, in small doses, he could and did make one think afresh. He was the ultimate court of appeal as to whether one was talking nonsense. Oh, yes, Wittgenstein took us right away from the cosy sceptics and utilitarians of the era of Moore. As a matter of fact, it was Wittgenstein who occasionally made one turn back to reading Sidgwick's essays.'

Wittgenstein was eventually made professor of philosophy in succession to Moore. As such, as will be seen later, he brought philosophy into the sphere of mathematics. It was he, along with Schlick and Carnap who formed the Vienna school of philosophy in the 1920s and founded logical positivism, which had many distinct links with mathematics. The Apostle quoted in the previous paragraph really hit upon the nub of Wittgenstein's philosophy when he said it raised the question of whether one was talking nonsense. For, to sum up his creed, one can say that any statement is either true, false, or meaningless, and it was in the area of meaningless where inquiry and debate should take place.

An Apostle who became a Fellow of King's in 1929 and a few years later as appointed Director of Studies in Classics was Donald William Lucas, brother of Frank Lucas. He also served as secretary of the Society for a period, and records show that he delivered some eleven papers. Between 1927 and 1929 some particularly outstanding new members

101

came into the Society. First among these was Alister George Douglas Watson, later yet another Fellow of King's, a brilliant mathematician, and later a secretary of the Society. Philip Dennis Proctor (later Sir Dennis Proctor) also joined in 1927 and quickly struck up a close acquaintanceship with "Goldie" Dickinson, by then a very sick man. Sir Dennis was present at a farewell gathering of Apostles to Dickinson in London in 1930, when the latter wistfully remarked that the Society was 'different from what it was in my youth,' though he added that, while he found the topics had changed, there was the same spirit of 'free, candid, uncompromising youth.' Dickinson had been asked to speak on the subject of 'Youth', but, using as a wry excuse that 'old age was second childhood', he spoke instead on old age and death.

'It wasn't intended as a farewell party,' said a member who was present, 'but it soon became clear to most of us that this was probably the last occasion on which we should see 'Goldie'. He wandered on and on when he spoke, sometimes as though he wasn't with us at all. A year later he was dead.'

The others who joined the Society in this period were Julian Bell, son of Clive Bell (who had never been an Apostle); Francis Crusoe, Anthony Blunt and Henry John Bevin Lintott. The last-named left Cambridge in 1932 to enter the Customs and Excise Department, eventually joining the Board of Trade, in which he served from 1935-45. After a spell as Deputy Secretary-General on the OEEC, he was knighted in 1957 and became first Deputy Under-Secretary of State the Commonwealth Relations Office and then British High Commissioner in Canada from 1963-68.

Up to about the end of 1930 the Society steered a relatively even course between what had become orthodox in the twentieth century and *avant garde* views of the late 1920s. There was a desire to investigate Marxist theories and concepts, but this impetus came from outside the Apostles rather than from within it at this stage.

Outside the Society there was widespread evidence of a leftward-cult which extended from serious support for socialism on the one hand to a commitment to a ritualistic Marxism at the other extreme. In the late 'twenties and early 'thirties this whole subject of 'how far left do we go?' was viewed fairly objectively by Society members. But, as first fascism, then nazism, progressed in Europe, so there was a closing of the ranks and a marked switch to the far left in political sympathies. Reality – the art of the practical in politics – was lost sight of in seeking ideological re-alignments. Instead of concentrating on the greater, or if one likes, the greatest evil, nazism, and isolating, or at least quarantining that political cancer, the error was made of attacking all authoritarian or nationalistic movements, thus driving them to seek alliances with Hitler.

Any deviation from this policy, any attempt to isolate Nazi Germany from such possible allies was denounced as appeasement. Yet, the real appeasement was conducted by those who failed to win friends among the moderate authoritarians and at the same time did nothing militarily to check the Nazis. That some of the so-called totalitarian countries had conquered unemployment, had established law and order and that Mussolini, for instance, had crushed the Mafia and brought stability and sound town planning to Libya were things which the intellectuals, with few exceptions, had totally failed to study.

The Apostles were not some kind of secret weapon of the Kremlin, or a subversive organisation. It would not even be right to say that the Society was infiltrated. The fact that a number of its members allowed themselves to become either deliberately conscious agents of the USSR, or to find themselves duped into serving the Soviet Union, was due in no small measure to the anti-Establishment traditions of the Apostles. It all began in the last century with the Society's desire to undermine the dominating position of the Church of England in university life. After that it was a question of finding an alternative *bête noire* to the Church of England. Imperialism, militarism and authoritarianism became the new targets, and out of this developed an illogical devotion to the Soviet Union which was in its whole political system imperialistic, militaristic and dictatorial.

But the influences which brought this about among some of the Apostles were outside rather than inside the Society. The most vehement and open supporters of the Soviet Union in Cambridge at this time were not members of the Apostles – men like J. D. Bernal, Maurice Dobb, James Klugmann, Patrick Blackett, J. G. Crowther and the socialist scientist Joseph Needham. These were the men who encouraged the Russians to start paying special attention to Cambridge and caused such recruiters for the Soviet cause as Meyer Trilisser, N. I. Bukharin and Samuel Cahn to enlist the aid of some Apostles. Cahn, the resident director of Soviet intelligence in Britain, played a leading role in first studying and then recruiting members of the Society.

It was among the scientist dons that pro-Soviet propaganda was most marked in this period. Those who lent close support to the National Association of Scientific Workers included Blackett, Crowther and Needham. Long before the 'thirties this had produced results beneficial to the Soviet cause. The physicist Crowther, chief of all fellow-travelling British scientists, had made seven trips to Russia in as many years, and, as a result, became one of the leading exponents of the USSR as being the embodiment of scientific progress. Crowther even went so far as to assert the super-high-power and high pressure steam turbines could only be used effectively under a communist system of production.

Joseph Needham was an altogether different figure, though in his way perhaps equally as valuable to the Soviet cause as the more extravagantly pro-Russian Crowther. Made a Fellow of Gonville and Caius in 1924, he was also a university demonstrator in bio-chemistry from 1928-33, with intermittent spells as a lecturer at Stanford, Yale and Cornell universities in the USA. Needham was that very dangerous combination – a scientist and a Christian Marxist – and he had been considerably influenced in his religious attitudes by the communist vicar of Thaxted in Essex, Conrad Noel. However, his talents as a scientist and his capacity for working long hours at a stretch lent added value to his pronouncements, especially among the younger scientists. His otherwise brilliant mind became intellectually curdled when he expressed opinions on political or aesthetic subjects. There was one essay of his, published in 1932, in which he discussed nude bathing and religion – 'a classless society of unascetic, uninhibited men and women in equal comradeship . . . would be in a sense a dialectical synthesis of the Greek and Christian ethos.' When addressing the Modern Churchmen's Union in 1937, when the Stalinist terror was at its fiercest, he blandly declared: 'the conception of the utmost cultural autonomy for different peoples, side by side with economic union, is a grand one and we owe it largely to the genius of no other than Joseph Vissarionovich Stalin.'

Of course, very many Cambridge scientists took totally different views, but it was the noisy and politically controversial minority who managed to make an impression on students, very much the same as was the case in the sphere of English, history and the arts generally. It would be totally wrong to suggest that the Apostles had gradually turned subversive, or pro-communist. Several contemporary members of the Society from Maynard Keynes downwards were strongly opposed to such trends. But, suddenly, in their usual investigative and inquiring style members came to equate Marxism and intellectualism and decided that therefore this was a subject for serious debate. The clue to this, of course, lay with the dictum shared both by Karl Marx and Lenin that modern communism was an intellectual creed, because there could be 'no revolutionary practice without revolutionary theory.'

In Society meetings in this period papers read were 'discussed rather than debated,' according to Michael Straight. 'The form in general was that a member would read a paper (which would go into the Ark, a procedure I never witnessed). It would then be discussed by all present. Keynes was plainly the intellectual leader and the most active senior member of the Society. He enjoyed all forms of intellectual exchange provided they were conducted with clarity and precision. His attitude toward the student radicals has been summarised by himself. His term 'amateur communists' seems to me now to be exact. That is, he regarded the commitment as shallow and transitory, an expression of a more enduring need, and as such, one to be accepted and understood, rather than as a permanent alignment with a hostile regime.'[1]

Another powerful, if restrained, critic of the ultra-radicals of these years was the late Sir Dennis Robertson. His interventions in discussions were always to the point, whether in combating pro-Soviet views, or even the occasional economic extravaganzas of Keynes. Robertson had come to Trinity from Eton and won the Chancellor's Medal for English Verse. He served in the 1914-18 War and returned to Cambridge in 1919, becoming a Fellow of Trinity and taking a keen interest in theatrical activities.

As a lecturer in economics he was very much opposed to the idea of reducing economics to mathematics and insisted that he himself was a 'literary economist'. His text-book, *Money*, published in 1932, included a number of quotations from *Alice in Wonderland*. For a time Robertson worked with Keynes, but gradually he came to the conclusions that Keynesian economics carried to the limit could be disastrous. Indeed, when he left Cambridge and went to London University he expressed the view that the Keynesian system was in effect 'no less rigid than that from which it was, or conceived itself to be, in revolt.'[2]

Sir Dennis Proctor left Cambridge to take up a post at the Ministry of Health. For a short while he was assistant private secretary to Stanley Baldwin, then a key man in the National Government. This led to his appointment as principal private secretary to Sir Kingsley Wood, wartime Chancellor of the Exchequer. At the same time he was a member of the American Philosophical Society.

Dennis Proctor and Alister Watson, two key members in the late 'twenties, were totally different types and from different backgrounds. Proctor, an arts man, went to King's from Harrow, and his interests remained in the field of arts despite his spell at the Treasury. Watson was a brilliant scientist who was to play a vital role during World War II first in the experimental department of the Admiralty Signal School, then in the naval radar establishment. Sir Dennis later became a trustee of the Tate Gallery, the editor of Lowes Dickinson's unpublished papers and an author in his own right with two books published during his retirement in the Vaucluse area of France. His interest in this region led directly to these works – *Hannibal's March in History* and *The Experience of Thucydides*.

Sir Dennis was a link with the Apostles' past, while Watson was an even more vital link with their future. As Sir Dennis said of his work on Hannibal's march, 'there is no new knowledge in this book, only some new thought on old data.' He also shed some new light on Maynard Keynes, providing the interesting theory, which many would dispute, that Keynes was at heart a man of humility. He spoke of Keynes's 'humility' in dealing with his junior colleagues, which may have applied to the younger Apostles, but he hastens to add 'maddening and exceedingly troublesome though he could also be.'[3]

Alister Watson not only contributed some nineteen papers to the Society – a high figure by any standards – but he was in two separate periods of office secretary of the Apostles. His nineteen papers compare well with Sheppard's and Braithwaite's eighteen each, and, as far as can be told, beaten only by G. E. Moore's twenty-five papers. Watson was a member of the Communist Party and, through the Apostles, a friend of Anthony Blunt. He was one student scientist who had been won over to the cause of international communism by the scientific dons who supported the Soviet Union. He became a Fellow of King's and, as such, continued to be an active member of the Society throughout the 1930s. Watson was one of the first to detect the incomparable genius of Alan Turing when the latter was awarded a scholarship to King's from Sherborne. The two men met for the first time in the Botanical Gardens at Cambridge, and Watson was fascinated by Turing's imaginative projection of the computer machine of the future, by which he pushed to its ultimate destination the calculating machine which Charles Babbage had first suggested in the earlier years of the previous century at Trinity.

However, the key man in attempting to use the Society for subversive aims in this latter part of the 1920s was Anthony Blunt who came to Trinity on a scholarship from Marlborough. The son of a Church of England clergyman, related to the present Queen Mother through his own mother, Hilda Violet Masters (before she married), Blunt, with his passion for the artistic world, would seem an improbable recruit for the Marxist cause. At Marlborough he had shown no interest in politics, but had actually founded his own society to discuss cubism. Louis MacNeice, the poet, who was Blunt's friend at Marlborough, said of him: 'Anthony had a flair for bigotry; every day he blackballed another musician; he despised Tennyson, Shakespeare, the Italian High Renaissance and Praxiteles, was all in favour of the Primitives, of Ucello, of the Byzantine mosaics . . .'[4]

Thus Blunt, despite his paranoid dislike of an earlier Apostle, Tennyson, once the hero of the Society, became a member of that élite group. Everything was in his favour: an acutely well-tuned and tough mind, tall, drooping, with his cold blue eyes and his half-amused, half-pouting personality ('it was the only way to describe Anthony,' said one of his contemporaries at Cambridge), he could boast of having a friendship with the late Duke of Kent and acquaintanceships with other important figures in the world outside of Cambridge. There is no evidence that he was recruited to the communist cause through the scientific network at Cambridge. From what one knows of him, he would have been contemptuous of their puerile expressions of Marxism. He saw that creed from a totally different viewpoint which had more in common with certain theorists in the artistic world than in either politics or science.

The great strength of Anthony Blunt as a recruiter to the cause of the USSR was that he was so fastidious, so aesthetic, so unpuritanically witty and charming that he never seemed to be what he was. Or, to put it another way, to those who had doubts about him, he was able to be completely disarming. In the autumn of 1928 Blunt founded an *avant-garde* magazine named *Venture*, introducing such left-wing writers as John Lehmann, Julian Bell and Louis MacNeice as contributors. By this time he was a confirmed supporter of international communism, though he was not known to have joined the Communist Party. During the 1930s Cecil Day Lewis (later to be made Poet Laureate) edited a collection of left-wing essays, entitled *Mind in Chains*, to which Anthony Blunt (later to be Keeper of the Soveriegn's Pictures) quoted approvingly Lenin's statement to Clara Zetkin that 'every artist . . . has a right to create freely according to his ideals, independent of anything. Only, of course, we communists cannot stand with our hands folded and let chaos develop in any direction it may. We must guide this process according to a plan and form its results.'

There can be no question but that Blunt was an increasingly powerful influence within the Society from his joining it until almost a quarter of a century afterwards. In 1932, after two years as a research student, he was made a Fellow of Trinity, largely because of a thesis concerned with Poussin. He remained at Trinity for eleven years, and therein lay his chances for recruiting new members of the Society to the communist cause. Not that he recruited more than a few, but those few wrought considerable harm in totality, if not individually. Yet throughout the whole of this period he was able to deceive many fellow members of the Society as to just how pro-Soviet he was.

A Crowther, a Needham could not have achieved such success in winning recruits. They would soon have been spotted. Lord Rothschild, who got to know Blunt about a year after he went to Trinity, states that 'Blunt seemed to me a somewhat cold and aesthetic figure, but with a sense of humour. He was an excellent conversationalist and a habitual party-goer . . . I remember, very vaguely, once thinking that an article about porcelain in the *Spectator* or *New Statesman* – I forget which – dragged in Marxism in a way I thought unnecessary and irrelevant.'[5]

So that was the way in which Blunt tried to win friends, never by doctrinal teaching, but much more by sheer charm, wit or, in some circumstances, homosexual seduction. Blunt himself put is somewhat differently. 'I became a communist, and more particularly a Marxist in, let us say, 1935-36. [Objective investigation would suggest it was much earlier.] The origin of it . . . I had a sabbatical year leave from Cambridge in 1933-4, and when I came back in October, 1934, I found that all my friends – that is an enormous amount of my friends and almost all the intellectual and bright young undergraduates who had come up to Cambridge – had suddenly become Marxists under the impact of Hitler coming to power and there was this very powerful group, very remarkable group of Communist intellectuals in Cambridge of which Guy Burgess was one, James Klugmann was another, John Cornford was another. It was a very remarkable group of enthusiasts, naive if you like, highly enthusiastic and highly intelligent, and of these the person I knew best, whom I already knew very well, was Guy Burgess. He had become a totally convinced Marxist and an open member of the Communist Party.'[6]

How many Blunt himself recruited to work for the Soviet cause is still a matter of conjecture. When he was questioned in 1979 by a team of journalists, he undoubtedly kept quiet on a number of matters. But subsequent articles in the press prompted him to reply in some detail and so it was that in November, 1981, he wrote: 'As far as I know there were no members of "the ring" beyond the three who had gone to Russia [Burgess, Philby and Maclean], Cairncross who had confessed in 1951, Straight who had named himself, and Long, whom Straight had named and whose recruitment I admitted.'[7]

This was almost certainly not the full picture, but it at least confirmed what many other people had claimed to be the truth. Yet not only is the verbal picture Blunt gave incomplete, it is also in some instances misleading and unfair, not least to the Apostles. For this reason it is important to spell out some of those facts which Blunt omitted, especially those relating to the Society. Of those he named, he himself, Guy Burgess, Leo Long and Michael Straight were members of the Society. Other Apostles who to a varying extent were either committed to the Soviet cause in some way or other, or were in favour of an anti-fascist front which included communists, he does not name. That was fair enough in that nobody else among these members had been positively confirmed as having betrayed any official secrets to the Russians, though a number of them had been interviewed by the Security Services and one or two had admitted that they might unwittingly have passed some information on to Blunt or others.

By his statement that he found 'an enormous amount of my friends and almost all the intellectuals and bright young undergraduates who had come up to Cambridge had suddenly become Marxists', Blunt played right into the hands of those who have asserted that the Apostles had developed into a subversive organisation. 'Communism and its merits' may have been touched upon in some papers read to the Society, but it would be wrong to suggest that, except for the few, support for communism was strong among students generally prior to 1931. Many Cambridge men of this era have echoed the view of Sir Jack Longland, who was at the university at this time, though not a member of the Society. He says 'My own lot, 1923-29, were in general a carefree, unpolitical and fairly uninteresting collection. I learnt to take politics seriously much later.'[8]

The real answer to all this is, not as Blunt suggests – an overwhelming support for communism and the USSR – but that a few activists by sheer audacity, determination and loud talking gave a minority much publicity and encouragement. More devious supporters kept silent about their activities. Blunt refers to Guy Burgess as though he was not only a convinced Marxist, but 'an open member of the Communist Party'. He omits the fact that at one period in the 1930s Burgess gave a very firm impression that he was pro-fascist and anti-communist as a cover for his secret work on behalf of the Soviet Union. At the same time he completely obscures the fact that his own attitude was ambivalent in the 1930s and that, apart from taking what seemed a somewhat trendy interest in applying Marxism to art, he deceived a number of his fellow Apostles and others in Cambridge by hiding from them his subversive plans. Certainly he gave no impression of being a communist. He sometimes flaunted his associations with members of the Royal Family, notably the Duke of Kent, whom he got to know in the days when his father was chaplain at the British Embassy in Paris. T. E. B. Howarth, one time senior tutor at Magdalene College, who was an undergraduate from 1933 to 1937, recalls Blunt as an unendearing personality – 'a cold fish, a snob, aloof.'[9] Lord Rothschild, who was a member of the Society in this period, has stated that when he was told by the authorities several years later that 'a former close friend of mine had confessed to having been a Soviet agent for many years, I found it hard to believe.'[10]

Then again, in his 1981 statement to the *Sunday Times*, Blunt tersely refers to 'Straight who had named himself, and Long whom Straight had named'. There was no reference to the fact that he had himself recruited both Straight and Long and persistently put pressure on them to aid the Soviet Union. This was certainly a departure from the E. M. Forster code of betraying one's country rather than one's friends, however repellent that might be to some people.

Michael Straight became a member in the latter part of the 1930s, so his part in the Society belongs to the future chapter. An American, filled with idealistic hopes for the future, he had come to Cambridge along with his brother, Whitney Straight, the motor-racing driver, after his mother had married Elmhirst, the creator of that *avant garde* school, Dartington Hall. Straight had committed himself to progressive left-wing views partly because he had felt inhibited by his family's wealth. He had visited Moscow and was quite open about his opinion, thus making himself an obvious target for the wiles of Blunt.

To put Blunt's statement in its proper perspective, it is essential in all fairness to Straight to give his own version of the subject to which Blunt refers. 'Burgess had been a member of the communist cell at Trinity,' wrote Michael Straight. He went on to say that Burgess broke with his communist friends in 1934 and worked with 'a Captain Jack Macnamara, a right-wing MP who had close ties with the Nazis . . . Guy would joke about the homosexual encounters he had taken part in with Macnamara and his Nazi friends. In his guise as Macnamara's secretary, Guy pointed to fascism as the 'wave of the future'. *He voiced such opinions in the meetings of the Apostles.*'[11]

The italics in the last sentence are mine, not Straight's, but they do perhaps underline how in this era friend deceived friend and later in a few cases how friend betrayed friend. Some Apostles in one way or another were fulfilling the role of Judas Iscariot. Then, on the subject of Straight having 'named himself' and others: he does not deny having named Blunt and Leo Long as pro-Soviet agents, but refuses any suggestion that he named Alister Watson. Various attempts were made to persuade Michael Straight to give information to Soviet agents – not official secrets, let it be made clear – but these were declined. Then in 1963, when asked by President Kennedy to be chairman of the National Council for the Arts, he told Robert Kennedy, the President's brother and Attorney-General in the administration, that he had been recruited for the Soviet cause by Anthony Blunt, even though he had not acted upon this. Having passed this information on to the FBI, who told MI 5, the British counter-intelligence organisation were given their first hard evidence against the Keeper of the Queen's Pictures.

The point that should be stressed here is that Michael Straight had been offered a post by the President and he did not wish to take this without warning the powers-that-be that he could be vulnerable if questions were asked. Apart from all this, though ardently in the forefront of those opposing fascism and Nazism, he had long since been convinced of the perfidy of the Soviet Union whatever his youthful optimism might have suggested. As to Leo Long and John Cornford, the former belongs to a future chapter and the latter was not an Apostle.

Up to about 1930 it was a question of investigating Marxism as a creed and a philosophy among some Society members. Only after that date did two, possibly three of the Marxist Apostles embark on attempting actively to recruit fellow members to the Soviet cause. It was very skilfully done and applied only to those likeliest to comply, and occasionally homosexual seduction was a technique employed. 'Helping the cause of international democracy' was often the ploy, or in some cases the plea that to help Russia was one way of keeping the peace. Britain was still enjoying peace, Nazi Germany was beginning to be a menace and a German-Soviet Pact something totally unimaginable to the intellectuals. To give a balanced picture, however, it is important once again to cite Keynes, who was forever hammering home to the Apostles his loathing for Puritanism and his belief that the British had a puritanical urge to adopt unpleasant solutions to their problems. 'When Cambridge undergraduates take their inevitable trip to Bolshiedom, are they disillusioned when they find it all dreadfully uncomfortable? Of course not. That is what they are looking for,' he wrote in 1934.[12]

At one meeting of the Society in a somewhat heated debate Keynes denounced Marxist economics as 'an insult to our intelligence.' Not that this deterred those who were stubbornly determined to enjoy their Marxist dreams. E. M. Forster may have propounded the need for developed hearts, but he allowed himself to be lured to support the undeveloped minds of communism when he was an Apostolic delegate to Willi Muenzenberg's International Congress of Writers for the Defence of Culture in 1935. Muenzenberg was a tremendous influence on the young and literary circles generally in those years.

# 11

# ANOTHER SPANISH ADVENTURE

'I have never seen a more sublime demonstration of the totalitarian mind which might be likened unto a system of gears where teeth have been filed off at random. Such a snaggle-toothed thought machine, driven by a standard or even a sub-standard title, whirls with the jerky, noisy, gaudy pointlessness of a cuckoo clock in Hell'

(Kurt Vonnegut, Jr.)

It was unquestionably the Spanish Civil War which provoked the most passionate, vehement and extremist elements of communism at Cambridge in the 1930s and, while there was undoubtedly a stolid support for the Republican side among the working class and trade unionists of Britain, this was muted and apathetic compared to the loudly enthusiastic backing of the intellectuals. There were a few evil and unscrupulous opportunists among the Civil War campaigners, but very many more were mistaken yet honest and compassionate.

All this must be seen against the steady rise of communist, or Popular Front, mythology in the universities since the early 'thirties. Much of this thinking was idealistic: it reflected a deep mistrust of the Establishment and politicians generally. What is more a number of those who joined up and fought on the Republican side and died were far from being bigoted communists. Perhaps their contribution was to show that pacifism did not work, that there came a time when one needed not only to stand up and be counted, but to fight as well.

Julian Bell was perhaps the epitome of the idealists of this era. Not only the epitome, but the standard-bearer, the committed soldier of the cause. An Apostle and also a poet, he never – at least not openly – became a communist. In 1925, together with David Haden-Guest, he used his car as a battering-ram against members of the Jesus College club who had been pelting anti-war marchers with rotten eggs and fruit. It has been suggested by some of his friends – notably Raymond Mortimer – that Bell 'always detested communism', and it is true that, unlike the average dedicated communist, Bell was jovial, slapdash and eager in the use of his reason to seek the truth.

Bell seems to have reacted instinctively against his education at that Quaker establishment, Leighton Park, taking an impish interest in war as an art. He went to King's where, from all accounts, he spent as much time falling in and out of love as in political activities and writing poetry. But in December, 1933, he wrote a letter to the *New Statesman*, which was to become for many people a testament for the future: 'In the Cambridge that I first knew in 1929 and 1930 the central subject of ordinary intelligent conversation was poetry [he could only have been speaking of his own circle at the university] . . . By the end of 1933 we have arrived at a situation in which almost the only subject of discussion is contemporary politics, and in which a very large majority of the more intelligent undergraduates are Communists or almost Communists . . . It would be difficult to find anyone of any intellectual pretensions who would not accept the general Marxist analysis of the present crisis.'

Julian Bell (elected 1928) beagled seven days a fortnight all winter. In 1929 he wrote that 'the most important event in my Cambridge life was being elected to the Apostles; this happened to me in my second year . . . The whole period was one of great expansion and a feeling of richness and possibilities in the world . . . The core of this was the Apostles – my first meeting – was terrifically impressive. I really felt I had reached the pinnacle of Cambridge intellectualism. Since then almost all my male friends have been drawn from the Society, and in general it has played a more important part in my life than any other institution.'[1]

Both he and John Cornford, were from an early date in the vanguard of activist movements against fascism. Cornford, a Trinity historian, the son of F. M. Cornford, a Fellow of Trinity, had become a charismatic figure for many left-wing students. His love of poetry was inherited from his mother, herself a poet and a one-time friend of Rupert Brooke. He was an overt communist and certainly the ablest of communist party organisers at Cambridge in this era. But his communist faith was leavened by a streak of pessimism about the future. In raising the Socialist Society at Cambridge from a membership of 200 to 600 and ensuring that it was dominated by the Marxists he showed great professionalism. He once told of 'waiting on Parker's Piece with a body of followers ready to deal with an expected Fascist descent one summer when Mosley's vans were making frequent appearances.'[2]

Meanwhile Julian Bell transformed his beaten-up Morris car into a military vehicle. The 'armour' of his car was mattresses, and his navigator was Guy Burgess. They made charges at 'the enemy' (mainly hearties who were against the anti-war demonstration of Bell and his friends on Armistice Day).

After Cambridge, Bell spent a year and a half teaching in the Wuhan

University in China. When the Spanish Civil War broke out, he returned post haste to England, determined to join the International Brigade in Spain. He reminded his Cambridge friends that he had always wanted to take part in a war. His pacifist-minded parents called on Guy Burgess to try to dissuade Julian from going to Spain. According to Burgess, a compromise was reached and instead of fighting with the International Brigade, Bell drove an ambulance, but was killed just the same.

It would seem that the majority of the active Apostles at that time (excluding some of the 'Angels' and those who only occasionally took part in the Society's business) were ardently on the side of the Spanish Republicans against the Franco forces. Michael Straight was president of the Socialist Club at Cambridge and helped to raise money for the Spanish Loyalists. On a brief visit back to Cambridge from the Spanish Civil War Julian Bell attended a meeting of the Apostles and read a paper praising the military virtues and identifying 'the soldier as his new ideal.' This meeting marked Bell's total break with the pacifism of his parents and those who belonged to the Bloomsbury Circle.

'I was shaken by what he said,' wrote Michael Straight, '. . . when it came to my turn to speak, I attacked Julian's paper, saying that the war in Spain called not for the soldier's detachment, but for the intellectual and emotional commitment of the partisan.'[3]

Bell was killed in the battle for Brunette.

This was a period of acute economic crisis right around the world, from which recovery was being made all too slowly. It had started with the Wall Street crash in the autumn of 1929 and banks shutting down all over the USA. All this had accentuated the extremist views of many at Cambridge at that time. Just how much extremism had triumphed over careful consideration of all the issues can be judged from John Cornford's outrageousness when he talked gleefully of the machine-gunning of 5,000 counter-revolutionary prisoners by the Bolsheviks during the Russian Civil War, and wrote blatantly propagandist verse about raising 'the Red Flag triumphantly for communism and liberty.' Cornford was killed in Spain on 28 December, 1936, the day after his twenty-first birthday.

Bell and Cornford were but two of a number of Cambridge men who took part in the Spanish Civil War. Trinity provided a strong contingent of volunteers for this conflict. Apart from Bell and Cornford there were Sir Richard Rees, ann Old Etonian baronet, and Malcolm Dunbar, who became chief of staff with the International Brigade. Rees, a close friend of George Orwell, had been an honorary attaché at the British Embassy in Berlin in 1922. He left to join the Cambridge University Press the followng year and was honorary treasurer and lecturer to the Workers'

Educational Association London District from 1925-27. In the Spanish Civil War he was an ambulance driver with Julian Bell. Rees, like Orwell, was greatly disillusioned by what he saw in Spain. He served in the RNVR in World War II and won the *Croix de Guerre*.

While Cornford was a poet and even in a mild way a romantic poet as is portrayed in his simple but unflamboyant love poems sent to his girl friend, Margot Heinemann, Julian Bell had that Apostolic mistrust of romantic poetry, which he described as 'a natural product of emotionalism and confused thinking'. F. L. Lucas wrote an obituary of Julian Bell in which he recalled him as one who 'right, or wrong, could think for himself, and, as time showed, act on it.' Then came Lucas's final appraisal of this tragic young man who had shown so much promise: 'He never let himself be rammed into a Marxist pigeon-hole. He was too vital and intelligent . . . He was a citizen of the future, in a world of blind newts that cannot look beyond the next frontier, the next dividend, or the next dog-race.'[4]

If Bell was the heroic activist of the Society in this period, Burgess and Blunt and one or two others remained the silent conspirators. All this was, of course, done outside the Society, but the all-powerful link of comradeship through membership was exploited whenever possible. What was sinister was the manner in which some of the people recruited to 'the cause', or 'our friends', as Burgess and Blunt would put it, were either told what jobs to take up, or were manipulated into them. This happened on a number of occasions, and, generally speaking, the instructions were to enter one or other of the key ministries such as the Foreign Office, Treasury and Home Office. Financial and economic espionage was at that time valued more than anything else. Michael Straight, for example, who had considered becoming a British subject, as his mother lived in the United Kingdom, was urged by Blunt to go back to the United States and supply just this kind of financial information – i.e. legitimate straightforward economic intelligence.

Guy Francis de Moncy Burgess was the son of a naval officer who had determined his son must follow in his footsteps and thus entered him for Dartmouth, the naval training establishment for cadets. Defective vision ended what had promised to be a successful naval career and Burgess left Dartmouth to finish his education at Eton, from whence he won a scholarship in history to Trinity. He was a great charmer who even had a knack of making himself agreeable to those who were his natural enemies. He had friends and acquaintances in all walks of life and he did not allow membership of the Apostles to keep him from mixing with many unApostolic types. Nor did his flirtations with communism and his communist friends stop him from becoming, apparently without anyone questioning his motives, a member of the right-wing Pitt Club at

Cambridge. It was Anthony Blunt who introduced Burgess to the Apostles.

Both Blunt and Burgess sought out new recruits for support of 'the cause' and attempted to plan their future careers. Burgess's technique and his ideal cover for many of his activities was his outrageousness: nobody knew whether to believe him when he made his extraordinary boasts. A man who claimed to be a communist one moment and a fascist the next could not easily be taken seriously. Burgess reminds one of the advice given by the President of the Central Anarchist Council in G. K. Chesterton's spy story, *The Man Who Was Thursday*: 'You want a safe disguise, do you? You want a dress which will guarantee you harmless, a dress in which no one would ever look for a bomb? Why then, dress up as an *anarchist*, you fool! Nobody will ever expect you to do anything dangerous then.' Not that Burgess ever dressed as an anarchist: his chatter was his best disguise. Nonetheless, he was a supremely brilliant talker and in many ways an original and serious historian.

Blunt, on the other hand, made discretion his policy and kept his Marxism under wraps by applying it solely – or so it seemed to some – to artistic questions. But there can be no doubt that he used the world of art as a means of expressing in code what he felt about politics. Thus when he went to Paris in 1937 to see Pablo Picasso's *Guernica*, he afterwards dismissed it in an article in the *Spectator* as 'a private brain-storm which gives no evidence that Picasso had realised the political significance of Guernica.' It is true that Blunt's enthusiasm for Soviet painting and left-wing literature had influenced him more than Marxist dogma. So it was with his criticism of Picasso: art must not just capture certain ideas and express them in an abstract form, but it must escape from its own abstract dreams.

Here one gets very close to some of the more debatable aspects of Wittgenstein's philosophy – Spartastistic, stoical, ascetic. Not that Blunt was ascetic in his mode of life. This attitude occasionally reflected itself in the discussions of the Society. 'Are dreams enough?' was one subject debated, and it was left to Blunt to demand the alternative of the new 'new realism.'

'He wanted us to forget Matisse and Manet as bogus, and to turn to the New Realism of the Mexico School of modern artists such as Orozco and Rivera. Yet we sometimes wondered why, if all this was true, he so adored Poussin. Of course, he always had an answer, but it was the kind of answer that seemed to elude the very truth he insisted was essential. It was too subtle for most of us. The idea that Poussin was the perfect Marxist artist was a little hard to swallow. Not that Anthony put it that way, yet the implication was there. One had the feeling he wanted to have the best of both lives – that of the dispassionate Marxist intellectual and the future Master of the Sovereign's Picture's.'

It was not only the students who became militant in the mid-thirties. Some of the elder pacifists among the Old Brigade changed their minds. Even Bertrand Russell said that 'Hitler's Germany was a different matter. I found the Nazis utterly revolting – cruel, bigoted and stupid. Morally and intellectually they were odious. Although I clung to my pacifist convictions, I did so with increasing difficulty . . . at last, consciously and definitely, I decided that I must support what was necessary for victory in the Second World War, however difficult victory might be to achieve.'[5]

Inevitably, with such flamboyant characters as Bell and Burgess, the Apostles were bound to attract some unwelcome attention to themselves in this period. They were not as secretive as they became at a later date as far as the world outside the Society was concerned. Reproduced in this book is a photograph of a group of Apostles taken by the local photographic firm of Ramsey and Muspratt (now Peter Lofts), which was started by Mrs Lettice Ramsey, widow of Frank. Nevertheless, secrecy was still the general rule. Sometimes outsiders invented ridiculous stories about the Apostles. Hugh Sykes Davies was once asked: 'Is it true that at your Saturday meetings the youngest member is stripped, made to lie face down on the floor and you use his back and buttocks as a table?' 'No,' he replied, tongue in cheek, 'we place him face upwards and he balances the main dish on his penis. Tell your friends to think up rather a better story next time.'

The above story shows just how sophisticated, humorous and blasé about the outside world members of the 1930s were. They could even joke about themselves, or, as one of their wits put it to me: 'entry to the Society was much more likely to be through the Homintern than the Comintern. Most preferred Sodom to Moscow and Gomorrah to Leningrad.'

Not strictly true, of course, but hyperbole made the point.

The idealism of those passionately committed activists from Cambridge in their support of Spanish republicanism was ruthlessly crushed in a later period of that war when the Soviet Union sought to impose its own terms on the Republicans, which meant destroying all those, especially POUM, a dissident Marxist party which was not totally committed to the cause of communism. So it was that in the 1930s the Apostles – or at least some of them – re-enacted the tragedy of the 1830s in Spain. It must be said that their determination, commitment and idealism were much more marked in the 1930s, but, despite this, once

117

again the result went against them.

Significantly, the more subversive members of the Society stayed outside this conflict. Blunt dedicated himself to the world of art, and Guy Burgess, who had taken a first in history and was tempted to become a don, as well as setting himself up as a financial adviser, turned instead to the BBC. Sir George Trevelyan, one of the 'Angels' and Regius Professor of Modern History at Cambridge from 1927-40, was persistent in urging the services of Burgess to a number of people, though not always successfully. He did his utmost to get Burgess made a Fellow of Pembroke, but failed. Unavailingly, too, he pulled strings on his behalf with one or two Ministries in Whitehall. When eventually Burgess got his job with the BBC, it was a telephone call from Trevelyan to the Director-General which clinched the appointment.

So Burgess joined the BBC Talks Department during the Spanish Civil War and soon made his influence felt both in choice of speakers and topics. It was not until 1932 that the Courtauld Institute had provided the first faculty for teaching the history of art in England and so paved the way for a memorable career for Anthony Blunt. He joined the staff of the Warburg Institute in London in 1937 and eventually became deputy director of the Courtauld Institute of Art.

An interesting aside on this period is that, certainly among a number of Apostles, the ancient hatred of Cambridge for all things and all people Oxonian and *vice versa* disappeared. This was particularly marked among the pro-communist faction. Some of these members of the Society set out to win allies in Oxford, sometimes in an effort to lure them into supporting what was at first vaguely referred to as 'the cause', but which, upon a firmer acquaintanceship, sometimes years later, clearly involved an invitation to provide worthwhile intelligence to the Soviet Union.

Cyril Connolly, a Brackenbury Scholar who had been at Balliol, was friendly with Guy Burgess. They had both been at Eton and Connolly had become a contributor to the *New Statesman*. 'To this generation communism made an intellectual appeal, standing for love, liberty and social justice, or for a new approach to life and art,' said Connolly in reference to Burgess.[6] It is quite incredible how naive some of these supposedly intelligent graduates could be: communism might have an intellectual appeal of a kind, but to assert that even at that time it could stand for 'love, liberty and social justice', was really another example of thinking in blinkers. Yet during the Spanish Civil War when Burgess was at the BBC, Connolly said that he 'seemed to have become a Fascist.' Later, however, in January, 1941, when Burgess was in the BBC propaganda department covering Europe, Connolly wrote: 'His position became one that greatly appealed to him, involving him eventually in

118

y Burgess

Michael Straight

Victor Rothschild, cricke[
and scientist

Wilfred Noyce, author a[
mountaineer

liaison work with the most secret organisations, until he was able to represent the Foreign Office'.

Then again Burgess was also a close friend of an Oxonian communist named Derek Blaikie, who was killed in World War II. They visited Moscow together in 1934. Blaikie was the author of a pamphlet which was a Marxist analysis of the modern literary scene, competent enough to attract a notice from Desmond MacCarthy. The influence of this 'Angel' had lasted for many years and it was still apparent in the 1930s, with MacCarthy often siding with the young left-wingers among the Apostles. There was rather more literary back-scratching in those days than now, unbelievable though this may seem, with Desmond MacCarthy writing to Bertrand Russell in 1937 to say that he was 'relieved that you thought my review likely to whet the public appetite: that is what I tried to do . . . I went to Trinity Commem. and dined in Hall Sunday night. I found the review was working there. What I am pleased is that I got G. M. Young to write about it in the *Observer*. He wanted to write about it in the *S.T.* [Sunday Times] & I got him, by grabbing the book from him, to offer his comments to Garvin.'[8]

MacCarthy, too, kept up friendly relations with people at Oxford University, though there was nothing whatsoever political in this. Much more positively political were Burgess's attempts at winning friends at Oxford. Apart from Derek Blaikie, he was on close terms with the late Morgan Goronwy Rees, who had become a Fellow of All Souls. Goronwy Rees stated that one day well before World War II Burgess told him: 'I am a Comintern agent and have been one ever since I came down from Cambridge.'[9]

Burgess added that, during his visit to Moscow with Blaikie, he was recruited as a Soviet agent 'at a long secret interview with Nikolai Bukharin.' Tom Driberg in his book about Burgess, based on long talks with the latter in Moscow in 1956, tried to refute this suggestion, saying that 'Bukharin did not, in fact, hold any important official position at that time, with the Comintern or any other organisation, and Guy did not meet him . . . as it was, all the meetings with Communists that Guy had in Moscow arose from introductions given by Rees to Blaikie and most of these introductions had in turn been obtained by Rees from Mr David Astor, whose mother, Nancy, Lady Astor, had visited Russia with George Bernard Shaw in 1931.'[10]

This appears to have been an attempt on Driberg's part to underline what he calls 'the respectability of the auspices under which Guy went to Russia,' but it could also have been an attempt to obliterate any links which Burgess may have had with Bukharin, who was liquidated in the Stalinist purges of the late 'thirties. For Driberg was quite wrong to suggest that Bukharin did not hold any important official position at that time, as he was not only a leading figure in the Comintern and a member of the Politburo, but a known recruiter of British talent. Apart from this he had been one of the leading lights on the Anglo-Russian Committee in the 1920s.

It was Burgess who told Goronwy Rees that Anthony Blunt was also an agent of the Soviet Union.

'We were not then at war, the Nazi – Soviet Pact had not been signed and I did not pay too much attention to what Guy said, knowing full well how he loved to exaggerate and to shock. I am sure it was an early attempt to sound me out, but it was only long afterwards that the truth dawned on me,' said Goronwy.'[11]

Mr Sean Day Lewis, son of the former Poet Laureate, has referred to the 'underlying confusions of the decade', of the 1930s.

'The Blunt revelations,' he has written, '. . . have shown again how dangerously blinkered the idealism of these public-school seekers after religion could become. My head tells me this. Yet my heart still romanticises the English of that generation and class who believed in something with what still seems to me an attractive and quite selfless innocence. It is romanticism so unreasonable and persistent that I, who have never been attracted to communism, could never quite bring myself to go with my family to Spain, where my in-laws then lived, while Franco was still in power.'[12]

One of the weaknesses of the Cambridge mind, if (*pace* Wittgenstein) one can use that phrase without being accused of saying something meaningless, is that in contrast to the Oxford mind it is much more reluctant to admit its mistakes and change course. Many Apostles have proclaimed certain doctrines and theories and stubbornly stayed with them long after they were disproved. But the Oxford mind is much more elastic, possibly less inhibited by Cantabrigian Puritanism of the unctuous kind. First-hand experience of the Spanish Civil War and the Soviet intrigues and brutalities of that period caused even Julian Bell to make clear his doubts on the situation, and it is all the more tragic that it was he who died who should have commented in the letter to Cecil Day Lewis, another Oxonian, that 'either one has the smell of the committee-room, the intrigues, wrangles, bigotry of doctrine, and squabbles on points of fact, or the worse noise, unreason and enthusiasm of the public meeting and street demonstration . . . Revolution is the opium of the intellectuals – pseudo-revolution.'

Yet the Oxonian intellectuals were on the whole the first to change

120

their minds positively and openly on the Spanish affair. W. H. Auden, of Christ Church, Oxford, after a quick visit to Spain, referred to the 'thirties as 'that low, dishonest decade.'

Bertrand Russell, though some of his philosophical precepts were being challenged and even denounced in the 'thirties, was as usual one of the keenest and most accurate observers of any Apostle of the international scene. One of his closest friends in Spain was Gerald Brenan, a survivor of the Bloomsbury Group who had for many years made his home in Spain. Russell spent part of one summer in the 1930s in Brenan's home in Malaga where he spent his days writing books and occasional poems. Brenan, who still lives in Andalusia at the age of ninety-one, was described by Senor Javier Torres Vela, Andalusia's regional councillor for cultural matters in June, 1984, as 'understanding us better than we understood ourselves.'[13]

From Gerald Brenan Russell received a letter in 1935, saying 'It is easy to sympathise with the destructive desires of revolutionaries: the difficulty in most cases is to agree that they are likely to do any good. What I really dislike about them are their doctrinaire ideas and their spirit of intolerance. The religious idea in Communism, which is the reason for its success, will lead in the end to a sort of Mohammedan creed of brotherhood and stagnation . . . I am opposed to this Communist religion.'[14]

Note that this letter was written very early on in the development of republicanism in Spain, a year before the Spanish Civil War broke out. Was Brenan's message passed on to the Apostles, I asked one contemporary member. 'A few of us were told about it,' was the reply, 'but unfortunately Russell was not around to put this over at meetings. You must remember that he had long since become an "Angel".'

One of the many unsolved mysteries of the Apostles is why the name of Gerald Brenan has been given to at least two other researchers into the history of the Society other than myself as having actually been a member. Now, as he never went to Cambridge, this would seem to be totally impossible. After leaving Radley, which he hated, he fought in World War I, and then immediately went to live in Spain, eventually becoming the foremost and most perceptive foreign writer on that country and its literature. I asked my Apostolic contact if he could say anything about this improbable suggestion.

'No, and I don't think I should, if I could,' was his reply. 'I'm sorry if that sounds unhelpful, but I will only say that I, too, have heard this story before and I think it emanates from the papers of the late T. H. Vail Motter at Princeton University. Without implying anything else, I would also add that Brenan spent the 1939-45 period back in this country.'

Was Brenan in some way made an honorary member of the Apostles?

It should be remembered that he was a friend not only of Bertrand Russell, but other Apostles such as Lytton Strachey, Leonard Woolf and Roger Fry. Alas, an inquiry to Brenan himself has drawn no response.

# 12

# APPROACHING WAR AGAIN

'We abandoned our political activities not because we in any way disagreed with the Marxist analysis of the situation in which we still both found ourselves, but because we thought, wrongly it is now clear to us, that in the public service we could do more to put these ideals into practical effect than elsewhere.'
(Guy Burgess in his statement to the press made in Moscow, 11 February, 1955)

It is probably true to say that a number, probably a majority of the younger Apostles, felt that they were already at war against Nazism and fascism long before war was declared in the late summer of 1939. To their credit, they faced up to the stark facts of life rather better than many of their elders. On the debit side, a few failed to discriminate between one enemy and another. The middle ground, as is so often the case, was disregarded by both groups. The young who favoured left-wing policies either failed to realise the truth or allowed themselves to be mesmerised by the Comintern, while the older generation either sought refuge in pacifism or pretended that the hard right in Europe was capable of being won over. A Metternich, or a Machiavelli would have sought out the soft right whether in Spain, Italy or the Ruritanian areas of the Balkans.

It was, of course, soon abundantly clear that the British Government of the day was pursuing a policy which only encouraged the Nazis and the fascists to employ even more aggressive tactics. A strategy of appeasement which lamentably failed to detach Mussolini from Nazi Germany was in itself disastrous. There seemed little more hope from the British Labour Party: it was filled with pacifists and it had run away from its responsibilities during the 1931 economic crisis. So some of the younger generation, disillusioned with British socialism in action, turned to communism. Kim Philby, who was not an Apostle, summed it up when he said that

'the real turning point in my thinking came with the demoralisation and rout of the Labour Party in 1931 . . . . Through general reading I became gradually aware that the Labour Party in Britain stood well apart from the mainstream of the Left as a world wide force.'[1]

Sir Stephen Runciman, a former King's man, records that he was not an Apostle, 'nor wished to be – I took the line that there was something ridiculous about a self-important secret society – and I still think so. Though I believe I was considered for membership, nothing, rightly, came of it. In my undergraduate days I would say that the Society was pretty secret. Though I knew that several of my friends belonged to it, one was supposed not to know who the members were; and they would never talk about it to an outsider. It was when the left-wing boys more or less took it over that secrecy was reduced. No one could expect Guy Burgess to be discreetly silent about anything – even about his politics: which makes his employment by the Foreign Office so extraordinary.'[2]

An abundance of new talent was apparent in the Apostles in the period covering the end of the 'twenties and the first year or two of the 'thirties, when a number of new members were initiated. Outstanding among these was Andrew Benjamin Cohen, who came to Trinity from Malvern. A powerfully built young man possessing enormous energy, yet with a dreamy idealism in his eyes, he swiftly made his mark in the Society. Like some of his Victorian predecessors, he said that the Apostles' dedication to 'enlightening the world on things intellectual and spiritual has stayed with me almost as a personal religion.'

Cohen's father, Walter Cohen, was formerly director of the Economic Board for Palestine, while his mother had been headmistress of Roedean before becoming Principal of Newnham College, Cambridge. 'He was very much one of the inner circle of younger Apostles,' says one of the early 1930s vintage. 'You would find him in constant contact with Llewellyn-Davies, Blunt and Alister Watson. They were always in each other's rooms. I would have said he was a liberal who was constantly looking some twenty years ahead of his time. I don't know how else quite to put it. Nothing doctrinaire, by the way. He was impatient, did not suffer fools gladly, but he was always ready to debate a new idea and help develop it.'

In 1932 Cohen joined the Inland Revenue, where he must have found the work frustrating for one of his essentially imaginative mind. The following year he was transferred to the Colonial Office where he soon proved to be a hard-working and dynamic personality. It was in the Colonial Service where he was ultimately to make his name, especially as an expert on African affairs.

Maintaining the father – son pattern which has sometimes been a feature of the Society was Richard Llewellyn-Davies, son of Crompton. Yet another Trinity Apostle, he subsequently became an architect with a flair for town-planning. It was he who first hyphenated the family name into Llewellyn-Davies. After leaving Trinity he spent some time at the Ecole des Beaux Arts in Paris, qualifying as an architect in 1939. It was, however, not until several years later that he was to become well known as a controversial figure in the architectural field not only in this country, but in Africa, the Middle East and South America.

Another star in the Apostolic firmament, was Victor, later the third Lord Rothschild, who went to Trinity from Harrow in 1929. He first distinguished himself at the age of eighteen by hitting thirty-six runs off Larwood and Voce when playing cricket for Northants. At Cambridge he made a name for himself as an inquiring scientist, with the emphasis very much on the inquiring. He became a Prize Fellow of Trinity from 1935-39 and was made an Honorary Fellow in 1961. His work in the scientific field has ranged from research into spermatozoa and biology generally to anti-sabotage measures, the last of which was to lead to some of his most outstanding work in World War II. Later his work in the scientific field extended from Cambridge to an honorary fellowship at Bellairs Research Institute of McGill University, Barbados, to an honorary fellowship at the Weizmann Institute of Science at Rehavoth, and he was elected a Fellow of the Royal Society in 1953 for his bio-physical research. Although never a left-winger, he joined the Labour Party under Clement Attlee's leadership in 1945.

There was a brief period during the 1930s when membership of the Society declined because elder members claimed they had encountered few young men whom they regarded as 'Apostolic'. It is far from clear as to whether some of them feared a take-over by the Left, or had other reasons for their doubts. After all, a majority of the elders were probably well left of Centre, if not positively left-wing. Michael Straight was made aware of this feeling of doubt among the elders when he was approached by David Champernowne (elected 1934), who became a secretary of the Society. Michael Straight quotes this letter from Keynes of 3 February, 1937:

Dear Michael,

For the meeting of the Society we fixed, I think, Saturday February 20th in my rooms; and I was to let you have some suggestions as to who might be asked.

For King's I suggest Sheppard, the two Lucases, Rylands, Richard Braithwaite and Watson; almost certainly Champernowne, if you can get him to Cambridge.

For Trinity – G. M. Trevelyan, G. E. Moore and D. H. Robertson, and of course the younger people such as Blunt, Rothschild and the others.

Then there is Sykes Davies from John's and quite likely there may be others I have forgotten for the moment.

Yours ever,

JMK.[3]

Hugh Sykes Davies, poet, novelist and brilliant lecturer, was one of the more gregarious and less secretive of all the Apostles. Perhaps this was why he had the supreme gift of being able to laugh at himself and make others laugh with him. The son of a Wesleyan minister, with a strict Nonconformist background, he went to Kingswood School, Bath, and from there won an entrance scholarship to St. John's. Arriving at Cambridge in 1928, he was awarded the Le Bas Prize in 1933 and then elected a Fellow of St. John's, eventually being appointed a university lecturer in English in 1936.

In many respects he was an original and unique teacher of English, covering literature from Chaucer to the present time. He took a keen personal interest in his pupils, even to the extent of taking an undergraduate into a public house to discuss English over a few drinks, if he felt this was the right way of doing things. As a result, some of the better writers of the 1970s, if not the 1980s, feel they owe a lot to Hugh Sykes Davies.

A delightful companion and conversationalist, Sykes Davies would have made an admirable historian of the Society, if he, too, had not been inhibited by advice from fellow Apostles. In 1982, at the request of the editor of the *Cambridge Review*, he wrote two 'Apostolic Letters' for that periodical, having been encouraged to write about the Society, presumably following certain revelations in the press. His fatal mistake was to show his proposed work to another senior Apostle who not only showed it to another Society member, but expressed his criticism of what he regarded as breaking 'a kind of unspoken contract.' For, quite untypically, Sykes Davies opened his 'Apostolic Letter' with a reference to recent press stories about the Society as having 'the appearance of being part of a well-orchestrated campaign against the University in general, and because they are published, not in the absolute gutter press, but in newspapers, magazines and even books which are not gutter in price, whatever value may be placed on their contents.'[4]

Now this reads as though Sykes Davies was writing with a tongue placed far out into his cheek, for no other Apostle had talked so freely about the Society (admittedly with some reservations) to members of the press and others, like myself, as will shortly be seen. He himself was able to take an objective view of all the changes in members' thinking from decade to decade, yet on this subject he said nothing whatsoever in his articles.

Though a left-wing socialist, he did not become a member of the Communist Party until 1937. 'It was Anthony Blunt who persuaded me to join the Apostles,' he said, 'but I didn't need much persuading. Later I joined the Communist Party, but had some difficulty in getting in because Anthony had been saying that surrealism was bourgeois. As I was a surrealist and an organiser of the 1936 Surrealist Exhibition, the Communist Party had misgivings about me.'[5]

In the late 1930s Sykes Davies went into a sanatorium in Switzerland for some months. Then, in 1938, he became prospective Labour Party candidate for the Isle of Ely, but his candidature was terminated when they discovered his Communist Party membership. He admitted that he had failed to tell the Labour Party he was a Communist, adding: 'Yes, it was a deception. I was deceiving a lot of my constituents as well as the Labour Party. It was a question of balancing the ethics of the things against the realities. We thought there was a war coming and that it could not be stopped. When they rumbled me, they were hopping mad. They sent Morgan Phillips down to get rid of me, and he did.'[6]

During World War II, as his tuberculosis had made him unfit for military service, Sykes Davies worked in the Ministry of Food, taking an administrative post which at times he found 'hilarious as well as time-consuming.' He was never recruited into the service of the USSR in any capacity, overt or covert, and indeed he very soon reverted from communism to moderate socialism. The fact that he was not a spy for the Russians was something which he joked about in December, 1981, after further revelations about Soviet spies among the Society membership. 'I was certainly never approached as a potential spook by anyone, least of all Anthony Blunt,' he stated at the time. 'I feel a bit insulted that nobody tried to put any such proposition to me, but then again,' he added with a wry smile and an invitation to another drink, 'they probably regarded me as not being serious enough. Then again, I wasn't a homosexual, but most positively committed to the female sex. Indeed, that could have told against me in their eyes. They would think the women around me would be hazards to a potential spy. Maybe they would have been right. I've been married four times and intent on taking a fifth wife even today.'[7]

Hugh Sykes Davies proved to be a valuable informant on the Apostles not because he revealed any real secrets, but that he knew how to convey the atmosphere of those days without betraying any of the friends of his youth. He bore out Michael Straight's contention that homosexuality in the 'thirties was not ostentatious in the Society – at least to the degree it had been in earlier decades. 'Nobody ever made a pass at me,' was his comment. 'After all, on my track record, there was no reason for any of them to have any hope.'

There was a pause and then he proceeded to say: 'You have got to remember that the Society felt from very early on that the Church had an altogether too authoritative grip on the university. This grip stifled them. So from one generation to another the Society felt it had to challenge the Establishment. This partly explains the secrecy. The 'thirties? Well, it wasn't all political. Surprised as you may be to hear it, romanticism played a part. Not with all: too many were only inspired by puritanical prejudices. But you must remember that on the artistic side there were many pointers towards a new outlook, slant, call it what you will, on art and life in the Soviet Union. At that time. It happened in the 'twenties and we learned about it in the early 'thirties. Probably it was totally snuffed out by the time we were absorbing it.

'I don't think in the 'twenties they would have regarded surrealism as being particularly bourgeois. The post-revolution decade was a time of experiment in Russia. At that time the inevitable ruthless and uncaring hand of communist realism had not taken total control. There was still a feeling – anarchist, perhaps, but still genuinely artistic – that the revolution could give new life to art and literature. Some of the musical and poetic ideas developed in this period were admirable and exciting. Mosolov developed Mussorgskian writing in his songs and the Russian film-makers paved the way to new techniques, new methods, films that were different.'

Hugh Sykes Davies died in 1984, but his career as poet, novelist and critic has still not been given its full due. Here was a major guide who could, with great, good humour and many illuminative comments, take one out of the rut of writing into the Elysian fields of enjoying the English language. He was at one and the same time a medievalist and a modernist, and added to this was his fluency in Italian and French. 'If one knew Sykes Davies,' said one Apostle of the 'sixties, 'one could forget Leavis and all that academic mish-mash. He really helped one how to write. His *Grammar Without Tears*, published in 1951, was brilliantly written and showed how English grammar had developed since Chaucer and without being bogged down by Latin principles.'

Sykes Davies is, in fact, almost worth a chapter in himself. He was a disciple and an admirer of Wordsworth and he wrote three novels, *No Man Pursues*, *Full Fathom Five* and *The Papers of Andrew Melmoth*. The last named was the story of a scientist who foresaw the destruction of the human race not through the actual H-bomb, but from fear of it. Sykes Davies developed a tubercular disease shortly after he took his degree and he went to Switzerland for treatment. 'There I spent some time in reflection about Surrealism, the Spanish Civil War, the even bigger war that was coming to us. On the day I left Switzerland, Hitler moved into Austria. It felt uncomfortably close. When I found my surrealist friends still at their happenings, their private views at midnight and so on, I urgently wanted to warn them that the game was up, that playing with bright images was over. The images had turned around. The new *Ars Poetica* was to be the art of cursing, and we had to learn it. My warning to my friends, and the curse on our enemies was published in the *London Bulletin*, the last remaining place for surrealist poetry. Perhaps the editor failed to understand that it was anti-surrealist.'[8]

It is a matter of minor importance, yet still of interest on the subject of the ultra-secrecy of the Apostles that Sykes Davies admitted that he 'never told my wife I was a member. As we always met on Saturday evenings, I had to think up some improbable reason for not being with her every weekend. What she thought I cannot imagine.'[9]

Two key figures in the Society in the 1930s were William Grey Walter and David Champernowne, who became the seventy-third and seventy-fourth secretaries of the Apostles. Both were King's men. Grey Walter was born in Kansas City in 1910, educated at Westminster School and eventually acquired his M.A. and D.Sc. at King's College. He was elected to the Society in 1933 and he soon became an influential member in a quiet, unassuming and non-controversial way. He was founder and foreign secretary of the Electroencephalography Society in 1942 and later president of the International Federation of Societies for Electroencephalography and Clinical Neurophysiology.

His interests extended way beyond those of medicine and psychology, though in Apostolic circles he was always anxious to bring discussions around to these subjects. In one debate he intervened to suggest that the subject under discussion should be changed to 'To live or to die?' One living member who recalls this comments that 'nobody really understood what he was getting at. But he had posed a vital psychological question on the will to live, or the too early acceptance of death. What Grey Walter stressed most was the need for the will to live, to project oneself, to improve the species, for all this to be turned into a positive philosophy of living. But, as Grey Walter put it over, this was much more firmly medically and psychologically based than any philosophical theory.'

Grey Walter was a Rockefeller Fellow of the Maudsley Hospital in 1935, and in 1949 he became a member of the WHO Study Group on the Psychobiological Development of the Child. But long before this, when at Cambridge, he became interested in the cybernetics movement and, with W. Ross Ashby, another neurologist, produced early and influential books on the cybernetic ideas. Walter made some motorised 'tortoises' which could recharge themselves when their batteries were low. His cybernetic 'tortoises' were on view at the Science Museum in South

Kensington in the Festival of Britain Year in 1951. He built his 'tortoises' at the Burden Neurological Institute in Bristol, where for many years he had a clinic and latterly became scientific director.

In almost every aspect of the arts of living Grey Walter was a pace-setter. Not only was he a philosopher and scientist, a co-founder of the International Association of Cybernetics, but a keen tennis player, a skin-diver and an adept in the art of gliding. Some years after World War II his son, Nicholas Walter, recorded that he was told by his father that 'the Security Services were still interviewing Apostolic suspects up to the 1970s . . . He told me several times that he was interviewed by MI 5 officers during the late 1960s, well after the Philby defection and Blunt confession, and that they were particularly interested in the social activities of the Apostles during and after the war, and were taking statements from hundreds of prominent men.'[10]

David Gawen Champernowne went to King's from Winchester and was a mathematics scholar. The son of the Bursar of Keble College, Oxford, he was elected to the Society in 1934. While still an undergraduate he had published a paper of great originality on Sierpinski, a Polish pure mathematician of the twentieth century. Afterwards he switched to economics.

Champernowne, like Victor Rothschild and Grey Walter, very much represented a new school of Apostles who joined the Society in the 'thirties and 'forties. Previously, the emphasis, when selecting new members, had been an interest in philosophy and the arts rather than science. Suddenly a whole new world of intriguing subjects and possibilities was opened up to the Society, though what evidence there is suggests it was not fully appreciated until at least one, if not two, decades later. But in their respective ways Rothschild, Champernowne and Grey Walter paved the way on a wide variety of scientific, statistical, biological, medical and other subjects, including the development of computerology.

How much computerology may have been hastened forward by discussions between Apostles it is not easy to say. One must remember that Apostolic influence was not confined to the Saturday night meetings: it erupted into informal talks between groups of Apostles in their own rooms. Yet it would seem that the influence of members of the Society on the development of computerology was considerable, and in some instances vital. One of the outstanding undergraduates involved in this field of research was Alan Turing, who, at the age of fifteen when he was at school at Sherborne, had discovered for himself, and without the normal use of elementary calculus, the infinite series for what is known as 'the inverse tangent function.' He gained a scholarship to King's and was elected a Fellow at the age of twenty-two. In 1937 he published a paper, entitled 'Computable Numbers', which summed up his most original development of an idea that had first been played around with by Charles Babbage, a Trinity man of the early nineteenth century – that of a sophisticated calculating machine.

Turing was not an Apostle, but he received great help and encouragement from members of the Society. Wittgenstein was greatly impressed by 'Computable Numbers' after Alister Watson had introduced him to Turing. For a while Turing was in Wittgenstein's class on foundations of mathematics. It was a stern test for the most dedicated of mathematicians, as Wittgenstein's method was to ask questions which tried to relate pure mathematics to everyday life and to show that the answers made total nonsense. That is, of course, an extreme way of explaining Wittgenstein, but his teaching technique was frequently so obscure that sometimes few understood what he either meant, or was trying to say.

Champernowne and Turing worked on a chess programme which they called the 'Turochamp'. According to Turing's biographer, this had a scoring system in which pawn mobility and castling and getting a rook on the seventh rank were included as well as captures.[11] The system was later adopted for poker. It is clear that Turing was looking far beyond even the present day system of computerology. Or, as he wrote at the time:

'The special machine may be called the universal machine: it works in the following manner. When we have decided what machine we wish to imitate, we punch a description of it on the tape on the universal machine. This description explains what the machine would do in every configuration in which it might find itself. The universal machine has only to keep looking at this description in order to find out what it should do at this stage. Thus, the complexity of the machine imitated does not appear in the universal machine proper in any way.'[12]

Two other Apostles who supported Turing's drive towards creating new and better computers were Professor Richard Braithwaite and Robin Gandy. Braithwaite, then Emeritus Knightsbridge Professor of Moral Philosophy at Cambridge, was known as 'King's philosopher of science' and became president of the British Society for the Philosophy of Science. A man with a tremendous zest for exploring new ideas, as his record of some eighteen papers to the Society suggests, he took the theme of a 'thinking machine' to its logical conclusion, arguing at one meeting that such a machine would need to be equipped with its own in-built, insatiable appetites for learning and doing. This thesis was developed much further when, in a BBC programme in January, 1952, Professor Braithwaite stated that people's ability to learn was determined by 'appetites, desires, drives and instincts, and that a learning machine would need to possess something corresponding to a set of appetites.'

Robin Gandy, who was reading mathematics at King's, struck up a friendship with Turing on account of their mutual interest in computerology and electronic encipherment work. Much later, as secretary of the Society, Gandy would have proposed Turing as a candidate for the Apostles, but at that time the Society's policy was to choose only younger men. Had war not intervened in 1939, it is more than likely that Turing would have been elected.

By the mid-'thirties Cambridge University in many respects led the world in a great deal of scientific research. It was Lord Rutherford who, after 1953, took the lead in opening up British academic life to Jewish refugees in the scientific field. Politics continued to occupy the minds of some scientists: '. . . a number of the young scientists became committed communists, or fellow-travellers,' recorded T. E. B. Howarth, 'and even a veteran like Gowland Hopkins was reported to be prepared to put his pen to the draft of any "progressive" letter to the press put under his nose.'[13]

The archives of the Association of Scientific Workers in these years show the dominance of the communists, especially those in the Cambridge branch. Referring to the Association's influence in this period, Dr Elizabeth Kay McLeod writes: 'Politically, it diverged from other organisations both in its explicit commitment to trade unionism and in its concern with the application of science in society. As such it attracted a new generation of politically aware scientists, many of whom were sympathetic to, or active in, some branch of the Labour movement.'[14]

One of these young men was Alister Watson, who died in 1983. Watson was later to pay heavily for his membership of the Communist Party during his Cambridge days, as this fact coupled with his membership of the Apostles and friendship with Blunt was sufficient to give the authorities cause to question him in the 1960s as a possible Soviet spy.

But, as Sir Alan Hodgkin, then Master of Trinity, told *The Times* in November, 1979, the role of the Apostles has been somewhat distorted in relation to these various charges of espionage.

'It is quite wrong to suppose it was a kind of crypto-communist cell. People have been ludicrously 'out' over this . . . The set-up was that it was basically an undergraduate debating society which had senior members come in.'[15]

Sir Alan went up to Trinity from Gresham's School, Holt, in

132

1932, and after obtaining his M.A. and doctorate in science, became a Fellow of Trinity in 1936. His political views were those of a Quaker with a social conscience and he became neither a Marxist nor a socialist while at Cambridge: he was much too intent upon both learning and achieving, especially in his own chosen field, that of biophysics and medicine. He was elected to the Society in 1936, when, briefly, its active membership had dwindled to two, himself and one non-Marxist economist. It is strange how quite often in its history the Society was been full of active members one year and then, perhaps only a few months later, suddenly down to a mere two or three. Only a year or so before this there had been 'eight or nine undergraduate members and a much larger number of Angels', according to Hugh Sykes Davies.[16]

Maynard Keynes, always keeping a wary eye on the Society even in his busiest moments, came to the rescue, said Sir Alan Hodgkin, 'and over the following two years resuscitated it, bringing it some good new undergraduates.'[17]

As war approached, Guy Burgess was already in the BBC. His greatest talent was that of ubiquity. He had influence all over the place, and not merely in one country. Greatly underestimated both as a scholar and as a highly-skilled intelligence-gatherer, his strength was that he operated on wide and disparate fronts: whether with British, American, French or German operators and politicians, Burgess somehow managed to ingratiate himself with all. As has been noted, Eddie Marsh gave him an introduction to Churchill, while at the very same time he was a frequent visitor to the London apartment of the Baroness Moura Budberg (Maria Ignatievna Zakrevskaia), the former secretary to Maxim Gorky and friend of Sir Robert Bruce Lockhart. In this connection it is apt to cite a statement from Robin Bruce Lockhart, Sir Robert's son:

'Members of our intelligence services and others who knew her well had strong suspicions that she was a Russian agent, some even believing that she duped my father in 1918 during the so-called 'Lockhart Plot' – not that I give any credit to this last suggestion. Certainly Well's [H. G. Wells] story of Moura's deception in 1934 tends to corroborate a categoric statement made to me earlier this year by a senior member of the Russian media in Moscow that Moura was quite definitely a Soviet agent. Further, she had stood side by side with Stalin at Gorky's funeral in 1936.'[18]

Burgess's contacts with Wolfgang Adler zu Puttlitz, a secret communist sympathiser inside the German diplomatic service in London, and with a close confederate of Daladier, the French Premier, were invaluable for his own contacts with Soviet Intelligence in this period. In

Burgess's favour it should be said that Puttlitz was genuinely opposed to Hitler and that he volunteered his services to the British and continued to offer them a supply of dispatches after he left London for the Hague. As a result of carelessness by two British agents in 1940 the Gestapo discovered Puttlitz's double-dealing and a warning message was sent to the German ambassador at the Hague. Luckily for him, Puttlitz was able to decipher the message before his ambassador saw it and so made his escape to London.

Meanwhile Michael Straight, who had returned to the United States, was in a dilemma. After John Cornford's death in Spain Anthony Blunt had asked Straight to call on him. Up to this time Straight had fully intended to become a British citizen as his brother Whitney had done. But Blunt indicated that it was Straight's 'duty' to carry on 'the good work started by John'. This did not mean taking up British nationality: 'some of your friends have other ideas for you,' added Blunt. 'You must return to the USA. Straight understood that the 'friends' meant people in the Communist International and that he was to work on Wall Street to provide appraisals.'[19]

'I went to an annual dinner of the Society in 1937,' Straight told the author, 'and I was attacked by a Treasury official who had prepared an 'extemporaneous' response to my speech (as the new member), denouncing me for my radical beliefs which he assumed were contrary to the values of the Society. Unfortunately for him my speech was conciliatory and gentle. Anthony Blunt, for reasons which were unclear to me, urged me to comply with the Treasury man's image, thus providing him with the context he needed. I declined, and the Treasury man went ahead and delivered his 'extemporaneous' response word for word, rather than appearing to be less clever but closer to the truth. Keynes among others was deeply offended by his brutal assault on me. I don't recall who he was, but I suppose he was one of the 'conservatives' who had heard that the Society had fallen into the hands of 'communists'. I was asked to recommend individuals for admission and, overcome by other matters as I was in 1937, I responded with the names of my friends who were radical but Apostolic. Most were admitted and they in turn brought in others.'[20]

Michael Straight was never happy about the proposition made to him by Blunt. On more than one occasion he asked to be relieved of any such chores. In his autobiography, *After Long Silence*, he has told of his private anguish wrestling with his conscience about a youthful radicalism that seemed somehow to have got out of hand, and how he was mysteriously approached by telephone in late April, 1938, by a foreigner who used the code-name of 'Michael Green'. The latter suggested that when any interesting documents came to Straight's desk, he should take them

134

home 'to study'. Straight replied that no documents came his way. Thus he continued to avoid committing himself and in due course told the American authorities the whole story.

Straight was the youngest member of the society in 1937 and as such was responsible for arranging meetings. He has paid tribute to the fact that Maynard Keynes gave him a great deal of help. 'Keynes was plainly the intellectual leader and the most active member of the Society,' he says. 'He enjoyed all forms of intellectual exchange provided they were conducted with clarity and precision. His attitude towards the student radicals has, of course, been summarised by himself. His term 'amateur communist's' seems to me now to be exact. That is, he regarded the commitment as shallow and transitory, an expression of a more enduring need, and as such, one to be accepted and understood, rather than as a permanent alignment with a hostile regime.'[21]

The truth was there was not much proselytising in Apostolic circles and discussions. This would have been wholly foreign to the spirit of the Society. Whatever attempts were made to convert members to support a particular creed or political belief were made outside the circle. Political issues were only occasionally discussed. Michael Straight adds this comment: 'No communist views were expressed in my presence at least in Society meetings. No indications of homosexuality were ever in evidence. Discretion on all counts was part of that world, and indiscretion was frowned upon as a lack of internal discipline. Individuals such as Burgess and Blunt were never proselytising communists; that was left to the foot soldiers; nor were exhibitionists welcome as far as personal behaviour was concerned.'[22]

Possibly this way the proselytisers were able to work more efficiently towards their long-term aims. The spade work, the putting forward of ideas in a reasonable manner, all this was done in Apostolic sessions with no emphasis on ideologies, but the gradual pressure for recruitment to a communist ideal, even if this meant disguising what it really was – all this was achieved through personal relationships outside the Society.

135

# 13

# APOSTLES AT WAR

'I met murder on the way –
He had a mask like Castlereagh –
Very smooth he looked, yet grim;
Seven bloodhounds followed him:
. . . One by one and two by two,
He tossed them human hearts to chew'
(*The Mask of Anarchy*, Percy Bysshe
Shelly)

These lines of Shelley can be applied to a variety of political incidents, and it is surprising how aptly they still ring out down the years. At the time of Munich, when Neville Chamberlain gave away so much to Hitler, in 1938, the then Lord Castlereagh wrote an article for the *Daily Telegraph*, pointing out certain resemblances between the foreign policy of Chamberlain and that of the first Lord Castlereagh after the defeat of Napoleon. Hugh Sykes Davies wrote a letter in reply to this, asserting that a rather better comparison would be the above lines by Shelley which 'seemed to me to be curiously apt for what Munich did for Czechoslovakia.'[1]

The comment was certainly apt and no doubt Sykes Davies regarded the fact that St. John's had been Castlereagh's college with some amusement. Shelley's *The Mask of Anarchy* has provided other and more frightening and horrific parallels than this as the years since 1939 have passed by. Munich, yes; Poland, yes; the barbarities of Belsen and Buchenwald, yes; but, not least, how first the United States under Roosevelt and then Britain began tossing 'human hearts to chew', not just 'one by one and two by two', but millions of Poles, Czechs, East Germans, Slavs and Russian prisoners-of-war back into the grips of the bloodthirsty tyrants of the Soviet empire. Much of the latter part of the 1939-45 war was spent in helping the USSR cover up their real intentions in demanding the forcible repatriation of more than two and a quarter million Russians from Western Europe.

Whereas it was the pacifist Apostles who were often most prominent in World War I and only a few of those who took active part in prosecuting the conflict like Sir Ralph Wedgwood, Rupert Brooke and Lucas

136

distinguished themselves, in World War II the position was reversed. Nearly all members of the Society played a part in fighting Nazism in one way or another, and many of them fulfilled tasks of incalculable value in winning the war.

Sir Alan Hodgkin worked on radar in World War II – such was the range of his scientific interests and accomplishments – and was attached to the Air Ministry and the Ministry of Aircraft Production from 1939-45. This work more than anything else reveals the kind of versatility which was so welcomed in Apostolic circles. It was, of course, far removed from his real interests as a pioneer of research into the physiology of nervous conduction and in measuring the electrical constants of nerve by square-pulse analysis. Sir Alan's experiments in this field enabled him (in his own words) 'to find out how nerves work, how they conduct messages, how pain and sensations reach your brain, and how they travel back to the reverse direction.'

As the 'thirties drew to a close and after war was declared the scientific element began to have increasing influence within the Society. These scientific links spread outwards from the Apostles into many fields and eventually led to important cooperation between members of the Society and scholars in the United States. This has been most marked in the fields of medicine, psychiatry and psychology. It is also interesting to note in the trans-Atlantic connection that in 1944 Sir Alan Hodgkin married Marion de Kay, daughter of the eminent American pathologist and cancer research pioneer, Dr Peyton F. Rous, Member Emeritus of the Rockefeller Institute for Medical Research. Dr Rous maintained this trans-Atlantic association by not only being a foreign member of the Royal Society, but an Honorary Fellow of Trinity Hall.

A pupil of Sir Alan's, Andrew Fielding Huxley, who was another of the Westminster School outflow to Trinity, also contributed substantially to the war effort with operational research for Anti-Aircraft Command from 1940-42, and for the Admiralty for the rest of the war. He became a Fellow of Trinity.

Dr Alister Watson worked as a government scientist in the Admiralty during the war, notably in radar. His research in this field was of enormous value. He continued in the service of the Admiralty after the war in what was a top security post. Inevitably, when MI 5 were searching for other possible members of the Cambridge network of Soviet spies, Watson's youthful membership of the Communist Party was noted. He was questioned at great length, but nothing was proved against him, and the only action by the authorities was to take away his top-security clearance and move him from a defence post in the 1960s to a job at the National Institute of Oceanography. Dr Watson himself denied allegations that he had made a confession to MI 5, and in November,

1981, he declared that he was completely innocent, though he admitted that British intelligence had good reason to suspect him. He added that he was 'never guilty of passing classified information to any unauthorised person. I am not and never have been a Soviet spy.'[2]

Some of the important developments in deciphering in World War II, in which the British lead was of incalculable value, actually came about through talks between Apostles and that remarkable genius, Alan Turing. There was a quite large contingent of Cambridge men at Bletchley who applied themselves to the unravelling of German ciphers with the aid of the Enigma machine, and members of the Society who played a part in this included Robin Gandy and the brothers Lucas. Frank Lucas commanded the unit's Home Guard at Bletchley.

Inevitably and sensibly, Alan Turing's talents were harnessed to the war effort, and for this he owed much to Apostolic influence. After a brief spell at Princeton University he was told to report to Bletchley Park in September, 1939. Here, in developing the Enigma system and, while feverishly working on the deciphering of German signals, young amateurs worked side by side with professional scientists and at the same time peered into the future to discover what computing machinery would offer to the post-war world. Robin Gandy followed Turing into the same kind of work in 1940, when he joined the Special Communications Unit No. 3 at Hanslope Park in Buckinghamshire.

Later Gandy became a lecturer at Leicester University for a while and Turing, having taken his doctorate, went on to publish his paper, 'Computing Machinery and Intelligence' in *Mind* in 1950. In this he posed a question which had been debated in the Society a long time previously – whether men and machines between them might not produce a 'thinking machine'. The logical development of this idea was announced in Japan in 1984 by Mr Kazuhiro Fuchi, director of the Institute for New Generation Computer Technology, when he described how Japan's plan was to build 'fifth generation computers' that could ultimately be more intelligent than human beings.

Though Dr Turing, who tragically committed suicide in 1954, was not an Apostle, subsequent research in computerology since the war has been aided, sometimes directly, sometimes indirectly by other Apostles. Both Professor Champernowne and Robin Gandy must take some of the credit, but there were others, too, both on the technical side and in the actual work of collating and assessing the intelligence gained. Non-scientists will often complain that computers fail to do all that is expected of them, though the real answer probably lies with the operators. There is, however, another side to this problem – statistics. For too long statistics as a subject requiring lengthy and imaginative study was neglected outside the academic world. Computers without expert and highly intelligent analysis of the statistics they throw up could continue to fail to do all that is expected of them.

It was as a statistician that Professor Champernowne played his role in the war. From 1936-38 he had been an assistant lecturer at the London School of Economics. He was then made a Fellow of King's and from 1938 to 1940 was University Lecturer in Statistics at Cambridge, being appointed to the Prime Minister's statistical department from 1940-41. This post was no dreary bureaucratic one: it entailed work in an entirely new department created by Winston Churchill himself.

'One of the first steps I took on taking charge of the Admiralty and becoming a member of the War Cabinet,' wrote Churchill, 'was to form a statistical department of my own. For this purpose I relied on Professor Lindemann, my friend and confidant of so many years. I now installed him at the Admiralty with half a dozen statisticians and economists whom we could trust to pay no attention to anything but realities. This group of capable men, with access to all official information, was able . . . to present to me continually tables and diagrams, illustrating the whole war so far as it came within our knowledge. They examined and analysed with relentless pertinacity all the departmental papers which were circulated to the War Cabinet, and also pursued all the inquiries which I wished to make myself.'[3]

Until Churchill entered the Cabinet on the outbreak of war in 1939 there had been no Government statistical organisation. Compiling of statistics was very largely (as it so often is in business and industry today) an amateurish, hit-and-miss mish-mash, with, as Churchill himself ironically commented, 'the Air Ministry counting one way, the War Office another.' A central body for statistical work was desperately needed. But it was not until Churchill became Prime Minister the following year that he was able to create a statistical department which would cover all governmental requirements. It was then that he wrote to Sir Edward Bridges, Secretary to the War Cabinet, arguing that 'the utmost confusion is caused when people argue on different statistical data' and that he wished all statistical information to be concentrated in a Central Statistical Office.

Professor Champernowne played a vital role in this new department until in 1941 he was appointed as assistant director of programmes in the Ministry of Aircraft Production. When war ended he became Director of the Oxford University Institute of Statistics.

The ever-questing mind of Victor Rothschild also proved to be of considerable value to the war effort when he joined the Intelligence Corps, acquiring the rank of colonel, and becoming a key figure in the highly dangerous task of dealing with and evaluating unexploded bombs, for which he was awarded the George Medal in 1944. An additional wartime chore was protecting Churchill from poison or other means of destruction, which even involved analysing a present of cigars from some unknown benefactor. He also received such honours as the American Legion of Merit and Bronze Star, as well as being described by US President Harry Truman as 'one of the world's greatest counter-sabotage experts.'

Andrew Cohen was dispatched to Malta in 1940 when he was given the task of organising food supplies for the beleaguered island. It was a highly successful mission and he made himself popular with the native population, not least because of his courage during air raids when he always made a point of being out and about. He was forgiven his many eccentricities on account of his hard work and devotion to duty. His reward at the end of the war was to be made Under Secretary in charge of African affairs at the Colonial Office.

Maynard Keynes, by this time Lord Keynes, after having displayed his investment skills for King's while Bursar and Fellow at that college, was often consulted on economic and financial matters during the war and he worked closely with the Governor of the Bank of England. He ended his career by leading the British delegation to Bretton Woods in 1944, and seeing the establishment of an International Monetary Fund to assist reconstruction. He also negotiated the American loan to Britain of more than £1,000 millions in 1945. By this time the whole of Britain's foreign investments had been sold and their proceeds spent, as well as Britain's reserves of gold and foreign currency.

Richard Llewellyn-Davies joined the engineer's department of the London, Midland and Scottish Railway in 1942 and was engaged on a programme of rationalising railway station construction.

But not all Apostles served in civilian posts during the war. Richard Guy Bosanquet, of King's (elected 1937), joined the Royal West Kent Regiment and, as Major Bosanquet, was killed in action in Italy in July, 1944. Peter Derek Vaughan Prince (elected in 1938), another colourful King's character, and Old Etonian, went out to Palestine to serve with the Royal Army Medical Corps. A Craven Student in 1939, he later ran a school for Christian and Jewish children in Jerusalem until the British mandate ended. He briefly returned to Cambridge as a Fellow in 1948.

Rather less fortunate initially was Walter Wallich (elected 1939), who, having been born in Potsdam, was interned as an enemy alien after taking his B.A. degree. However, he was eventually released and joined HM Forces, taking a commission in the Royal Artillery. When war ended he was appointed to the Control Commission for Germany, handling the so-called 'de-nazification' of journalists, actors and musicians. During this period he helped to set up the Berlin Broadcasting Station of NWDR, after which he returned to Britain and joined the BBC German Service.

One of the most attractive and popular of Society members in the late 'thirties was Cuthbert Wilfred Francis Noyce (elected 1934). The elder son of Sir Frank Noyce, a member of the Council of the Viceroy of India, he was head of school at Charterhouse before winning a scholarship to King's. Climbing was Noyce's passion as an undergraduate. In this he was encouraged by Professor A. C. Pigou, the economist of King's and the generous patron of many young would-be mountaineers. It was Pigou who introduced Noyce to the Alps. At Cambridge Noyce once climbed King's College Chapel at the bidding of the Dean to remove a chamber-pot which had been placed on one of the turrets. On another occasion he was unable adequately to explain to the magistrates why he had been found on top of a lamp-post on Guy Fawkes night.

When war broke out Noyce joined the Friends' Ambulance Unit at Edgbaston and then worked with them in hospitals in the East End of London. After Dunkirk, however, he shelved his pacifist inclinations and became first a private in the Welsh Guards and then a subaltern in the King's Royal Rifle Corps. Richard Holmes, of Jesmond, confirms how when he and Noyce were stationed not far from Cambridge during the war, the latter took him to meet Pigou in his rooms at King's: 'The beer, brewed on the premises, was the strongest I have ever tasted . . . It certainly loosened our tongues . . . There was no doubt about the rapport which existed between Pigou and Noyce and –, especially on the subject of the Soviet Union, which they constantly praised and drank to . . . Pigou and Noyce clearly worshipped one another.'[4]

Later in the war Noyce was a captain in the Intelligence Corps in India. He even managed to do some climbing in the Himalayas in this period and became chief instructor at the RAF Aircrew Mountain Centre in Kashmir. After two more terms at Cambridge after the war Noyce worked as a schoolmaster, first at Malvern, then at Charterhouse. In 1953 it was Noyce who, with Sherpa Annullu, opened the way to the South Col in the successful ascent of Everest by Sir John Hunt's party on the eve of Queen Elizabeth's coronation.

On 30th July, 1962, it was announced from Moscow that Wilfred Noyce, together with another British climber, Robin Smith, had been killed after a successful ascent of Mount Garmo in the Pamir Mountains on the borders of Russia and China. Noyce had already indicated that the expedition which he had led at the age of forty-one to Trivor in the Karakoram was his last, but when the Russians agreed to an Anglo-Soviet project, he felt such an opportunity 'of helping to breach the Iron Curtain was an imperative call . . . with this in mind I accepted the invitation.'

Noyce was an idealist in a very special sense of that word. In many respects he was a knight in quest of chivalrous and dangerous deeds, the type of man who might have been conjured up in the mind of 'Sapper'. On the other hand he was down-to-earth, practical, gregarious, devoted to achieving world peace and with a genuine desire to seek an accord with the Russians in any way possible – even by mountaineering. The party he joined to climb the Pamirs comprised twelve British and six Russians.

Like many mountaineers, Noyce was also something of a romantic, and this was eloquently revealed in one of the last papers he wrote: 'When, in August of 1960, I was sitting on the summit of Trivor in the Karakoram, I noted mechanically the line of fairy summits away to the north-west. Mechanically, I realised that the Pamirs of Russia were before me. But I felt no emotion, no zeal for a Promised Land. Even when I knew that an expedition was being organised, it did not occur to me that I could or should go with it. And when it came my way, I was filled with doubt.'

> 'What moves a man who sits brooding over an invitation? . . . To me, brooding seemed that mountaineering had hitherto been a private adventure, a self-seeking . . . To be with those who thought and spoke quite differently, yet on common ground and with common aims – this might be a bridge, not only of my understanding of other men's motives in the sport of mountaineering, but perhaps even, in a small way, of the gap separating East and West over all fields of thought. With this in mind, and of course for the more obvious reasons, too, I accepted the invitation to join the British – Soviet Expedition to the Pamirs.'[5]

In telling the story of the Apostles down the ages one tends to linger on the name of Wilfred Noyce. For here in this more recent cavalier of the mountains are echoes, even if each in different ways, of Tennyson, of Hallam, of William Smith O'Brien, of Julian Bell. Even on the subject of mountaineering Noyce felt there needed to be a purpose behind it. He did not accept the theory of most mountaineers that 'I climb because I like it'. In his book, *The Springs of Adventure*, he stressed how many tough trail-blazers were physically frail as children and sometimes emotionally and mentally complex people. Noyce found at the core of man's need to turn his back on the easy life and attempt the impossible – what he found within himself – was a search for 'the state of awe', for 'greater purpose and reverence.' Perhaps it was a search for God.

There is no question about Noyce's sincerity in this attempt he made to analyse some of his own motives. Maybe he realised this only towards the end of his life, but clearly in this book he was concerned with the mystical aspects of adventure. Again and again he records his intense feeling that at all times when life was most dangerous, *someone else was there*. His approach to mountains was always that of the poet, and his books were all about mountains – even his mountaineering novel, *The Gods are Angry*.

Leo Long was yet another member of the Society who had joined the Cambridge Communist Party in the 1930s. This occurred when he was at Trinity studying languages. It was his talent in this direction which led to his joining MI 14 when war broke out. This was the branch of the War Office which dealt with the deployment of German forces. His work in MI 14 involved processing thousands of decrypted signals transmitted by the *Wehrmacht* and the *Luftwaffe* in what they believed to be total security, but which were actually read by the British deciphering teams at Bletchley. It might be argued that if any of this information was passed on to Russia after she became an ally, it would enable her to cope better with the Nazi onslaught in the east, whereas if the USSR went under, all Germany's might could be turned against the United Kingdom. But the vital requirement was that Germany should not find out that Britain was reading her signals, and the more people who knew this, even among allies, the greater the risk of this happening. In fact Russia was not entirely starved of the fruits of such intelligence. It was known in London that Soviet signals intelligence was then relatively poor and the USSR was actually given some of the material provided by the deciphering, though its source was skilfully disguised.

Long, who held an important post in military intelligence on the Allied Control Commission after the war, was named to British Intelligence as a suspected Soviet agent in 1964, and he made a full statement when questioned, admitting his part in passing information. In referring to this in November, 1981, he declared that 'The only force in the world that seemed to stand four square against Hitler was the Soviet Union, about which we had fantastic illusions.'[6]

But perhaps this unhappy business is best summed up by the text of the Prime Minister's statement in the House of Commons on 9th November, 1981:

'When Mr Blunt made his confession in April, 1964, he admitted to having recruited Mr Long before the war and controlled him during it. Mr Long was then seen by the Security Service. He asked for immunity from prosecution; this was refused, but he was told that he was not likely to be prosecuted if he cooperated in the Security Service's inquiries. He then made a detailed confession.

143

'. . . While at Cambridge he was recruited by Anthony Blunt as a potential Soviet agent . . . He had access to analyses based on intelligence derived from secret sources, but not to the sources themselves. He passed information obtained from these analyses to Anthony Blunt, knowing that Mr Blunt would pass them to the Russians . . . I have been able to give this answer today about Mr Long because he has publicly admitted his guilt.'

Meanwhile Blunt and Burgess, while working in MI 5 and the BBC respectively, were both serving Soviet interests to the best of their ability. From January, 1941, Burgess operated for the BBC in their propaganda for Europe. This was the kind of work which appealed to him, enabling him to keep some kind of liaison with the Foreign Office. 'He helped . . . to remove the anti-Russian bias from Poles whom we were training for sabotage,' wrote Cyril Connolly, 'and in 1942 he attempted a mission to Moscow which got no further than Washington, where he remained for a few weeks.'[7]

Burgess, of course, in recruiting people to aid 'the cause', sought far outside the Society as well as in it. Cambridge, Oxford, London University, Bohemia, Soho and Bloomsbury . . . Burgess had contacts all over the place. Cyril Connolly writes of Burgess's 'Etonian convert to Marxism who became one of the Californian Communist leaders and died there.' Equally he was in close touch with a Canadian named Herbert Norman at Cambridge, a man who later joined the Canadian Diplomatic Service and who, while he was ambassador to Cairo, was recalled to Ottawa to answer questions raised about his past relations with the Communist Party which had come to light following inquiries in the USA. Back in Ottawa, Norman jumped to his death from the roof of the apartment block where he was living.

Blunt's aid to the Soviet Union not only went much deeper, but involved more ruthless treachery. Not only did he manipulate MI 5 so that he was assured of the maximum amount of useful intelligence to pass on to the Russians, but he also used his links with both the Foreign Office and Military Intelligence to ensure that thousands of Tsarist fugitives who had never lived in Russia, but had fled their country in 1919 as allies of the British and Americans, and who were not in consequence covered by the Yalta Agreement, were surrendered to *Smersh* in Austria under an arrangement so secret that 'exceptional circumstances are still employed to suppress the evidence.'[8] This statement refers to File No. 383.7-14.1, which is not available to researchers because the Ministry of Defence has withheld it on the grounds that it is 'personally sensitive.'

It was Anthony Blunt who played a considerable role in stifling criticism of the proposed wholesale repatriation of such persons to the Soviet Union. One Special Operations Executive (SOE) officer, Major L. H. Manderstan, who had been born in Riga and was a fluent Russian speaker, was sent to France shortly after D-Day to question Russian prisoners captured by the British. Major Manderstan felt that many of these prisoners had been coerced into working for the Germans and that some deserved asylum if they wished for it. Later he put this view forcibly to the Foreign Office. His reports seem to have been totally ignored. Sir Geoffrey Wilson, who was then serving in the Russian Department of the Foreign Office, referred to 'SOE's mysterious refusal to allow the NKVD a prior interrogation of the volunteers [sic]' and added that he was not surprised the Russians would not cooperate: 'I doubt if Colonel Chichaev [the NKVD officer in London at this time] has a very high opinion of Major Manderstan.'[9]

The man who helped to sabotage Manderstan's work was Blunt. He kept a close ear open for all that Major Manderstan said and did. Not only was this all reported back to the Russians in London, but, as a result of Blunt's information, there were two attempts by the NKVD to assassinate Manderstan. Fortunately neither of these succeeded. 'I have no doubt that the man behind my troubles was Blunt,' Major Manderstan told the author. 'Nobody else could have known so much detail about me and my movements. But nobody seemed to believe me when I reported these facts. Nor did they seem to care about the fate of the prisoners.'

However, on the other side of the Atlantic, Blunt's friend Michael Straight, had been whole-heartedly supporting the war effort without allowing himself to be entangled with Soviet subversion or manipulation. From 1938-39 he did his best, in a series of forceful memoranda, to push the State Department towards an active role in Europe in defence of the democracies. It was an uphill task, but he made some impression. Between 1941 and 1943 he managed to reverse the isolationist stand of the *New Republic*, which in those days was a highly influential periodical. He was able to be a voice for the young men in the preparedness programme aimed at driving up military production despite the resistance of sections of American industry. Straight's war effort may have been low key, but it was certainly effective, and the important thing to remember is that it was carried out prior to American involvement in the war.

# 14

# THE FITFUL FIFTIES

'What worried me in 1958, as it does now, was the way in which the sentimental Left occupied all the same positions and rehearsed all the same arguments that I was just old enough to remember from twenty years before.'
(Professor Donald Davie, Stanford University)[1]

Though Cambridge briefly regained something of its pre-war elegance in the early 1950s, with the reappearance of May balls and other festivities, something of the inbuilt austerity in thinking and teaching remained, and there was a refusal to face up to the mistakes of some pre-war teaching. Professor Donald Davie, who went from Barnsley Grammar School to St Catherine's, perfectly summed this up in the quotation given above. He, too, was irritated by the Leavis dogmatisms, but, as he says, after four years in the Navy, he was horrified by the 'manifest inability, on the part of students and their teachers, to learn the plain-as-a-pikestaff lessons of recorded recent history.'[2]

What went wrong at that time with both teachers and students, he argued, was 'something that was going wrong with the whole national life in those years – the 1950s and 1960s. This I discovered to my cost in 1964 when I left to help found the ill-starred University of Essex.'[3]

Antagonism to and disgust with Leavis continued. By the 1950s the revolt against him was in full swing. Raymond Leppard, the University lecturer in music and subsequently conductor of the BBC Northern Symphony Orchestra, referred to 'F. R. Leavis, of whom we became heartily sick on behalf of friends who read English and had all their enthusiasm by his powerful, ascetic, critical theories.'[4]

Raymond Leppard was never a member of the Apostles, though in a letter to the author he says that 'after a few years of belonging to the Stuart Dining Club called 'The Family', I was invited to join. I was dissuaded by a friend, and if further dissuasion were necessary, Anthony Blunt's somewhat frequent presence at High Table – I knew he was a member – was enough to clinch it . . . a most disagreeable individual.'

There were also signs of revolt on the philosophical front. Students began to feel that they were in danger of 'being conned by the oldies', as one of them aptly put it. 'We felt that many of their theories were a mere outdated fad or fashion, and Wittgenstein and Moore were seen by us in much the same way as a long since forgotten fashion in neck-wear.' This revolt was slow in coming because the tradition of the Apostolic philosophers like Moore, Russell, Wittgenstein and others had become deeply entrenched. Lecturers put over their theories as though these earlier path-finders were Holy Writ, often to the point of playing down the very continental philosophers from whose ideas they had so heavily borrowed, often not altogether effectively. Piers Paul Read, now at Stanford in USA, recalled that he had 'tackled Russell, Ryle, Moore and Wittgenstein without understanding more than a fraction of what they were talking about. If, before my tutor, or among my fellow students, I mentioned Plato, Kant, Nietzsche, Marx or Sartre, I was treated with a pained smile, or a scoffing laugh . . . Such speculative, continental fun-philosophies were considered quite outside the bounds of serious study.'[5]

However, though, such problems indirectly affected some of the newcomers to the Society in the 1950s, they certainly did not influence members of the 'forties. Among those members there was still a marked devotion not only to Leavis, but to Far Left viewpoints. One such member was Dr Arnold Kettle, of Pembroke, who both in meetings of the Society and in a pamphlet he subsequently produced argued that in place of conscription there should be a voluntary system of military training organised through the trade unions. Kettle was a vehement opponent of conscription.

Dr Kettle, who subsequently became Professor of Literature at the Open University, was the editor of *Shakespeare In A Changing World*, a series of essays contributed by twelve Marxist, or near-Marxist, critics who wanted their readers to believe that Shakespeare was really one of their ilk. He even urged in his own essay on *Hamlet* and *King Lear* that Lear's 'madness is not so much a breakdown as a breakthrough.' Unlike many Apostles who abhorred Leavis, Dr Kettle went out of his way to acknowledge his debt to both Mr and Mrs Leavis, though admitting the limitations of their roughshod 'take-it-or-leave-it: I am the light and the resurrection' style of teaching. But the worthy Dr Kettle himself borrowed something of the Leavis technique of nagging, insisting on his own righteousness and allowing little room for honest doubt.[6]

Writing on 9 March, 1940, the veteran Cambridge don, A. S. F. Gow, commented on the 'awful lot of German refugees in Cambridge, and I am constantly hearing scraps of Hunnish in the streets . . . Another consequence of the arrival of London in our midst is the growth of undergraduate soviets of one sort and another, fostered, I fancy, largely by the London School of Economics, whose left-wing predilections incline them favourably to soviets.'[7]

This was, of course, a considerably exaggerated picture of events in Cambridge at this time, as the LSE, who were evacuated to Cambridge, had quite a few right-wing economists among their numbers. But war changed the university's atmosphere, as it did in other places, and the Apostles suffered from the departure of dons to war work as well as the fact that fire-watching and other part-time war services curtailed some Society activities.

Bertrand Russell foresaw the Cold War which was to follow the victory of 1945 as early as 1941 when he wrote: 'I cannot think the Nazis will survive. America will dominate, and will probably not withdraw as in 1919 . . . There is good hope that the militaristic regime in Japan will collapse, and I do not believe that China will ever be really militaristic. Russia, I think, will be the greatest difficulty, especially if finally on our side. I have no doubt that the Soviet Government is even worse than Hitler's and it will be a misfortune if it survives.'[8]

This was a remarkably perceptive prophecy of events, the more so as it was written before Germany invaded the Soviet Union and so brought Russia in on the side of the Allies.

King's rather than Trinity continued to claim more new members of the Society even into the 'forties, and in this connection it is perhaps worth quoting what Professor Eric Hobsbawm, an Apostle and a King's man, has to claim for his college: '. . . a reputation for bourgeois unconventionality, a taste for the arts and intellectual pursuits not necessarily resulting in major achievements, for personal relations, non-soldierly behaviour, rationalism, music, homosexuality, and a great tolerance for people's eccentricities, including their opinions. While its ambience was liberal and its politics, if any, left of centre, it was as unlikely to breed social revolutionaries as Bloomsbury itself.'[9]

On the whole this seems to be a fairly accurate picture, though it would be fair to add that its very tolerance of eccentricities often led to some intellectual perversity, sometimes merely because of a desire to be perverse. One former King's man and Apostle of this era told the author:

'We were much more interested in philosophical than political arguments and social revolution of any kind would have been a bore. But I would add that for a not insubstantial minority, their politics was Far Left rather than left of centre.'

Professor Hobsbawm's sharp, analytical mind and economic yet distinctive style have for many years made him one of the leading communist intellectuals and interpreters of Marxist principles in this country. He joined the British Communist Party in the mid-1930s, and, unlike some of his fellow dons and many of his pupils, he stayed with that party. Probably no other living Marxist intellectual has received such extensive praise and favourable reviews in almost all sections of the serious British press. His devotion to his creed is puritanical and he is, for the type of King's man he portrays, singularly intolerant himself of some other people's points of view, even ruthlessly criticising the work of a fellow communist, the late James Klugmann's history of the British Communist Party and asserting that he 'wasted much of his time' in writing such a book.

Certainly Professor Hobsbawm provided arguments within the Society for a closer and more intellectual and philosophical examination of Marxism. But it has been as a teacher and historian after he left Cambridge that his impact has been greatest, though a rider must be added that, though such work has been distinguished, it has sometimes become discursively obscure in places. After a lengthy spell as lecturer at Birkbeck College of the University of London he was appointed Professor of History at that college, and in 1973 he was made an honorary Fellow of King's. He has also taken a prominent part in the annual Communist University of London, a regular feature of the academic calendar started in 1968 as a summer school to give students a series of courses from the Marxist viewpoint and with the aim of developing 'a distinctive British Marxist tradition.'

In 1949 an exceptionally large number of Apostles and 'Angels' attended the annual dinner of the Society which on this occasion was somewhat unusually held in a private room at the RAC Club, surely a most unApostolic venue. Guy Burgess presided and the principal speaker was Desmond MacCarthy. Altogether some twenty-five to thirty people were present. Michael Straight recalls finding himself sitting beside Eric Hobsbawm. 'We had a furious argument and Hobsbawm made it clear that he had not given up his beliefs in the Communist movement of which he had been a member when a student at Cambridge. But even he was capable of engaging in small talk and in voicing sophisticated views on a variety of subjects.'[10]

However, when Straight referred somewhat bitterly to the Soviet occupation of Czechoslovakia, Professor Hobsbawm commented that there were 'more political prisoners in the USA today than there were in Czechoslovakia.'[11]

No doubt this was a hyperbolic comment and what Hobsbawm had in mind was the large number of innocent victims of Senator Joseph McCarthy's virulent and ridiculous anti-communist campaign. Hobsbawm is given to such hyperbole as, for example, when he recently commented that 'as a government of the Right, Thatcher has no parallel, at least in twentieth century Britain. Every historian will confirm this.'[12]

It was after this dinner that Guy Burgess and Anthony Blunt took Michael Straight on one side and asked: 'Are you still with us?' When they received a negative answer, they put yet another question – 'but you are not totally unfriendly?' Among civilised people, however much they might have differed on questions of politics or morals, the fact that they had been friends surely precluded any other answer than that which Michael Straight gave – 'You know that I'm not.'[13]

In short, what Straight was saying in effect was that, at that stage and in those circumstances, while he was not prepared to betray his country, neither did he wish to betray his friends – a rather better balance of moralistic judgement than that of E. M. Forster. Those circumstances completely changed when there came the offer of a post from his country's government some years later. Then he revealed his past associations with communists and any matters which might pose future problems.

Meanwhile the Society had begun to concentrate rather more on sociological as well as philosophical problems. In the late 'forties a number of new members of some distinction arrived, such as Arthur Boyd Hibbert (1946), Robin Gandy (already mentioned), Peter David Shore (1947), Stephen Edelston Toulmin (1947), Noel Gilroy Annan (later Lord Annan, 1948) and John Murdoch Mitchison (1949).

Hibbert went to King's from Alderman Newton's Boys School, Leicester and his reward for a number of academic distinctions was a Fellowship in 1948. Toulmin, who went from Oundle to King's, had worked in the Ministry of Aircraft Production from 1942-45, and he returned to King's to become a Fellow in 1947. Professor Toulmin, as eventually he became, was a university lecturer in the philosophy of science at Oxford from 1949-55, and then, after terms at Melbourne and Leeds Universities, was appointed visiting professor of philosophy at New York University and later Director of the Nuffield Foundation Unit for the History of Ideas. His *Philosophy of Science: An Introduction* was published in 1950 and instantly attracted much attention in America as well as over here. This was followed at intervals by his three volumes of *The Ancestry of Science* and other works. At the time of writing he is engaged in the work of the Committee on Social Thought at the University of Chicago.

Peter Shore arrived at King's via Quarry Bank High School, Liverpool. He took a degree in history and, as Simon Hoggart has noted, his speeches are sometimes reminiscent of 'the more florid passages from the old Arthur Mee's *Children's Encyclopaedia* . . . Phrases like 'this

Sir Alan Hodgkin,
Nobel Prize winner

Lord Annan, lecturer
and patron of the arts

Peter Shore, former Labour
Minister

Jonathan Miller, outstandingly
talented and versatile modern
Apostle

island race' and 'one thousand years of history' tend to march from his lips fully armed . . . Here you feel is yet another man of destiny.'[15]

But it is Shore's sense of history which underlines much of his political thinking, not least in his opposition to Britain entering the Common Market. He is more of a planner than a rigid socialist. Going up to King's as an exhibitioner in 1941, his university career was interrupted for three years when he served as a navigator/bomber in the RAF, ending up as a flight-lieutenant in India. Returning to King's, he joined the Society in the late autumn of 1947, but had no further dealings with them after the summer of 1948, when he came down with a second in history.

He joined the Labour Party in the year he left Cambridge and contested the Cornwall seat of St Ives in 1950 and Halifax in 1959, but it was not until he stood for Stepney that he became a Member of Parliament. Working in the Labour Party's research department, he was very much influenced by welfare state protagonists such as Richard Titmuss, Brian Abel-Smith and Peter Townsend. Always apt to take an independent line even as a Labour Minister in later years, it is worth noting that in 1955 he joined with an American academic, A. A. Rogow, in writing a critical survey entitled *The Labour Government and British Industry 1945-51*. It dealt with what was alleged as the failure of the Attlee government to impose its own planning priorities on private industry because of the skill with which industry had managed to neutralise bureaucracy.

Peter Shore feels the EEC robs Britain of much of its sovereignty, something which actuates him rather more than economic objections. On careful reflection, he would probably agree that the influence of his former headmaster at Quarry Bank School, an Old Etonian who had been a housemaster at Shrewsbury, R. F. Bailey, was still a potent influence in his early life. For, whatever his own brand of socialism may be, Shore is still both a traditionalist and a patriot.

It may well have been that Peter Shore, either at that time or later on, was influenced by another Apostle of this era, Professor Harry Johnson. Here was yet another of the Society's links across the Atlantic Ocean, for Johnson was a Canadian who graduated with honours from the University of Toronto in 1943, taught at St Francis Xavier University, Nova Scotia, served in the Canadian Forces in Europe and then went to Cambridge after the war. Johnson was a complex character who in turn both loved and hated Britain and Canada for various reasons. His excuse was that he was an internationalist. Yet he opposed Britain's application to join the Common Market, as his sympathies were more to an Atlantic than a European alliance.

Professor J. M. Mitchison, who is the son of Lord Mitchison and Naomi Mitchison, the writer, went to Trinity from Winchester. From

1941-46 he was in Army Operational Research, returning to Trinity at the end of his war service as a Senior and Research Scholar and becoming a Fellow of Trinity in 1950. He writes that

'I have practically no memory of what we babbled about. My vague recollection is that the subjects were philosophical rather than political and that there was comparatively little science except at a very broad level. Undergraduates talk about the infinite at midnight coffee sessions, and long may they continue to do so. My memory of the Apostles is that they did much the same. Morgan Forster encouraged us at intervals by what I would call a strictly non-interventionist approach.'[15]

John Mitchison became Professor of Zoology at the University of Edinburgh in 1963, and for some years afterwards was a member of the Council of the Scottish Marine Biological Association.

Morgan Forster (E. M. Forster) was still an active figure in the Society and among undergraduates generally even at this late stage of his life, despite the fact that his health was far from good and his eyesight impaired. The hilarious story is told that when he was a guest at a marriage party he bowed low before a gigantic wedding cake in the firm belief that he was making obeisance to Queen Mary, then the Queen Mother!

While the cult of secrecy surrounding the Society was preserved to some extent by Forster himself this did not prevent him from writing a novel obliquely touching upon it in 1907. This was *The Longest Journey*, which was recently re-issued in a special edition with editorial introduction, appendices and explanatory notes.[16] Into this work Forster put much of himself and quite a good deal of some of his Apostle friends. He writes of his chief character in this book that Cambridge 'had taken and soothed him, and warmed him and laughed at him a little'. This is in essence the tale of how one Rickie (so named because he was 'rickety and lame') was elected an Apostle and became friendly with another Apostle named Ansell (remarkably like Leonard Woolf). In 1907 Forster could not have hoped to get away with an overtly homosexual theme in a novel without facing the risk of prosecution. So, much of the book is symbolic and it requires deciphering. Rickie is lame and this is a symbol of homosexuality, and in coded writing Forster develops the theme of a man who is an Apostle and a homosexual and who breaks away and marries. And it is in tackling this theme, for which Forster was hardly qualified by experience, that he reveals his inherent weakness as a novelist. It is the weakness of man who twists life to make it fit into his own misshapen patterns. 'Little by little,' he writes of Rickie's wife, 'she would claim him and corrupt him and make him what he had been; and the woman he loved would die out, in drunkenness and debauchery.'

In many respects Forster's novel cannot compare with a later novel (1911) by Max Beerbohm. In *Zuleika Dobson* Beerbolm draws a delightful and evocative picture of a similarly exclusive Society at Oxford (the Oriel Noetics?), throwing light on the extent of the influence that a female can exert on the membership of such a Society.

An influential Apostle in the longer term was Noel Annan, who went from Stowe to King's. During World War II he had served in the War Office, the War Cabinet Office and in Military Intelligence from 1940-44. He has not been included in the chapter on 'Apostles at War' for the simple reason that he was not elected a member of the Society until 7 February, 1948, when he returned to King's after his war service. Yet it was his experiences and postings during the war which played no small part in determining his advancement in the days of peace. 'The war broadened Noel's mind, woke him up to new horizons,' is the comment of a fellow Apostle. He played a role which was complementary to what was being done at Bletchley – helping to track down German troop movements. He worked both in France and Germany, becoming GSOI in the Political Division of the British Control Commission from 1945-46.

Back at Cambridge, where he already had had close links with George Rylands and Lord Keynes, he was made a Fellow of King's, first as a lecturer in politics, than as the youngest Provost in living memory at the age of thirty-nine. Gradually, Annan became one of the chief talent-spotters and recruiters of talent for official circles since Trevelyan. Perhaps he had this in mind when he wrote *The Intellectual Aristocracy* (in *Studies in Social History: A Tribute to G. M. Trevelyan*). In this book he showed how élitism had developed out of middle-class families who had passed on the torch of learning from one generation to another, but gave a glimpse of how this had worked in the ranks of the Apostles, too.

From the mid-'fifties onwards Lord Annan (he was made a life peer in 1965 under the Wilson government) was a figure whose influence extended far and wide, from being a Romanese lecturer at Oxford to chairman of the Departmental Committee on Teaching of Russian in Schools and on the Planning Board of the University of East Anglia; with such varied posts as Senior Fellow of Eton College, trustee of Churchill College, Cambridge, Director of the Royal Opera House, Covent Garden, a member of the Gulbenkian Foundation, Fellow of Berkeley College, California, and very many other offices of note.

Possibly because he personally is almost aloof from politics, though sometimes anxious to support claims made by both Right and Left, he has been accused of being a manipulator and place-maker. There were some critics who, somewhat unfairly, after he was made a life peer, suggested that he was 'in the pocket of No. 10 Downing Street.' The truth is that, as far as can be ascertained, he never took a Whip from any party while in the Lords. Yet he himself sometimes gives a curious impression of ambiguity. For example, when referring to his friendship with E. M. Forster, he said:

'He [Forster] emanated a kind of wisdom: he hated class and anything that stood against tenderness or sensitivity, but he was a demanding friend. Both he and Keynes were *hard* Liberals, not soft: they believed in duties as well as in rights.'[17]

It is extremely difficult to imagine Forster anything other than a very soft and impractical Liberal. In many respects Lord Annan has been a lone crusader against a certain type of reprehensible élitism among many British intellectuals – those who regard trade and industry with contempt and complete lack of interest, something which, he feels, has too often permeated academic life. He takes the view that this attitude has been largely responsible for the decline and stagnation of British industry and trade. In 1982 he indicated that he intended to write a book on this very subject. In particular he mentioned Evelyn Waugh and George Orwell as displaying that contempt for money and trade which he believes has permeated the attitudes of the ruling classes and helped to undermine the British economy.[18]

Simon Raven, author, critic, dramatist and soldier, who was at King's in this period, writes that

'Early in 1949, when King's was still a proper college with proper people in it, I was summoned one night by Noel Annan to drink claret in his rooms after dinner. Round the fire was a crew of ill dressed and ill made and prematurely decaying young men, who made an odd contrast with the wholesome Etonians one usually saw in Noel's rooms and indeed with Noel himself (then, as now, a picture of zestful well being). Nobody seemed to be saying anything much, so I myself launched into some trivial anecdote about the Army (from which I had been recently released). The anecdote was not really out of order, as I had heard someone mutter something about style (*le style, c'est Rhyl*) and my tale was about how cunningly Army methods of instruction taught chaps to write clear, brief, accurate and sometimes even elegant English. My story was received with naked hostility, whether because it was indeed rather light-hearted, or whether because it was about the Army, or whether because it revealed that I myself had been, both by situation and temperament, an officer, I never found out.

'Some months later I told the story of this gruesome evening to Dadie Rylands, who said that it had almost certainly been an 'Apollo spotting party', which it had (presumably) been Noel's turn to give. Needless to say, I was not recruited – nor ever could have been, come to that. I can't think why Noel ever invited me – unless he himself (being of incorrigibly cheerful disposition) had hoped for an element of light relief.'[19]

For some while the reference to 'Rhyl' puzzled me. Simon Raven described him as 'a philosopher, more celebrated in the 40s and 50s than now, I think, for his elegant style.' I was inclined to suspect a hoax, not least because my birthplace was Rhyl. But it eventually dawned upon me that Rhyl must be a mis-spelling of Ryle and refer to Gilbert Ryle, the Oxford logical positivist, author of *Plato's Progress* and *The Concept of Mind*. Now however much Ryle may have had his admirers in some circles in the Society, he was regarded as – to quote another Apostle – 'uncivilised, since his example of an artistic experience in one of his books started off "if I got to a concert to hear a military band".'

By the late 'forties and early 'fifties the Cold War had begun on several fronts – not only in Europe, but in the Far East from Korea to Indo-China and from Malaysia to Hongkong. The European borders of this new, undeclared and silent conflict was aptly described by Churchill in his Fulton speech of 1946 as 'the Iron Curtain.' To those who could look back dispassionately and consider the lessons of history and weigh them against actual experiences of living in Europe it seemed unlikely that there was any other solution than patience to face a prolonged psychological war built on military strength and testing the nerves of civilians on both sides. Safety in equality of strength, the very lesson which history showed had been neglected by many governments in two previous world wars.

To a few on the Right, but chiefly in the USA, newcomers to the kind of horrors Europe had become used to, the real risk of a Third World War seemed imminent. Some then believed that a short, sharp preventive war fought at a stage when the West had a distinct advantage in nuclear weaponry might be the answer. It was the possibility of such action, however remote from reality, which a few on the Left feared, and because of it, wanted an accommodation with the USSR at all costs. Certainly this view did not appeal to the Labour Government of Clement Attlee, who had in his Foreign Secretary, Ernest Bevin, a man of sound commonsense as well as being one of the most forthright opponents of communism of all time. But it was a view which was held by all the

Soviet-committed members of the Society as well as by some who were indecisive in their politics.

Both Burgess and Blunt kept in close touch with fellow Apostles who shared their views and attended the annual dinners of the Society. In 1944 Guy Burgess had switched to the News Department of the Foreign Office and in 1946 had become assistant to Hector McNeil, Ernest Bevin's political aide. Then in 1948 he had been moved to the Far Eastern Department of the Foreign Office. Later came his disastrous appointment to Washington, his return to London and, ultimately, defection with Donald Maclean to Russia. For the record, it has often been suggested that Maclean was an Apostle: my own researches suggest that there is no evidence whatsoever to support this claim.

Anthony Blunt had by this time left his war-time work in Intelligence and been appointed Keeper of the King's Pictures and director of the Courtauld Institute. Andrew Cohen had used up his phenomenal energy and his intellectual gifts in pressing hard to get the Labour Government of the day, and afterwards the Conservatives, to speed up the granting of independence to African colonies and dependencies. In this respect he was rather more the political policy-maker than the civil servant, sometimes being criticised for this by those in the Commonwealth Relations Office. It was a period when some in the Labour Government, more especially Patrick Gordon-Walker, hoped to stabilise relations between Africa north, west and east with South Africa by creating a Central African Federation including the two Rhodesias (north and south) and Nyasaland. This was not at all how Andrew Cohen viewed the future.

James Griffiths, then Colonial Secretary, appointed Cohen as Governor of Uganda, but this led to a conflict with the hereditary ruler, the Kabaka. There had been riots in Uganda between the end of the war and 1949 and the relationship between the Buganda tribe and the protectorate was most unsatisfactory. The peasants were angered by the Indian population's monopoly of the cotton ginneries. Boom conditions in that period led to Cohen introducing a number of radical reforms which delighted the African peasants, left the Europeans hostile and apprehensive and the Indians extremely doubtful about their own future in Uganda.

Then in 1953, Cohen, who had received a knighthood in the previous year's honours list, issued a statement withdrawing recognition of the Kabaka of Buganda under the auspices of a Conservative government. It was a hasty and ill-conceived action largely based on Cohen's belief that territorial and tribal chiefs were an anachronism. Yet Sir Edward Frederick William Mutesa II, the Kabaka, had been educated at Magdalene, Cambridge, and was an honorary lieutenant-colonel in the

Grenadier Guards. That single action of deposing the Kabaka was to lead to more than a quarter of a century of misery, strife and degredation for Uganda. Ever since then conditions in that territory have steadily deteriorated towards anarchy; crime and terrorism have increased, the Indians have been forced to emigrate, and poverty and famine have predominated. Such, alas, was the legacy of Andrew Cohen's dreams of a new and enlightened Africa.

It was in this same period that Richard Llewellyn-Davies made his name as an architect, and ultimately in 1963 became the first member of his profession to be made a life peer. Having graduated as an engineer and then turned to architecture, it is not surprising perhaps that he became very much a technocratically-minded architect. To his fellow architects in Britain he remained something of an enigma and quite often he was out of step with their thinking. This sometimes led to the criticism that in his architectural designs he carried utilitarianism to excess. Yet Llewellyn-Davies' achievements were considerable by any standards. In 1953 he was appointed by the Nuffield Foundation to be director of the Investigation into the Functions and Design of Hospitals set up by the Foundation. In planning a model for the hospital of the future one of his fact-finding experiments was to put pedometers on nurses in the old Victorian-built hospitals. He discovered that they walked a surprising number of miles in a day and so conceived the modern hospital in which the central services could be situated in the centre of the building from which the wards radiated outwards. He successfully designed a number of hospitals both in Britain and overseas before being appointed head of the Bartlett School of Architecture in London university. The *Guardian* newspaper commented on this appointment in 1959 that it was

'likely to bring the Renaissance twilight that has lingered around the School of Architecture to an abrupt end. The new professor – like Bertrand Russell – never went to school. He took an engineering degree at Cambridge and went on to the Architectural Association School.'

Llewellyn-Davies' work ranged from the master plans for Washington New Town, County Durham, and Milton Keynes to the experimental village of Rushbrooke in Suffolk. He often argued that any technical knowledge gained in a school of design risked being out of date by the time the student was in a position to use it. What he never seemed to stress was the question as to how much this was due to the way in which the demands of the workers resulted in a lowering of standards.

At the same time he built up a thriving practice as an architect in the firm of Llewellyn-Davies, Weeks, Forestier-Walker and Bor which produced plans for a new centre of Tehran, for developments in Karachi and for the redevelopment of the Menninger Campus, Topeka, Kansas. One of his most important interests was the World Society of Ekistics, the organisation concerned with the theory of human settlements that had been founded in Athens by Constantinos Doxiadis. Llewellyn-Davies was elected as the first president, while one of the vice-presidents was Dr Margaret Mead, the American anthropologist, and Professor Buckminster Fuller, the American experimental engineer, as well as M. Roger Grégoire, the French administrator and former director of the French Civil Service.

It was in this latter interest of his that Llewellyn-Davies was at his most perceptive and constructive. What emerged from the setting up of the World Society of Ekistics was this statement:

'Pressures – of population, of technology, of economic transportation – are not self-correcting. Urban spread can threaten, as in south-east England, to submerge the whole region. In many developed cities, visual monotony, lack of satisfying urban design, pollution of air and water, are among the elements which reduce man's pleasure and pride in his urban setting. At the same time our institutions are becoming less adequate to deal with the pace and scale of change. Such problems cannot be dealt with locally since they cut across most of the customary lines of authority.'

It was in this last sentences perhaps that the World Society of Ekistics held themselves open to criticism, for they added that tired and repetitious proposal that 'the emergence all round the world or regional agencies and systems – for planning, for administration – is a symbol of striving to match our new environments with appropriate institutions controlling the area and necessary to achieve the purpose in view.'

Somehow we seem to have heard all this before – that remote planning commissions know so much better – and yet it has never been proved to succeed. If ekistics means anything at all – and by definition it is quite clear what it should mean – it is that we learn from the past as much as from the present, that we may find answers in primitive settlements as much as in modern ones, in the highlands of Ecuador and the communes of Outer Mongolia as much as in modern town-planning.

Cambridge remained in a state of flux for some years after the war due to a variety of influences. The revolt against Leavis was well under way and an increasing number of people, lecturers and undergraduates, were nauseated by his teaching. On the other hand the strident Marxism of Maurice Dobb was still rampant and powerful and other opinionmoulders were Canon Charles Raven, Mervyn Stockwood, a disciple of Stafford Cripps, and John Robinson, later Dean of Trinity and Bishop of Southwark as well as being the author of *Honest to God*. The Apostles never seem to have been infected by the direst symptoms of the Leavis cult, but John Vaizey (later Lord Vaizey), who was at Queens' from 1948, wrote of it that 'intellectual ruthlessness has appalling effects on the manners and emotions, but excellent results on the intellectual morals of the Cambridge young. Of course, it has its destructive effects on morals in the wider sense. Leavis, who may be seen as the representative in this great tradition in a lean period, became a cult figure . . . a movement I was on the fringe of, since the people whom I much admired and liked included some of his pupils.'[20]

On the other hand Vaizey also commented that he had seen pupils under Leavis' supervision who had married and watched their marriages 'intensely entered into, intensely wobble and crash, as the necessity to bare feelings, to analyse motives, to tell the truth without fear or favour had put the marital structure of compromise and accommodation to the test.'[21]

In this somewhat indeterminate viewing of Leavis – his contributions and his zeal for destruction – one can perhaps see why Vaizey did not become an Apostle. Therefore, on Leavis and the murky trail of extirpatory literary criticism which he spewed out in torrents of abuse, perhaps the opinion of an Apostle who declines to be named is apt: 'Leavis took all the sparkle, all the challenge, all quixotry out of debate and life. His bloody-minded criticism killed one's enthusiasms. One just hoped he would hurry up and drop dead. I really hated the man and all he stood for.'

# 15

# THE RESTLESS SIXTIES

> 'There is beginning (it still has a long way to go) a
> movement of discontent among undergraduates . . . It
> takes many forms: agitation against the rule requiring
> students to wear gowns after dark . . . demand for courts
> of appeal against disciplinary measures.'
> (Eric Ashby writing in the *Clare College Association
> Annual, 1966*)

From the fitful 'fifties Cambridge, like many other universities, erupted
into the restless 'sixties. There were many reasons for this eruption and
there will still be many disagreements as to what they really were. An
Apostle puts it guardedly, but reasonably accurately, like this: 'In science
we had already evolved from the 'forties and nobody could say we were
left behind in any respect whatsoever. It was in the arts and other fields
that the 'fifties simply had not evolved from the 'thirties. There had been
lags on the left and lags on the right in these fields, and suddenly in the
'sixties some people realised that something approaching a revolution
was needed. That revolution went right, left and still in some cases
consolidated in the centre: the point is wherever it manifested itself it was
at last related to the decade. 'Fifties teaching had lagged behind in the
arts, English, and allied subjects. Not that I'm sure it has yet caught up
in all fields. But the 'fifties was a mindless decade.'

That's one viewpoint, and this particular Apostle added that 'we had
one debate in 1959 which centred on the question 'have we learned
anything in the 'fifties' The result of the poll was a draw – sometimes, I
feel, all for the wrong reasons on both sides.'

One cannot, however, dismiss the 'fifties in discussing how the Society
reacted to the 'sixties. As in the past membership was still predominantly
drawn from King's and Trinity, and in many respects members had not
changed much: philosophical discussions were still given priority. But in
a philosophical sense one relatively new subject had raised its head in
Apostolic debates – sociology, a science which still means different things
to different people.

In the 1950s sociology as a tripos subject had not been introduced at

160

Cambridge. One early Apostolic exponent of sociology in a truly
scientific sense was W. G. Runciman, the son of Viscount Runciman,
who went from Eton to Trinity and became a Fellow in 1958. It was in
the 'sixties that he made his impact as an authoritative and lucid
interpreter of the whole sociological scene. No doubt this was enhanced
by the fact that between 1953 and 1955 he had done his National Service
in the Grenadier Guards. In understanding the sociological facts of life,
National Service was an admirable apprenticeship. Personal experience
in this field often counted more than the semantics game – inquiring too
deeply into the real meaning of meanings – and possibly even more than
the new doctrine of sociometry (the measurement of social relationships
in school, factory, work groups and individuals). One of Runciman's
first literary efforts, however, was philosophical rather than sociological –
*Plato's Later Epistemology*, published in 1962. This was an analysis which
charmed with its occasional unorthodoxy, but convinced with its
essential moderation.

It was in the 'sixties and 'seventies that Walter ('Garry') Runciman came
to the fore as both prophet and practical applier of the often abused subject
of sociology. While many social workers and directors of what is often ill-
advisedly called 'social work' were often misapplying this relatively new
science, Runciman was trying to put it in perspective. *Sociology in its
Place*, which he published in 1970, was an admirable example of this. In
a single sentence, perhaps, one could fairly sum up his views on
sociology: that he believes much more efficient use should be made of
statistics and the emphasis should be put on obtaining rather better
scientific explanations of social phenomena. Or, to put it another way,
even though this over-simplifies what is really much more complex,
Runciman believes in Max Weber rather than Karl Marx. Indeed, he has
gone on record as saying that 'without wishing to assert categorically that
Weber is right where Marx is wrong, it is strongly arguable that Weber's
analysis of social stratification and of the relation between ideology and
economic structure is more subtle, more acute and in practice more
useful than that of Marx.'[1]

In 1970 Runciman was visiting lecturer in sociology at Harvard
University, and two years later he became treasurer of the Child Poverty
Action Group. His contribution to new thinking on a whole range of
social problems has been considerable and deserves much wider
attention than it has yet received. In his work, *Social Science and Political
Theory*, he not only opens up discussion of many unsolved problems, but
poses new lines of inquiry for future students. His argument is that it is
vital for all of us to 'continue to ask how societies ought to behave as well
as how they behave', but that these two questions are essentially
interrelated.[2]

If in this chapter considerable attention is paid to the Runciman theories, it is because from a period in the late 'fifties and early 'sixties the Society took rather more interest in the problems he posed, though not necessarily accepting his views. But, apart from what members of the Society may or may not have accepted, the Runciman teaching on sociology is a positive contribution to everyday life. It is also interesting to note that as his continued work on sociology has often been delayed by his combining an academic career with the chairmanship of several companies, he modestly observes that 'the extent to which I am a better sociologist for being at the same time a practising capitalist should be left to my readers to judge rather than to me.'[3]

A number of post-World War II members of the Society made a name for themselves in literature, the stage and journalism. Karl Miller, who was the author of *Poetry from Cambridge* in the early 1950s, was one such member while at Downing College. Though he started his career as an assistant principal in the Treasury in 1956, it was in journalism where he first made his reputation, as literary editor first of *The Spectator* and then *The New Statesman*, and from 1967-1974 as editor of *The Listener*. He is now Lord Northcliffe Professor of Modern English Literature at University College, London.

Another Apostle who has made his name both in journalism and literature is John Gross, who was awarded the Duff Cooper Memorial Prize for his book, *The Rise and Fall of the Man of Letters*, an ambitious project covering English literary life since 1800. Here was a case of an Oxford man (he was at Wadham College) who became an Apostle when he was appointed a Fellow of King's, Cambridge, where he taught from 1962-65. His first job was working as an editor for Victor Gollancz, after which he returned to academic life, first at London University, teaching English, and then at King's. It was when he became editor of *The Times Literary Supplement* in 1973 after a spell as literary editor of *The New Statesman* that he made a revolutionary change of policy – the introduction of signed reviews. For many years literary criticism in the *TLS* had been anonymous, and sometimes this anonymity had been abused. Gross decided that the principle of personal accountability should override arguments for retaining anonymity. There can be little doubt that he was absolutely right, especially from the viewpoint of posterity.

Gross summed this up admirably when he explained his policy: while admitting that there were 'respectable arguments on either side', he cited one earlier English editor, Richard Cumberland, of 150 years ago. Cumberland made the point that

'everyone must confess that there is a dangerous temptation, and an unmanly security, an unfair advantage in concealment . . . A piece of crêpe may be a convenient mask for a highwayman, but a man that goes about an honest errand does not want it and will disdain to wear it.'

This is another important example of Apostolic thinking and influence in modern times. If one lingers on the name of John Gross it is because his influence has been considerable in many fields of literature and journalism. After resigning from the editorship of the *TLS* he spent some time in publishing. Now that he has joined the *New York Times* his talents are being appreciated on both sides of the Atlantic. His high degree of dispassionate criticism is exemplified by his declaration when editor of the *TLS* that 'one's mail in any one day can bring evidence of distinguished, even daunting scholarship at its best, also the squalor of the academic mind at its most disagreeable.'[4]

For some years after World War II E. M. Forster occasionally attended Society meetings. But increasingly he appeared to the younger members as a remote, geriatric figure, pathetically wanting attention, but whose last work which was published in the late 'sixties was *Marianne Thornton*, a biography of his great-aunt. Gradually there was a healthy departure from previous Apostolic tendencies to worship certain of their senior members. True, this had never been anything approaching unanimous, but it had from time to time stunted the growth of new ideas. Even when a member showed outstanding talents and an ability to mesmerise his fellows with some show of brilliance, much greater caution was displayed and there was a feeling that each was equal to the rest. Hero-worship was discarded even if élitism still existed.

Even the legend of élitism tended to come from outside rather than from within the Society. If Cambridge University Communist Party used the Apostles as a hunting-ground for recruits in the 1930s (never, let it be said, as an instrument of policy or any other kind), in the 'fifties and 'sixties they regarded it with contempt.

Neal Ascherson, for many years a correspondent of *The Observer* in Germany and a specialist in Eastern European affairs, and who was a member of the Society in the post-World War II period, says that 'I suspect most members of the University Communist Party at the time weren't even aware of it [the Society]. Leftists in my day treated the Apostles with derision and steered clear of them.'[5]

In 1967 Mr Ascherson was elected as president of Berlin's 83-member Foreign Press Association. The author of an outstandingly perceptive study of King Leopold II of the Belgians (*The King Incorporated*), he has always taken a distinctively individualistic approach to the situation in Eastern Europe since 1945. Hindsight, it would seem, has caused him to revise his opinions on the Polish situation: in *The Polish August: The Self-Limiting Revolution* (1981) he wrote '. . . For anyone who travelled around Poland with John Paul II, it took time to become normal again. In dreams one walked still over strewn flowers, in the glare of the sun.'

Yet, like a majority of Apostles, Ascherson has a respect for revolutions which are based on rational principles even if in the beginning they seem to become imbued with illiberal tactics, and he certainly has an understanding of them. This understanding, however, led him to give the impression that the Cold War was started by the Americans and to argue that if the Poles had been more inclined to go along with the communist experiment, they might have been better off today. This view, which should not be regarded as in any way pro-communist (however dangerous some of us may see it), can be summed up as a twentieth century form of Robert Browning's optimism – that is to say, the view of those who believe that the communist system can eventually reform itself. True, this can happen and Neal Ascherson could point to China as a prime example, but the reverse can also be true when one bears in mind that Gomulka withdrew many of the reforms which he introduced in Poland (under pressure, let it be noted) in 1956.

Neal Ascherson was one of the earliest supporters of the Free Communications Group in 1969. This group established links with others in the United States, France and Germany. Its objectives could not easily be defined, but, whereas one could say there was a marked divergence of opinion among members, the one policy which united them was that the means of communication should be controlled by those employed in them. Ascherson's own view was that 'the only guarantee in a situation in which editorial control is being merged in a large pattern is that those who actually write and film and print it must take a larger part themselves . . . Communications cannot be a limb of democracy unless they are themselves democratic.'

Perhaps the most brilliant and in the long run the most versatile of all Apostles of this period and the one who had so much to contribute to contemporary life in philosophy, medicine, psychology, the arts as a whole and especially the stage was Dr Jonathan Miller. Had he been born in Edwardian times he would undoubtedly have been put upon the kind of Apostolic pedestal that was – not always justifiably – reserved for Moore, Strachey and others. His original and quietly authoritative mind had a widespread potency. Dr Miller went to St John's College from St Paul's School, and he wrote that 'the smart thing in Cambridge in the early 'fifties was to be queer – rather wittily queer: and therefore people feigned queerness as a way of escaping, or seeming to escape, from the austerity. I was a privileged young man with a decent public school education and nothing to complain about, and therefore wasn't angry or annoyed. I was slightly *nettled* by things, but that was because I was amused by them rather than really outraged.'[6]

Though it has frequently been asserted that Jonathan Miller made his acting reputation with the Cambridge Footlights, he himself has said 'I can hardly remember anything about theatre in Cambridge. It played a very small part in my life. I wasn't a member of either Footlights or the ADC.'[7] However he was soon to stamp his almost larger than life personality with his loping gait and eccentricity of gesture on what rapidly became a new conception of that old form of dramatic art – the revue. Out of this was born *Beyond the Fringe*, which, under Miller's authorship and imaginative direction, became an instantaneous success, and, first in London, then in New York, was hailed as marking the revival of stage satire. Yet while all this was going on Dr Miller spent much of his time travelling to the London Hospital to carry out post-mortems.

There was something unique about Miller. Here was a serious scientist and pathologist with a great sense of both fun and theatre, who had the talent to pose all manner of sociological and medical questions. As far back as 1961 he was stating that

'I want to study people's attitudes to madness: what is the point at which acceptable, eccentric behaviour passes into what people consider looniness? Nobody's ever studied this. I'd like to write a book on it.'

This is the kind of versatility which makes for an outstanding Apostle. One has the feeling that Dr Miller misses nothing, that he makes use of the seemingly irrelevant in an entirely new way, that the most improbable incident in life or literature can teach him something, though he makes the proviso that it all depends upon the environment. The point is that Dr Miller admits this, while most of us would pretend otherwise.

Miller on God is tersely informative. In 1969 he had a discussion on BBC Radio 4 with the Dean of King's, the Reverend David Edwards. Jonathan Miller told the Dean that he was

'a godless Jew' and that to him the word 'God' was 'a blockish word' which had never meant anything to him at any age. On the other hand he admitted that he was drawn towards churches during Advent and believed that man was 'essentially a ritualising animal' and that football crowds and pot-smoking parties were not a satisfactory substitute.[8]

165

He has directed Shakespeare, been appointed a visiting professor of drama at Westfield College, London, joined the Arts Council, brought a touch of his own magic to the filming of *Alice in Wonderland*, and out of his television series, *The Body in Question*, he produced a book about the human body which enlightens through the infra-red lucidity of his metaphors. Indeed, it is hard to find a sphere in which he has not won distinction, so that one tends to forget that he has spent much time researching mesmerism and phrenology, written a critical book on McLuhan's theories of 'media mottoes' and even taken an active hand in production of *The Marriage of Figaro* for the English National Opera Company. When he directed the film of Kingsley Amis's story, *Take A Girl Like You*, he revealed the mind of the neurologist, doctor and philosopher combined when he summed up the film as

'it's a serious redescription of why certain young girls hold their virginity as something of value. Nowadays virginity is thought of as something rather laughable. Or else it's held on to with a sense of automatic virtue. The fact is that virginity and its surrender is a somewhat existential issue. When someone decides to change status and go from a virgin to a deflowered girl, she's actually making a decision about choosing a new character for herself. The moment at which the body is enjoyed by someone else is a moment in fact of great gravity and it's not actually as trivial as we make out.'[9]

As the 'sixties advanced, so the Society turned its attention to many new subjects, or rather, as one 'sixties member put it, 'we turned to new views on old subjects and pretended we had invented new ones. I think we had that old Apostolic knack of turning something upside down just for argument's sake. If sex appeared to be a kind of free-for-all, let's try anything, exaggerated permissiveness, we would occasionally – and I don't want this to be misconstrued – argue the opposite way in just as an extreme manner.

'Don't think we adapted any anti-permissive stance. We just questioned those consensus views which seemed to us to be getting out of hand. You could call us anti-consensus to a limited extent. So once there was a discussion on 'Is sex necessary?', not a very original title as there was once a book so called.'

A keen interest in looking at philosophy from such strictly scientific angles as those of psychologist, neurologist and psychiatrist, fields in which the Society had produced a number of members in recent years, resulted in discussions taking on personal problems. 'We talked about personal relationships in an exhaustive manner and there wasn't much I can remember of any political or scientific interest,' says another member of this period. 'By discussing our personal problems, or even our fantasies and eccentricities we were able to understand what was genuine and what was bogus in philosophy and psychiatry. Wittgenstein has always insisted that Freud was not a scientist. And while some of us thought Wittgenstein was an outdated crank, others felt Freud was really making a literature of fantasies out of his theories of psycho-analysis. There was something to be said for each school of thought.'

One or two Apostles of those days have asserted that as much, if not more, value was obtained from informal discussions between groups of fellow members than in Society debates. 'Out of the chats between three or four members in a member's rooms, or sometimes even between just two members, came much material for Society discussions,' said one. 'Sometimes as few as three of us would debate such an off-beat theme as 'did Freud explain children to writers?' commented the same member.

This struck a chord in the author's memory, though it was a long time before the subconscious message could be deciphered. Suddenly I recalled that Jonathan Miller had written something resembling this and eventually I found it tucked away in an article he wrote in the 1960s: 'Freud simply carried into childhood, and into the fantasy of the world of dreams, the same imaginative sensitivity which other writers had expended on the world of waking adults. It was not so much that he brought science to bear on adults as the fact that he enlarged the scope of *literature* to include the world of dreams and children.'[10]

If the influence of the early post-World War II Apostles was beginning to make a strong impact in many fields in the 1960s, that of the pre-war Apostles was still considerable. Sir Andrew Cohen, who had been strongly criticised for some of his actions and policies in Uganda, was for a brief period permanent United Kingdom representative on the trusteeship council of the United Nations, after which he became Permanent Secretary of the Ministry of Overseas Development. He was at the ministry when it was presided over by Mrs Barbara Castle, a coincidence which led some wit to refer to them as 'the Elephant and Castle'. It was not an inapt nickname: I have personal memories of hearing an elephantine noise of feet pounding down a staircase at the old Colonial Office in the early 1950s and smartly stepping back into the wall as Sir Andrew dashed past one, taking two stairs at a time, his hat brim between his teeth and files under each arm. Sometimes, half an hour later, he would be seen chatting to journalists in a café in Whitehall.

He made it a duty to know what journalists were thinking and writing about the territories with which he was concerned. In 1948 he had also inaugurated a Colonial Service summer conference at Cambridge where, sometimes at Queen's, he initiated seminars on colonial administration. People from the Colonial Service and the Colonial Office, some members of the University and a few administrators from Belgian, French and Portuguese dependencies would discuss all manner of problems, usually including some highly controversial papers prepared by Cohen himself. Kenneth Bradley has discribed how Cohen was at his best on these occasions – 'no longer intimidating, restless or "difficult". He used to sit there, hunched and overflowing on a very small chair, smiling and benign. And he never missed a trick. Always on the alert for good ideas, when one came up he would be on it like a flash, throw it like a ball into the air, and toss it back into play again. From those ideas . . . policy was born, and friendships, too.'[11]

Sir Andrew turned his summing-up of the lessons learnt in nearly twenty years in the Colonial Office and his term as Governor in Uganda into four lectures which he delivered at the Northwestern University in the United States. Tragically, his last few years were marred by cross-examination by MI 5 officers who were concerned about his association with the 1930s members of the Society, several of whom were subjected to questioning not necessarily about themselves, but quite often about others. He died in 1968 following a heart attack.

It was in the 'sixties that, following the Philby defection to the USSR, Sir Anthony Blunt, as he then was, came under questioning by MI 5, and these interrogations eventually led to a confession and the revelation of other names among the Apostles, or their close acquaintances. Cohen had been a close friend of Blunt, a friendship for which he paid the price like several other of Blunt's acquaintances.

On the other hand the long-suffering peoples of Uganda and Tanzania paid an even greater price for Cohen's policies. In these countries were perpetuated the most glaring and blatant electoral irregularities almost any country has ever witnessed following the coming to power of Milton Obote, the man the Kabaka regarded as unfit to rule. Cohen's arrogance was in fact one of the main reasons for Britain's steady loss of influence in Africa because of his insistence on imposing his notions of good government and good form on Africans who were indifferent to either concept. As Mrs Huxley in her work, *Four Guineas*, clearly warned, the decline of British influence in Africa had been due to the fact that worthy officials backed by missionaries incapable of learning the truth actually *bored* the natives. Africans believe in fun and laughter rather more than in work. Organised boredom, as Mrs Huxley pointed out, was, with Africans, one way of losing an empire.

Several Apostles were questioned by the Security Services about this time, and similar inquiries were carried out on the other side of the

Atlantic with the result that the Federal Bureau of Investigation in the USA built up a considerable dossier on the Apostles and their links both in America and Canada. It should perhaps be stressed that in many of these inquiries the search for more detailed information was often not so much on members of the Society, but on their friends. These included people like Herbert Norman, the Cambridge-educated diplomat who committed suicide after being questioned about his contacts with the Soviet Union, and the late J. V. ('Peter') Murphy, formerly of Magdalene, a left-winger who was a close friend of Lord Mountbatten who frequently found him a place on his staffs. Murphy, too, had contacts in the USA.

Sir Dennis Proctor, interviewed in 1981 by Harry Longmuir in Marseilles, admitted that

'I was suspected by MI 5 as a Soviet agent. They were convinced that because I was a personal friend of Guy Burgess and Anthony Blunt I must have been a member of Blunt's espionage ring. But I was not a spy. Like many hundreds of others at Cambridge in those days I was a Marxist. A colonel chap in MI 5 asked to visit me in 1966, two years after Blunt confessed to being a spy. The questioning went on and on. He had with him a copy of a letter which Guy Burgess had sent me from Washington. Guy was a good friend of mine. I knew he was homosexual, but he was good lively company and I had no idea at all that he was an agent for the KGB. But I am telling you, as I told the man from MI 5, that I never at any time consciously betrayed my country. It has been reported that I said I had no secrets from Guy Burgess. It is very true. But I had no real secrets to give.'[12]

That may, or may not be true. He was investigated by MI 5 in 1966 and, according to Anthony Blunt, he 'provided Burgess with one of the best sources he ever had.' Certainly Proctor's sources of intelligence extended far beyond the Treasury and he had many contacts within the SOE organisation in World War II.

Alister Watson was another of those questioned in this period and, coincidentally, he died in the same year as Sir Dennis Proctor. Meanwhile Guy Burgess, so often accused by friend and foe alike of being outrageously indiscreet, maintained a silence in Moscow about his associations with the Society. When Tom Driberg (later Lord Bradwell) was in Moscow researching his book, *Guy Burgess: A portrait with background*, he sought some information on the Apostles, but admitted 'I was unable to persuade Guy to tell me who his fellow-members were.'[13]

Outstanding among Apostolic achievements in the 1960s were those of

Sir Alan Hodgkin. Having been appointed Assistant Director of Research in Physiology in Cambridge in 1948, he carried out researches on the nature of nervous conduction – on which he had previously worked at the Rockefeller Institute of Medical Research in New York. Then in 1963, Professor Hodgkin, as he then was, shared the Nobel Prize for Medicine with two other physiologists for their work on nervous impulses, Professor Andrew Huxley and Professor Sir John Eccles.

Another Apostle who came to the fore in the 'sixties was Professor Geoffrey Lloyd, professor of ancient philosophy and science, who is Fellow of King's. Another Old Carthusian, he was Senior Tutor at King's from 1969-1973, after which he became Bonsall Professor at Stanford University, as well as a Fellow of the Japanese Society for the Promotion of Science. In 1966 he published *Polarity and Analogy*, swiftly followed by *Aristotle: the Growth and Structure of his Thought* and in 1979 the fascinatingly provocative *Magic, Reason & Experience*.

It would seem that gradually the younger members of the Society dominated proceedings and that the elder members attended less regularly. 'The serious discussions were mainly attended only by the younger members,' an elder Apostle told me, 'though there were occasional social occasions to which older Apostles were invited. Although there are official minutes of discussions, there is a strong disposition to couch these in frivolous terms involving puns and obscuring what was discussed.'

As to the attitude of members to the 'Roby curse' and initiation rituals in the 'sixties, the situation would appear to be somewhat ambiguous. One Apostle tells me by letter: 'As for the Roby curse – I can't recall anyone saying anything about it. In fact I'd never heard about it until you mentioned it.'

Another member of the same decade replied to my inquiry as to whether this custom was still kept up: 'The ritual jargon did, I think, continue to be used, albeit with irony.'[14]

170

# 16

# IN PURSUIT OF TRUTH

'The one thing you never admit to in Cambridge is
wealth. For me it's not simply Puritanism, but political
Puritanism. It's the history of the Diggers and Levellers
. . . In Oxford, by contrast, people don't behave as if
they're guilty. They're much more Cavalier . . . Here
it's important that you should be in pursuit of the truth.'
(Professor Istvan Hont)[1]

One of the most remarkable facts about the 1970s in Cambridge was
that, while almost everyone admitted that there had been a change in
outlook, few agreed as to exactly what that change was. In retrospect,
however, it would seem to have been not just a change in any one
direction, but an altering of course by people of varying opinions. The
right wing swung more positively to the right and this became more
marked as the decade drew to a close, the Far Left became strangely
élitist (strangely in the sense that it was élitist while vehemently denying
this), and those some way in the middle became politically apathetic and
much keener on just trying to achieve something on their own account.

Maybe this is not an ideal, or a statistically proven picture of the 1970s,
but it is at least a glimpse of what emerges after talking with both
Apostles and non-Apostles, lecturers, Fellows and students. It is, of
course, a somewhat bewildering picture and one which is rejected by
those academics who like to think of Cambridge in terms of crisp
summaries. But Professor Hont got somewhere near the truth in his own
comments made at the beginning of this chapter; there was a more
serious and deeply probing quest for truth, not unlike the doubters of
Sidgwick's time.

'King's had the edge in those days,' said one member of the Society.
'Not my college, but we all knew that somehow King's quietly controlled
things, or at least so it seemed to be. Too claustrophobic for me, which
was perhaps the reason I was always rather sceptical about the reasons for
our existence as a Society. Oh, yes, I remain silent on certain matters, but
I feel I can honestly be critical if only to enlighten to a modest degree
those who may follow. Nobody ever worshipped Marx in my brief time

as an active member, or, if they did, it was under some other name or ism. They were much more influenced by Noam Chomsky, the professor of linguistics at Massachusetts Institute of Technology, the inventor of transformational grammar. The Society had got itself into the world of words, semiotics, or whatever else you like to call it. They kept on analysing what words really meant. Quite right in a way, so very many words are wrongly used today, and the subjunctive is on the way out.'

Later this same member summed up the situation by saying: 'It may all sound different, perhaps, but in fact nothing had really changed. We were still chasing essentials in a pursuit of non-essentials.'

This was perhaps a cynical member's view. In many respects a very great deal has changed. Which all goes towards showing how members' views have differed down the ages. A member who has had considerable influence in the last few decades both inside and outside the Society is Professor Quentin Skinner, of Christ's College, where he became a Fellow in the 1960s, and was a lecturer in history and political science. It was he who, together with Peter Laslett and W. G. Runciman produced in 1972 their joint work, *Philosophy, Politics and Society*, and who later in the 1970s spent some time working in the United States. Here, while at the Institute for Advanced Study at Princeton University, Professor Skinner became greatly influenced by such American colleagues as Clifford Geertz, Thomas Kuhn and Albert Hirschman.

A new style of Apostolic thinking was introduced in the 'fifties and maintained up until the 1970s by Professor Harry Johnson, a Canadian member. He had known Maynard Keynes and the highly controversial members of the Cambridge Economics Faculty. After a spell at Toronto and Harvard, where he obtained his doctorate, he went to King's College. Afterwards he moved swiftly around the academic Establishment, first as Professor of Economic Theory at Manchester, then at Chicago University, and from 1966 to 1974 he held a chair at the London School of Economics, spending half the year in London and the other half in Chicago. He was above all else an Atlantic man and a dedicated internationalist, highly suspicious of Establishments everywhere and devoted to encouraging people from all universities, even perhaps especially those other than Oxford and Cambridge. Such encouragement he was able to substantiate in a practical form when he was editor of a variety of economic journals, especially that of the *Journal of Political Economy*, that outstanding Chicago journal which he edited until his death at the early age of fifth-three in 1977.

In 1974 Professor Johnson resigned from the London School of Economics and announced that he was ceasing to be a British resident and would in future be based in Chicago. In his letter of resignation he referred to the fact that owing to

IN PURSUIT OF TRUTH

IN PURSUIT OF TRUTH

'new developments in government policy . . . the prospects look even bleaker for the future in terms both of the development of graduate work and of the economic position and rewards of the academic career in Britain.' He added that 'there is the doubt about whether Britain will remain in the European Community, or at least whether there will be a Community in any significant sense . . . Secondly, it is clear that the standards of living of senior academic personnel will be reduced through both increased taxation and control of pay scales, as part of government policy for dealing with inflation.'

In June, 1971, Professor Johnson gave the presidential address of the Apostles' annual dinner, and, in doing so, he brought in all the traditional jargon of the Society in his opening sentences: 'I must confess to you that the farther away one gets from the *hearthrug*, both temporally and spatially, the more difficult it is to think of a suitably interesting subject. The essence of *the real world* is that subjects considered unthinkable need to be thought about, and that answers are far less important than questions. The *phenomenal world*, unfortunately for itself and us, works the other way around; the unthinkable is defined as inconvenient to think about . . . And if one has lived with the *phenomenal world* long enough – especially if one has lived in the United States – it becomes very difficult to think of a significant question, other than the question implied by an answer one already believes.'

One question he posed in his address, referring to earlier discussions on the subject, was 'what has the Cambridge homosexual tradition contributed to and subtracted from British public and intellectual life?' Professor Johnson went on to mention 'our late brother Strachey's attack on the ponderous pretentiousness of the sturdy Victorian society in which he grew up', saying that while this attack was justified, 'the absence from Strachey's work of a positive alternative suitable for mass consumption may well have contributed to the loss of self-confidence in British society that has led in our times to the determination on self-immolation in a fictitious "European" identity.'

He also had comments to make on other Apostles of an earlier era. There was an implied criticism of Keynes when he reminded members of the latter's dictum that 'in the long run we are all dead', which he described as 'a counsel of economic expediency that has tremendous political appeal, but that no-one responsible for rearing the next generation could or should take seriously as a guide to action.' On the other hand he paid tribute to 'the ability of Brother Keynes to break the crust of orthodoxy and come up with a contribution to the theory and practice of economic policy that places him in the category of modern greats along with Marx, Freud and Darwin; and in the field of literature, the ability of our late brother Morgan Forster to grasp and present the essence of the relation between the British and the Indians in India in a way enlightening to both . . . and also to appreciate the complexities of the relationship between the sexes, though it was perhaps unreal of him to rely on the novelist's conventional identification of one copulation with one conception.'

These reflections, asserted Johnson, suggested another question –

'has our permissive society unwittingly sacrificed the social value of the homosexual fringe by making it a legitimate part of the social fabric? Our brother Annan laboured long to get the laws against homosexuality changed in the cause of human freedom. The results are undoubtedly to create a more humane and acceptable society. But is it a better society? One suspects that it will turn out to be more tolerable, but less interesting and exciting. Indeed, one suspects that, now we have more or less disposed of nationality, race, religion and colour as grounds for discrimination and oppression, the only place to which we can look for social criticism and new ideas and under-standing is the one surviving area of discrimination in our society, discrimination against women. And if ever women achieve equality with men, our culture and society will be a dead duck.'

The introduction of female members to the Society after 1970 became almost inevitable after many of the senior colleges, including that erstwhile male precinct of King's, gave places to women. No society, élitist or otherwise, could hope to survive without making such a concession in the light of the long overdue consensus on the need for parity between males and females at the University on all levels.

Professor Johnson said at the 1971 dinner that

'the second subject that I thought of as the subject for my paper tonight, is the position of women in our society, in both the narrow and wide sense of the term "society". It is a particular pleasure to me to welcome our first "sister". Before I graduated to the status of angel, we had many discussions of the eligibility of various of our female colleague undergraduates for membership in the Society: and some of those whose names we discussed have demonstrated by their subsequent careers that we were wrong not to have elected them . . . The closest we came, in thought at least, was a speech at the dinner by our brother Hobsbawm, a speech in which he passed in review the great ladies of history and attempted to decide which were apostolic in character and which were not. So far as I can recall, Madame de Maupassant passed the test brilliantly, but Cleopatra was consigned to the outer darkness.'

174

One of the first female Apostles was Juliet Annan, daughter of Lord Annan. Her tutor was Dr N. O. A. Bullock, a member of the Architecture Department. Miss Annan took up residence at King's in 1974, obtaining her B.A. in 1977 and her M.A. in 1981. There have been two other female students from King's who have been elected to the Society in the last few years, but women generally are still in the minority. Miss Heather Glen, of New Hall, was another much welcomed English scholar member of the Apostles in the 1980s.

The main theme of Professor Johnson's presidential address was posed in the question: 'in real world terms, is the phenomenal world beyond redemption; or, in more prosaic terms, has the quality of life deteriorated beyond the point of tolerability?' 'When I first read our brother Keynes's paper on "My Early Beliefs",' he declared, 'I was struck by the supreme arrogance it displayed – here was a small group of gilded youth in Cambridge shielded by inherited social position from the expediencies of the phenomenal world that confronted everyone else, when virtually everyone else was preoccupied with the struggle to stay alive.'

Then came a revolutionary proposition by Apostolic standards: 'if one were re-forming the Society today, one would select perhaps two people from Cambridge or Oxford, one from Manchester, one from Aberdeen, and one from Exeter or Sussex – and, if one really knew, one from India or Africa or even from a remote college in the United States. There are people all over the world who have the true apostatic [sic] spirit.'

There were many things in contemporary society against which Apostles should rebel and Johnson summarised these under the headings of professionalism, pollution and privacy. On privacy he posed the question whether this was a private right or a public danger. On pollution he commented that 'we have told business firms to produce as cheaply as possible and to pay as high wages as possible, and one of the results has been that our air, water and food have become noxious to a degree that we resent. There is a serious problem here, that of striking a balance between the demand for civilised behaviour on the part of our businesses, in the sense of retaining an environment in which the rest of us can live, and the needs of business for a working environment in which it can produce efficiently and competitively and generate incomes that will permit the rest of us to have a satisfactory material standard of living.'

On what he called the 'crucial question of professionalism', Johnson said that the individual had become useful to society, not because he was

'a good person, but because he is an expert on something; and he is less useful the more his personality and individuality get in the way of the impersonal performance of his expert functions. The central problem that modern society poses is how to reconcile the liberty of the human spirit with society's need for people who can be trusted to perform an expert function in an expert and impersonal way.'

In a rare public statement in October, 1981, Professor Quentin Skinner, described as 'this year's president of the Society', said that:

'Secrecy is an extremely strong convention of the Society. When you join, you accept that convention . . . There are still weekly meetings, but I have not attended those for ten or fifteen years. Invitations to the annual meeting are sent out to all living members both here and abroad.'[2]

The annual meeting of the Society on that occasion was held in the Old Combination Room at Christ's College, and there was somewhat of a shock when it was discovered that a member of the *Cambridge Evening News* staff was seeking information. The latter's comments were that 'members began arriving at the Old Combination Room at about 7 p.m. and began to drift away soon after 11 p.m. They refused to comment and seemed taken aback when they were asked about the Society.'[3]

By the early 'seventies, according to most reports, nobody ate or drank anything at the Society's meetings which lasted 'only as long as they were interesting,' according to Professor Skinner.[4]

Something which reflects Professor Johnson's thinking about expanding and exporting the Apostolic spirit has been the informal and entirely individual exchange of views and ideas between members of the Society and the American and Canadian academic fraternity in the 1970s. There sprang up a happy and inspiring relationship of Cambridge Apostles and specialists in political science, the history of ideas, economics and in many other branches of thought across the Atlantic, all of which has helped to consolidate what might broadly be called Western thinking. One fascinating by-product of this was Professor Skinner's book on *Machiavelli* (1981), and Harry Johnson weighed in with such tomes as *Further Essays in Monetary Economics* and *Economic Policies Towards Less Developed Countries*.

Ronald Bryden, who was at King's and a member of the Society, after a spell as a dramatic critic, eventually took up a post at Toronto University. Dr David Wooton, one of the rare Peterhouse members of the Society, who took his M.A. in 1976, after a spell at Westfield College, London University, went to the Department of History at the Dalhousie University, Halifax, Nova Scotia.

The 'seventies was an age of swift change, switching allegiances, swopping jobs, moving around the world, and, because of this, it was less easy to keep trace of what some Apostles were thinking and debating. Brilliant shooting stars of the University came into the Society, attended about six meetings and then shot off again – sometimes to another university in the United Kingdom, sometimes overseas, frequently into an unexpected post. The 1970s members were totally different from those of the past. They felt less need for roots, they wanted to experiment, to 'do their own thing' to a much greater extent than previously.

Meanwhile some of the older Apostles were still influencing life in many fields in the 1970s. Lord Rothschild had been invited by Edward Heath, then Prime Minister, to become the first head of the Government's 'Think Tank', or Central Policy Review Staff as it was called officially. 'I had no idea what it was intended to be or to do,' declared Lord Rothschild. 'Nor did anyone else seem to have much idea . . . We spent quite a time during the first six months arguing about what we were supposed to be doing . . . From the start it seemed to me that our job was to analyse problems and proposals.'[5]

The CPRS was in many ways the type of organisation admirably fitted to some Apostolic thinking. But the CPRS has always suffered from lack of governmental direction and, because of this, governments following the Heath administration tended to blame the 'Think Tank' rather than themselves. Governments failed to lay down adequate guide-lines, or to show a proper concern for the vital necessity for such a body, and so it has tended to have its wings clipped and to remain somewhat amateurish, never being given enough scope for purposeful development. In Tokyo the value of a 'Think Tank' has been increasingly appreciated by each succeeding Japanese government so that today there is not just one organisation of this type, but several, all covering different subjects ranging from specific areas of the world to such closely defined matters as the environment and anti-pollution measures.

But if the 'Think Tank' project appears to be less favoured in Britain today, one can in no way blame Lord Rothschild. The 'Think Tank' was stopped largely because successive governments could not make up their minds exactly what they wanted the CPRS to achieve. They also failed to pay sufficient attention to some of its warnings.

One of these warnings was given by Lord Rothschild himself, when in September, 1973, he clearly cautioned the Government by declaring that unless Britain stopped acting like a rich nation, it would become one of the poorest in Europe by 1985. This warning was given in a speech to the Letcombe Laboratory of the Agricultural Research Council at Wantage, and it was well outside the terms of reference given to him by the Prime Minister, Edward Heath. What in effect he was saying was that, though Britain was a very pleasant country to live in (a view shared by people of many nationalities) the future was bleak unless there were many changes in policy.

An important point to make, if only to counteract the incredible complacency of the government of that day in the face of rapidly growing inflation: within two years it was approaching thirty per cent per annum. But it was in a remarkable address which he made on the occasion of becoming an Honorary Fellow of the Imperial College of Science and Technology on 24 October, 1975, that Lord Rothschild supplied what might well have been a Saturday night Apostolic peek into the future. He warned of the need for finding a solution to the problem of a world-wide population explosion: 'if we assume that people will go on having babies at the present rate, by the year 3700 the weight of all the human beings on earth will equal the weight of the earth.'

Possibly, with tongue slightly in the cheek, Lord Rothschild also posed the prospect of a 'pleasure-giving' pill, Extasin, which would 'be issued free, to a limited extent, on the health service, every Saturday morning', while the opposite of this drug ('Miserin: a drug to produce symptoms of intense misery') would need to be produced as a substitute for prison sentences. 'Law Court computers may decide, not only for public expenditure reasons, that cancellation of Extasin should replace the present archaic system of prison sentences. If one is used to intense pleasure every week-end, it will be an intense punishment not to experience it.'

War in the future, he added, 'may well be left to the anti-chemists. So it will be a race between the dejection and anti-dejection chemists, just as it is today between the SAMs with their changing gadgetry and the electronic countermeasures in the aircraft of ICBMs to be shot down.'

There were perceptible changes in Marxist thinking in the middle of the 1970s, some of them amounting to Marxist revisionism, some even to a rejection of certain aspects of Marxism. In Chinese communist circles a severe and highly critical appraisal was made of how Marxism had been taught. It first started relatively secretly in Peking where senior party members were told that Karl Marx's ideas were outdated and should not be taken too literally. Some of this thinking, though not necessarily in the same drastic form, percolated to Cambridge. At the University – not least at King's – there was a new theme among left-wing thinkers: Eurocommunism. Meanwhile at the International Congress of the Historical Sciences held at San Francisco in August, 1975, both Eastern and Western scholars argued, sometimes bitterly, about ideological controversies. The 83-strong Soviet delegation went out of their way to lay stress on the progressive nature of the American revolution, while at the same time insisting that their own 1917 revolution was the model for all future revolutions. Professsor Hobsbawm, who spoke at great length at this conference, attempted to cover all the many revolutions of the past 300 years, reminding his audience that Latin America alone had some 115 revolutions in the nineteenth century. But Soviet dogmatism was severely criticised during the conference, with Professor Fritz Stern, of Columbia University, declaring that 'the dogmatic assertion that Leninist history is beyond criticism, beyond conflict and the highest dispensation of truth is disheartening.'[6]

It was in the early 1970s that research scientists all over the world began to acknowledge their debt to Sir Alan Hodgkin. In his quest for the secrets of the complex internal system of communication essential to all forms of life, he had turned his attention to the shore crab. For the shore crab, in spite of its anti-social habits, has a special feature in the size of its nerve fibres. His achievement in isolating the individual nerve fibre had made possible significant progress with the communication of an electric impulse as it travelled along it. From the crab he had turned to the squid of the genus *loligo* because of its giant nerve fibres and its remarkable gift for swimming backwards at an enormous speed. However, in 1972 Sir Alan began to take an interest in much broader issues, not least when, as President of the Council of the Royal Society, he submitted a critical memorandum on the question of a partnership between the Government and the scientific community. This memorandum was presented to the House of Commons Select Committee on Science and Technology. It is interesting to note that this represented somewhat of a clash between two Apostles, as in effect Sir Alan was commenting on a report made by Lord Rothschild.

A few years later Sir Alan was criticising the reluctance of the Government to appoint a scientific adviser to the Cabinet in his retiring speech as President of the Royal Society. On this occasion he might almost have been addressing a Saturday night meeting of the Society for much of his speech was in true Apostolic tradition: 'The need for central coordination would become acute if the country were faced with a sudden crisis involving science and technology, as most crises do. Suppose, for example, there was a major epidemic of rabies in this country. The Government would have to deal with a number of awkward questions, involving a mixture of science and politics, which did not fit easily into the remit of one research council or ministry.

'For example, should all the foxes (or even dogs) be destroyed? How widely should innoculation be used? Should it be compulsory? Such questions involve the Ministry of Agriculture, the Medical Research Council, the Nature Conservancy Council, the Department of the Environment, the Home Office and the Ministry of Defence.'

Going on to urge the creation of a scientific adviser to the Cabinet, Sir Alan said that while such a person 'would probably know little about rabies or foxes, he would know his way around Whitehall, and he would know how to get the best scientists to work, both inside and outside Whitehall.'[7]

It has been noticeable throughout the period in which the Apostles have existed that, while a tiny minority of them have gone into politics, in the main they have preferred, or been content to exercise power and authority behind the scenes in Civil Service, diplomatic or advisory and even experimental capacities than to take part in government. That behind-the-scenes influence has often been extremely effective. Sir Alan's most valuable role was perhaps his bringing together of industry and science in a Cambridge experiment. He had been impressed by the effectiveness of technology in Germany and Japan due to the very close relations between industry and the universities and polytechnics, and the fact that in the United States there were some 82 science 'parks', of which nineteen were wholly restricted to research-related industry. In July, 1975, he saw a dream come true, the opening of Cambridge Science Park, a £650,000 Trinity College venture planned to attract science-based industry to the university environment. Its aim was clearly laid down as achieving 'a moderate growth of science-based industry in Cambridge in order to take maximum advantage of scientific expertise, equipment and libraries available in the area and to increase feedback of all kinds from such industry to local research laboratories.' The experiment proved to be highly successful.

In 1978 Sir Alan Hodgkin was appointed Master of Trinity College in succession to the late Lord Butler of Saffron Walden. There was at first some mystery in 1984 when Sir Alan failed to win re-election at the age of seventy, and retired from office. This might be partly explained by the desire of some senior University figures to seek a non-science man as Master, though there could be no doubt that the services Sir Alan had rendered both his college and the University itself were inestimable. There had, however, been a tradition at Trinity for the Mastership to go alternately to a humanist and a scientist. Interestingly, yet another Apostle, Walter ('Garry') Runciman was tipped for the post by many.

Across the Atlantic Ocean Michael Straight, who had been a significant force in opposing Senator Joseph McCarthy's obsessive and virulent witch-hunts of alleged communists in the 1950s, had distinguished himself in various fields. For three years he had served as national chairman of the American Veterans' Committee, while at the same time founding the United States section at Amnesty International. From 1969-78 he was deputy chairman of the National Endowment for the Arts, playing a considerable role in raising appropriations from six million to one hundred million dollars in those nine years. This was a tremendous achievement and there can be no question that in this decade the aesthetic consciousness of the American people were raised, the arts flourished and, to everyone's surprise, public funds were provided without censorship.

Michael Straight's books have also made an impact, ranging from such novels as *Carrington* and *A Very Small Remnant* to *Trial by Television* (his work on the McCarthy indictments) and *Make This the Last War*, a serious attempt (in the author's own words) 'to short-circuit time and to build on the world created by the last war.'[8]

When the revelations in the British Parliament and media concerning the links established by some Apostles with agents of the Soviet Union were made in the 1979-82 period there were some remarkable displays both of humbug and the British disease of obsessive secrecy among some of the older members. They took the view that the Society was very much a private affair and that nobody should invade that privacy. As has so often been the case, the media and especially the newspapers were blamed and attacked, as seen in Hugh Sykes Davies' Apostolic Letters to the *Cambridge Review*, when asked by the editor, Dr Brewer, to write on the Society. These 'Letters' read as though he, too, had been put under some duress from fellow 'Angels'. They could almost have been called *Non-Apostolic Letters*. Certainly some members of the Society (mostly the older ones) criticised Dr Brewer for suggesting such an article.

The view of these Society critics seemed to be that privacy was what the Apostles sought and that until then there had been an unspoken contract between the Society and outsiders to respect this. What they conveniently overlooked were two vital points: (1) that it was originally some of the members who had broken this secrecy in memoirs and books over very many years; and (2) that the fact that Blunt, Burgess and Long had been members in the same period could hardly be overlooked by any responsible journalist. To suggest otherwise was sheer hypocrisy.

However, in the light of these revelations there was, of course, a case for tightening up security within the Society for a period if only to obtain some privacy. An Apostle of the 1970s put it this way: 'What happened in 1979 and the few years afterwards was a blow. But the reason for the maintenance of secrecy was two-fold. Firstly, as had always been the case, we wished to prevent people offering themselves as members. Secondly, the Security Services and many journalists were anxious to discover the identity of recent members. The motives of those wishing to know the membership list are not always pure.'

It is also true that some members were unfairly smeared by implications that they, too, might have been Soviet agents. Some of them

181

were interviewed by MI 5 not because they were regarded as suspects, but in quest of information about fellow-members.

The structuralist controversy in the Cambridge English faculty in 1980 barely touched the Society. Perhaps the reason for this was the influence of the new generation of doubters. This generation, influenced to some extent by the philosopher Apostles of the 'sixties, took rather a pessimistic view of the relationship between philosophy, politics and society. Without ever admitting it, what some of them were doing was to escape from what might be described as a Wittgenstein miasma, to borrow a phrase from Professor Lakatos. There was a desire to escape from ideologies, to admit past diagnostic errors and to cast doubts over a very wide area. This was somewhat unfairly summed up by one of those anonymous *Times Literary Supplement* reviews prior to John Gross's editorship by this criticism of *Philosophy, Politics and Society* by Peter Laslett, W. G. Runciman and Quentin Skinner:

'Their present way back to ideology is programmatic and abstract – it does not actually offer an ideology, it merely tries to clear the ground of objections against the principle of the thing – and tends to do this by casting doubts on the very existence of value-free facts. Well, this would leave us without ideologies or facts. That appears to be the moral.'[9]

This massively incomprehensible piece of criticism should in itself be a justification for ending the anonymity of critics. It bore no relation in this author's opinion to what the trio were saying. Quite simply, Messrs Laslett, Runciman and Skinner were trying to put us all back on course.

The Cambridge tradition to a considerable extent has always been for putting conscience above loyalty, even if this meant being against one's country. Professor Skinner has pointed out that the danger of this is that 'once you take away the religious base of Puritanism, you get 'conscience before loyalty' without any reference point.'[10]

Recent generations of undergraduates have been quietly and effectively questioning their teachers. The lip service paid in the past to many of the philosopher dons and their followers, the sociological-statistical dons, has been called into question. There is now grave doubt among many undergraduates as to what they can be legitimately expected to accept. 'There is much disillusionment on the subject of statistics,' declared one young Apostle. 'They are now regarded by a majority – a cynical majority, I might add, consisting of Apostles and non-Apostles – as liable to be twisted, and those triposes which do include a statistical element, use it to teach students how to twist them to answer a particular question, or to make a particular (political) point. There is widespread cynicism about the value of statistics among the more questioning undergraduates, and this includes a few Apostles. We prefer to debate on non-statistical, empirical topics. There was once even a question posed for debate on 'Are statistics really necessary?' Frivolous, perhaps. But where have statistics got us in the quest of how to get the best out of life? Have we misused them or have statistics bamboozled us?'

In November, 1984, it was reported by two university proctors, commenting on student life, that there was political apathy among many students. Dr John Marks, of Girton College, and Dr Michael Tanner, of Corpus Christi, made the criticism that:

'We have been faced with only one demonstration involving violence, a feature which must be deplored, particularly in one of the premier centres of learning and free speech. On the other hand, we have been disappointed at the very small amounts of peaceful dissension that we have seen this year, and we are concerned about current political apathy on the part of the students in the presence of numerous national and international problems.'[14]

To which Mr Christopher Thornton, president of the Cambridge Students' Union, replied:

'I think the increasing apathy results from more pressure to get a good degree these days in order to get a good job when you leave here. There is also more pressure from parents on their children to do well because of the parental contributions in grants.'

Another reason for the ultra-secrecy of present day Apostles may well be that they wish to keep strictly apart from the many new (some of them self-debunking) societies which have sprung up in the University in recent years. Many of these societies have been critical of the idea of secret societies within the University. Not only do they oppose secrecy, but equally élitism and pretension.

'The Apostles certainly will not have been hit by the number of other societies around now,' says one undergraduate. 'The University is very much an élitist institution however much some may say they hate élitism. The majority of students would jump at the chance to join an "élite within the élite", which the Apostles are very much seen as.'

This is undoubtedly one reason why the Society has lasted for so long, while many other University societies fade out after a few years. There was the Cambridge University Raving Loonies, which disappeared in

1982. They went on a night raid to Oxford, stole all the toilet rolls they could find in the city and made a bonfire of them. There was also Tarquin Fintinlimbin f'tang ole biscuit Barrel, who stood against Mrs Shirley Williams in a by-election at Crosby. He was a Trinity mathematician. It is curious how the more lunatic-farcical elements, who have died away over the last two years, seem to have been mainly mathematicians.

'Cambridge humour is now a lot more sick,' was another Apostolic comment. There was a refusal to enlarge on this remark other than to say that this 'is visible in the content of Footlights revues. To some extent we have all lost a sense of farce in its classic setting.' One was left with an unanswered question: was this reflected in the left-wing and political 'Alternative' school of comedy in some Apostolic thinking?

'What effect has the Aphra Behn Society had on female under-graduates?' I inquired.

The Aphra Behn Society at Cambridge, named after Mrs Aphra Behn, the sixteenth century playwright, is supposed to consist of the twelve 'most beautiful and dynamic' women in the University.

'No more effect than that of the Get Little Claire Society or the Jomsborg – Fantasy Society,' was the evasive reply. 'The Aphra females are all hair gel and ultra-messy hair styles and I don't know anyone who wouldn't agree that if you took away their money and their hair gel, they would be an unremarkable group.'

Some modern societies at Cambridge have been more of an excuse for a giggle than anything else. The Get Little Claire Society has claimed that it was 'formed to warn the outside world of the existence of a miniscule but menacing young female who answers to the name of Claire.' The Jomsburg-Fantasy Society has been in the habit of meeting fortnightly to discuss such authors as Tolkien, Garner, Peake and Italo Calvino.

Miss Julia Bucknall, of King's, comments that many of these societies are for 'a mysterious and largely segregated breed who, for relaxation escape into science fiction, children's literature or wargames with the same fervour they accord to their studies . . . These bands of merry men and women give themselves some spurious title for various reasons – some to mock the pomposity of more traditional Cambridge clubs, while others do it just for a laugh.'[12]

In many respects Cambridge is at the cross-roads today. Some dons will deny this, but the truth is that there is consolidation on the Far Right and on the Far Left. Anything in between is regarded either with downright disfavour and irritation or sheer boredom, even though the Social Democratic Party has gained some adherents. A very large number of present day students look upon consensus politics as 'shuffling the same old pack of political cards,' as one student put it, 'and just hiding the fact that they have neither ideas, nor principles.'

An Apostle stated:

'There is large-scale cynicism about the so-called 'Real World' and the statistics which are said to sum it up. There is a strong move back to theory. So-called reality is doubted, not least statistics as they are presented. There is a return in popularity to what might be termed 'Grand Theory', especially the more modern writers – Foucault, Althusser, the Structuralists – obviously Levi-Strauss – plus people like Barthes. Sartre and its cronies are out, as is straight Marxism, Stalinism and the Heaths, Gilmours, Pyms and Priors of this world. The new debate is (or should be) between the New Right, represented by dons such as Maurice Cowling and Edward Norman at Peterhouse, John Casey at Caius, and the New Left, represented by Bob Rowthorn and the Professor of Sociology, Tony Giddens, both of King's.

'When Francis Pym launched his ridiculously named 'Centre-Forward' group, the Cambridge University Conservatives Association put forward a motion calling for his resignation as their president, and a number of students demanded the resignation of another "wet", Robert Rhodes James, a vice-president. So you see "wetness", especially when it is so irritatingly without any honest alternative policies, is almost totally disregarded, even when it hypocritically pleads compassion.

'If you want to interpret all this, or try to give some glimpse of Apostolic thinking of today (and I doubt if you will altogether succeed), then you must understand that the civilised world is faced with a number of seemingly intractable crises. That tends to make us bend over backwards to see another person's point of view far more than in the past. You cannot possibly compare us with our predecessors of the 'thirties. Nor, when one speaks of Left and Right would it be true to say we were neatly divided into such compartments. What you could say is that few of us now are other than highly critical of much of what Karl Marx had to say and of his relevance to the modern world. This goes for some of the Far Left just as much as the Right. Our Far-Lefters tend to create world-views of their own.

'Take Tony Giddens. He rejects the original Marxist conception of "class" as the be-all and end-all of society, and incorporates some of the Weberian elements of "status" in the determination of social stratification.'

This appears to the author as being as much an attempt to baffle as to inform. But it is nevertheless a most useful contemporary statement.

There is, of course, no such thing as concerted 'Apostolic thinking', only the assorted view of the Society's members. As to how it is possible to end the threat to civilisation as we know it, the comment of an Apostle of the 1930s is apt: 'Now that know-how about atomic and chemical weapons is so widespread we are all faced by the prisoners' dilemma and even with the most astute and well-meaning of political leaders, it is very hard to see how the risk of some crazy fanatic eventually starting a holocaust is to be eliminated.'

Does the suggestion that we must all bend over backwards to see another person's point of view mean that one solution of solving intractable problems is to surrender to the other person's viewpoint, or at least compromise with it? The answer is inconclusive because my young Apostolic contact says: 'Yes and no. Yes in some areas of the world, no in others. Yes on the subtly changing Far Left, or New Left as some of them call themselves, but emphatically no on the soft middle-of-the-roaders in politics and especially to the 'Charter for Jobs' campaign. The latter is nothing less than political wankerism, me-tooism and the canonisation of 'Rab' Butler and the late Edward Boyle. All this is heads-in-the-sands politics. We all know only too well that, with technology rendering so many jobs redundant, what we need to aim for is to educate everyone in the country to be able to tackle at least two, and preferably three jobs efficiently. Then we could have a nation comprising workers doing half-time there and half-time there to make a full week, or even a third here and two-thirds elsewhere.'

There does emerge a picture of at least some Apostles being on the right track. Yet, despite what some of them say, talk of a move to the Right in some quarters should not be interpreted as a move to the kind of Hard Right which has been attacked in some of the University student magazines. There are two kinds of 'New Right' – the Hard Right which is also concerned with the dangers of immigration and over-population and the Thatcherite – Libertarian Right which has more in common with nineteenth century Liberalism.

However, it would seem that a much keener and critical look is taken at the global field of economics by the Society of the 1980s. 'Books and economics are subjects upon which we concentrate,' said one 1980's member. 'Who are your literary heroes?' is a question which members will put to one another. Each tries to find a writer of whom the other has never heard of. A quest for truth, if you like, and that's one way of finding it. Discussion of a philosopher such as Heidegger is common-place. And even Nietzsche is still popular. Proust, Joyce and Lawrence are still avidly studied.

'Of course, you must understand that it is not only a question of discussions by the Society as a whole, but also of congenial groups of members between themselves who have special interests. Such interests are much more diverse than they were, though there are still some taboos. Astronomy and any philosophical discussions developing out of a new look at recent theories would be desirable for some, but the paranormal, by and large, tends to make members yawn. People who want to discuss and argue about the paranormal tend to join either the University's Psychic Research Society or the Sceptics. The Sceptics may be great doubters, but, while they attack the pseudoscientifics of today, especially those who support theories about UFO's, they appear to have an open mind on some matters of the paranormal, as they maintain links with the United States-based Committee for the Scientific Investigation of Claims of the Paranormal (CSICOP).'

But these are Apostolic viewpoints and, as such, may well be meant to tantalise and bemuse an historian of their Society as much as to educate him. On the whole I accept such evidence, given in confidence and with a feeling of mutual trust, as supplying the main outlines of a picture of the Apostles in the 1980s. The only way in which such evidence could be accurately tested (and even then, who knows?) would be for the author to be permitted to sit in at one of the Society's meetings. Such a request was made through an elder Apostle and I received the answer 'My impression is that you would have no chance of being admitted to attend.' And even if I should be granted such an unheard-of privilege, surely it would show a total lack of humour on my part if I did not suspect that on such an occasion my leg would be pulled unmercifully. Occasionally, such clichés have the effect of bringing one back to reality!

While I get the impression that the emphasis is on fast flowing, witty conversation rather than debate today, it would also seem that there is much less of the scornful arrogance once found among Cambridge intellectuals. Sex, I am assured, in all its aspects, is still a subject for frequent discussion, not in the same way that it was in the past, but it is regarded as – again I quote – 'an important but touchy subject.'

A non-Apostle, who is a close friend of an Apostle, has this to say:

'They talk about sex, but in a fairly abstract manner, or necessarily about other people's experiences – be it gay or heterosexual sex. For them this is an important but touchy subject. Their lack of experience of any kind with the opposite sex is in fact a major worry for the King's Apostles.'

This last sentence in reference to thinking on sexual matters in the

187

1980s may seem almost unbelievable, but I have no reason to doubt that it is sincerely held by some. Various spontaneously put counter-questions confirmed this feeling.

'Sex has been presented in such dreary, outrageous and boring terms in literature, drama, etc. today that discerning people are actually being turned off it. They feel the magic has gone out of it and that this ruins real life relationships.'

The female friend of an Apostle has this to say on the subject:

'I think you will find that the King's-orientated philosophers have had a considerable influence and especially a group which calls itself the Thursday Club. This was formed to meet each Thursday and to discuss a paper written by one of its members. I feel sure that they had some links with the Apostles. One or two Thursday Club members may have been Apostles as well.'

But economics is the subject most discussed by Apostles of the 1980s, to some extent due to the fact that one member is 'a very bright and lively economist', I was informed. One interesting subject debated by members in recent years was 'should we all share unemployment?' I am not privileged to have had details of how this debate was conducted, but a few members put forward the theme that, to avoid the tragedy of prolonged unemployment, there should be a system by which some of those who were in employment should have a compulsory spell of unemployment (presumably on some basis of pay) while the unemployed took on their jobs, if only for a few months. This is not as irrational as it might appear at first sight. It is realistic in that unemployment is more likely to increase than to decrease, and it avoids the middle-of-the-roaders' nonsense of creating unproductive jobs temporarily at increasing costs which can in no way be a long-term solution to the problem. However, I was warned: 'Don't make too much of this idea. We haven't really worked it all out yet and some do not go along with it. But it has not only some attractions, but a degree of logic behind it. What's more – on a more flippant level – the compulsory period of unemployment periodically could have some of the advantages of a sabbatical even if it was on much less money. Give one a chance to re-think one's life and how to plan it.'

As an historian approaches the present day it is vitally important that he should record what people still living can tell him. If he fails to do this in considerable detail, he is either in danger of getting the record wrong, or of lacking any feeling for the present.

This particularly applies in writing about the Apostles, even though it is exceedingly difficult to persuade many members to talk. It should not matter, therefore, whether one necessarily believes all one is told, or hears, or even if one thinks it is trivial, it is one's duty to record it, leaving some future historian of the Society in the next century to amend the records as, and if, he sees fit.

For example, one present day Apostolic comment which at first seemed hardly worth mentioning, was to the effect that 'relatively recently we have even swopped stories about our boarding schools. We rather like to look back and see where they were right and where they went wrong.' I queried the phrase 'boarding schools'. 'Yes,' was the reply, 'boarding schools, not necessarily public schools, though they are included. The point is such discussions still seem important.'

Virginia Woolf, who criticised the Apostles' apparent neglect of music and painting in the early 1900s, would have been delighted to know that in the mid-1980s one paper delivered at an Apostolic meeting was on the subject of Cezanne's influence on Braque. Impressionism still triumphs.

To sum up, the Society has probably had a considerable influence in the lives of very many people and could well continue to do so. In retrospect, it seems wrong to suggest that such influence in the sphere of philosophy has had anything like the impact claimed for it in the past, though in a less flamboyant manner it is having rather more potency today. Frankly, except in the case of Bertrand Russell, Apostolic philosophy prior to World War II was so unrelated to everyday life that it was insignificant compared with that of continental Europe.

In the outside world the influence of members has over the past forty years been more significant in science, medicine, economics and technology than in any other fields. Membership of the Society may well have encouraged feelings of élitism with some, and, what is worse, privileged élitism. Some Apostles, such as Harry Johnson, have acknowledged this. As we all suffer from ill effects of counter-élitism in its worst forms today, I should be the last to attack élitism, while still condemning privileged élitism. But in the long run, as I hope this book will have proved, the cut-and-thrust of debate, and arguments of such societies as the Apostles have in very many instances paved the way to better things and justified their existence.

So, if as an outsider, one may raise one's glass, 'To the Apostles, and may they long continue.'

189

# NOTES

## 1  Conversazione

¹*The Autobiography of Bertrand Russell: 1872-1914*, vol. i.

²John Punnett kept copies of many of his letters, and this particular letter is quoted from by permission of Miss C. F. Punnett, a descendant of the writer.

³An article entitled 'The Family', stating that it was in existence in 1834, was published in one of the periodicals of this year. Unfortunately, though a clipping of the article is extant, there is no clue as to the name of the journal. A complaint is made about the introduction of 'pipes and spitting boxes' at dinners held by The Family. A. S. F. Gow, a Fellow of Trinity, was a member of The Family in the 1920s.

⁴*Reminiscences of the University, Town and County of Cambridge: 1780-1820*, Henry Gunning, 1854.

⁵*Unreformed Cambridge*, D. A. Winstanley.

⁶Cited by Nesta Webster in her book, *World Revolution*, Constable & Co., London, 1921.

⁷*The Life of Frederick Denison Maurice, Chiefly Told in His Own Letters*, 2 vols, London, 1884.

⁸Arthur Hallam in a letter to Gladstone, 23 June, 1830, British Library Add. MS 44352, folios 158-9.

⁹Letter from Spedding to W. H. Thompson, of Trinity, 2 June, 1832, Thompson MSS, Papers of W. H. Thompson in Trinity College, Cambridge.

¹⁰Letters from Trench to Donne, 11 December, 1831, in the Johnson MSS (papers owned by Miss Mary Barham Johnson).

¹¹Letter from George Wrangham to Adrian Worship, 23 June, 1839.

## 2  The Lotus-Eaters

¹This letter was shown to the author as a result of an appeal for any documentary evidence of the earlier Apostles. There is the date '18 June, 1832' and the address 'Trinity', but no other clue as to the recipient ('Dear & Beloved Friend'), or the sender. Francis Garden was at Trinity in this period and was a great friend of one, Robert Monteith, another Apostle.

²Cited in *The Unquiet Heart*, R. B. Martin, 1984.

³*Joint Compositions*, E. L. Lushington & G. S. Venables, 1840.

⁴*Tennyson: A Memoir*, Hallam, Lord Tennyson, 1899.

⁵*Ibid.* See also *The Unquiet Heart*, Martin.

⁶*The Cambridge Apostles*, Frances M. Brookfield, 1906.

⁷Letter dated 11 November, 1834, in the Houghton MSS.

⁸This is a quotation from a letter from Buller to Edward O'Brien (another

Apostle) shown to the author when he was researching *The Temple of Love*, which concerned such strange sects as the St Simonians and the Agapemonites.
[9]*Leslie Stephen*, by Noel (Lord) Annan.
[10]*The Autobiography of Bertrand Russell*, vol. i.

## 3  Insurrection

[1]*Joint Compositions*, Lushington & Venables.
[2]*Collected Essays*, Graham Greene, 1969. See essay on *The Apostles in Spain*.
[3]*Tennyson: A Memoir*, Hallam, Lord Tennyson.
[4]*Life of John Sterling*, Thomas Carlyle, 1851.
[5]*The Cambridge Apostles*, Brookfield.
[6]*Personal Recollections of the Insurrection of Ballingarry*, Philip Fitzgerald, 1861.

## 4  The Curse on Henry Roby

[1]*Some Early Impressions*, Leslie Stephen, *National Review*, 1903.
[2]*Five Years in an English University*, C. A. Bristed, 2 vols, New York, 1852.
[3]*Life & Letters of F. J. A. Hort*, A. F. Hort, 1896.
[4]Article in *The Nation*, 28 February, 1907, entitled *The Cambridge Apostles*, by William Everett, See also *Life of Hort*, A. F. Hort.
[5]*Henry Sidgwick: A Memoir*, A. & E. M. Sidgwick, 1906.
[6]*Reminiscences of My Life & Work: For My Own Family Only*, by Henry J. Roby, privately printed, Cambridge University Press, 1904-14.
[7]*Autobiography*, vol. 1, Russell.
[8]*Ibid.*
[9]*Cambridge Between the Wars*, T. E. B. Howarth, 1978.
[10]*After Long Silence*, Michael Straight, 1983.
[11]*Ibid.*
[12]*Dictionary of National Biography.*
[13]*Apostolic Letter – Part I*, Hugh Sykes Davies, *Cambridge Review*, 7 May, 1982.
[14]Letter from J. J. Cowell to Lord Houghton (Richard Monckton Milnes), Houghton MSS, Trinity College, Cambridge.
[15]*Some Early Impressions*, Leslie Stephen.
[16]Statement made in an interview with Brian Silk in the *Daily Telegraph*, 7 December, 1981.

## 5  The Wish to Learn

[1]*Henry Sidgwick: A Member*, A. & E. M. Sidgwick.
[2]*Sowing: An Autobiography of the Years*, Leonard Woolf, 1960.
[3]*Maynard Keynes, vol i. 1883-1920*, Robert Skidelsky.
[4]Johnson MSS Papers.
[5]*The Strange Case of Edmund Gurney*, Trevor Hall, London, 1964.
[6]Cited in *The Occult*, Colin Wilson, Hodder & Stoughton, London, 1971.
[7]*Autobiography*, Russell, vol i.
[8]*Die Rothe Internationale*, Dr Zacher, & *Anarchism*, E. V. Zenker.
[9]*Leslie Stephen*, Noel (Lord) Annan.
[10]*Clarence: the life of the Duke of Clarence & Avondale*, KG, 1864-92, Michael Harrison, W. H. Allen, London, 1972.

[11]*Virginia Woolf: A Biography*, Quentin Bell.
[12]*Granta*, 13 February, 1891.
[13]*The Cambridge Review*, February, 1891.
[14]*Leslie Stephen*, Lord Annan.
[15]*Autobiography*, vol. i., Russell.

## 6   The Higher Sodomy

[1]*Minnermus in Church*, William (Johnson) Cory.
[2]*Life & Letters of Raymond Asquith*, John Joliffe, London, 1980.
[3]*Autobiography and Letters of Charles Merivale, Dean of Ely*, edited by Judith Anne Merivale, Oxford, 1898.
[4]*On the Edge of Paradise: A. C. Benson, the Diarist*, David Newsome, John Murray, London, 1980.
[5]*Maynard Keynes*, Skidelsky.
[6]*Autobiography of Lowes Dickinson*, edited by Sir Dennis Proctor, 1973.
[7]*Ibid.*
[8]*Ibid.*
[9]*G. E. Moore*, Paul Levy.
[10]*E. M. Forster: A Study*, Lionel Trilling, 1967.
[11]*A History of the Modern World: from 1937 to the 1980s*, Paul Johnson, 1983.
[12]Cited in an article entitled *The Cambridge Apostles*, *New Review*, viii, 1893.
[13]*Autobiography of Lowes Dickinson*.
[14]*Ibid.*
[15]*The Letters of Sidney & Beatrice Webb*, edited by Norman Mackenzie, Cambridge & London, vol. ii, 1978.
[16]*Autobiography*, vol. i. Russell.
[17]*A History of the Modern World*, Johnson.
[18]*Lytton Strachey: A Critical Biography*, Michael Holroyd, 1967.
[19]*Ibid.*
[20]See *Lytton Strachey*, Holroyd, and *Maynard Keynes*, Skidelsky.
[21]*Lytton Strachey*, Holroyd.
[22]*George Steiner: A Reader*, George Steiner, Penguin Books, London, 1984.

## 7   God and the Devil

[1]*Autobiography*, vol. i, Russell.
[2]*Ibid.*
[3]*Lytton Strachey*, Holroyd.
[4]*E. M. Forster*, Trilling.
[5]*What I Believe*, 1939, printed in *Two Cheers for Democracy*, E. M. Forster, 1951.
[6]Article entitled *George Moore & Modern Art*, Roger Fry, *Cambridge Review*, 22 June, 1893.
[7]*Variety of Men*, C. P. (Lord) Snow.
[8]*Autobiography*, vol. i, Russell.
[9]*Edward Marsh: Patron of the Arts*, Christopher Hassall, 1959.
[10]*Autobiography*, vol. i, Russell.
[11]*Lytton Strachey*, Holroyd.

[12]*Roger Fry*, Virginia Woolf, 1940.

## 8  The Keynsian Influence
[1]*Maynard Keynes*, Skidelsky.
[2]Review of *G. E. Moore & the Cambridge Apostles*, by David Williams, *Sunday Telegraph*, 1979.
[3]*The Common People*, by Cole & Postgate, chap. xxiv.
[4]*Sowing*, Leonard Woolf, See also *Rupert Brooke*, Christopher Hassall.
[5]*Rupert Brooke*, Hassall.
[6]*Edward Marsh*, Hassall.
[7]*Maynard Keynes*, Skidelsky.
[8]Personal statement to the author.
[9]*Edward Marsh*, Hassall.
[10]See *Rupert Brooke & Edward Marsh*, Hassall.
[11]*Essays in Biography*, J. M. Keynes, 1933.
[12]*The Times*, 2 January, 1934.

## 9  After Armagaddon
[1]*What I Believe*, E. M. Forster.
[2]*Essays in Biography*, Keynes.
[3]Letter to the author from Professor F. A. Hayek, 28 January, 1985.
[4]*Lytton Strachey*, Holroyd.
[5]*Autobiography*, vol. ii, Russell.
[6]*Cambridge Between the Wars*, Howarth.
[7]*Autobiography*, vol. ii, Russell.
[8]*Ibid*.
[9]Archives of the NUSW & AScW, Warwick University.
[10]*Ibid*.
[11]*Writers At Work: the Paris Review Interviews*, edited by George Plumpton, Secker, London, 1985.
[12]Article entitled *Our Century of Humbug*, by Dr A. L. Rowse, *Daily Telegraph*, London, 5 February, 1980.
[13]*On the Edge of Paradise*, Newsome.

## 10  Investigative Marxism
[1]Personal statement to the author in a letter from Mr Michael Straight.
[2]Sir Dennis Robertson: biography in the *DNB*.
[3]Article entitled *The Essential Values: No. 3*, by Sir Dennis Proctor, *Times Literary Supplement*, 2 May, 1975.
[4]*The Strings Are False*, Louis MacNeice, Faber, London, 1965.
[5]*Random Variables*, Victor (Lord) Rothschild, Collins, London, 1984.
[6]*The Times*, London, 21 November, 1979.
[7]*Sunday Times*, 22 November, 1981.
[8]Letter from Sir Jack Longland to the author, 24 November, 1984.
[9]Cited in *Now Magazine*, in an article entitled *The Spy Scandal*, 23 November, 1979.
[10]*Random Variables*, Lord Rothschild.
[11]*After Long Silence*, Michael Straight.

[12]Letter from Lord Keynes to the *New Statesman*, in 1934, cited by T. E. B. Howarth in *Cambridge Between the Wars*.

## 11 Another Spanish Adventure

[1]*Essays, Poems & Letters*, edited by Quentin Bell, 1938.
[2]See *David Guest: A Scientist Fights for Freedom*, by Carmel Haden Guest, Lawrence & Wishart, London, 1938.
[3]*After Long Silence*, Michael Straight.
[4]*Cambridge Review*, October, 1937.
[5]*Autobiography*, vol. ii, Russell.
[6]*The Missing Diplomats*, Cyril Connolly, Queen Anne Press, London, 1952.
[7]*Ibid.*
[8]*Autobiography*, vol. ii, Russell.
[9]*A Chapter of Accidents*, Morgan Goronwy Rees, Chatto & Windus, London, 1972.
[10]*Guy Burgess: A Portrait with Background*, Tom Driberg, Weidenfeld & Nicolson, London, 1956.
[11]Personal statement to the author by Morgan Goronwy Rees.
[12]Article entitled *A Decade, 40 Years On* by Sean Day-Lewis in the *Daily Telegraph*, 31 December, 1979.
[13]*Andalusia's Favourite Author Goes Home*, by Richard Wigg, *The Times*, London, 21 June, 1984.
[14]*Autobiography*, vol. ii, Russell.

## 12 Approaching War Again

[1]*My Silent War*, Kim Philby.
[2]Statement to the author, 3 December, 1984.
[3]*After Long Silence*, Michael Straight.
[4]*Apostolic Letter – Part I*, Hugh Sykes Davies, *Cambridge Review*, 7 May, 1982.
[5]Article entitled *Is this the secret of the Moles*, by Sharon Churcher & Andrew McEwen, *Daily Mail*, 5 November, 1979.
[6]Statement made in an interview with Brian Silk in the *Daily Telegraph*, 7 December, 1981.
[7]Statement made by Hugh Sykes Davies to the author.
[8]Article entitled *An Epilaugh for Surrealism*, by Hugh Sykes Davies, *Times Literary Supplement*, 13 January, 1978.
[9]*Daily Mail*, 5 November, 1979.
[10]Letter from Nicholas Walter to *Private Eye*, 30 November, 1979.
[11]*Alan Turing: The Enigma*, by Andrew Hodges, Burnett Books, London, 1981.
[12]*Ibid.*
[13]*Cambridge Between the Wars*, Howarth.
[14]*Archives of the NUSW & AScW*, Warwick University.
[15]*The Times*, 22 November, 1979: article entitled *The Apostles with different creeds*, by Roger Berthoud.
[16]Statement made by Hugh Sykes Davies to the author.
[17]*The Times*, 22 November, 1979.
[18]Letter to the *Sunday Telegraph* from Robin Bruce Lockhart, 7 October, 1984.

[19]*After Long Silence*, Straight.
[20]Letter to the author from Michael Straight, 15 November, 1984.
[21]*Ibid.*
[22]*Ibid.*

## 13 Apostles at War
[1]*An Epilaugh for Surrealism*, by Hugh Sykes Davies, *Times Literary Supplement*, 13 January, 1978.
[2]Article entitled *MI5 forced me to talk*, *Sunday Times*, 8 November, 1981.
[3]*The Second World War*, vol i, Churchill.
[4]Personal communication to the author by R. J. C. Holmes, of Jesmond, Newcastle-upon-Tyne.
[5]*The Last Words of Wilfred Noyce*, *Sunday Times*, 19 August, 1962.
[6]*The Times*, 3 November, 1981.
[7]*The Missing Diplomats*, Connolly.
[8]*The Victims of Yalta*, Count Tolstoy.
[9]Public Record Office: FO 371/43382 138-42.

## 14 The Fitful Fifties
[1]*My Cambridge*, edited by Ronald Hayman, 1977.
[2]*Ibid.*
[3]*Ibid.*
[4]*Ibid.*
[5]*Ibid.*
[6]*Times Literary Supplement*, 16 May, 1952: review of *An Introduction to the English Novel*, vol. i., Arnold Kettle.
[7]*Letters from Cambridge*, A. S. F. Gow.
[8]*Autobiography*, vol. ii, Russell.
[9]*Tinker, Tailor, Soldier, Don*, by Eric Hobsbawm, *Observer*, London, 21 October, 1979.
[10]Letter to the author from Michael Straight, 15 November, 1984.
[11]*After Long Silence*, Straight.
[12]Cited in *Daughter of Genghis Khan*, *Sunday Telegraph* 15 April, 1985.
[13]*After Long Silence*, Straight.
[14]Article entitled *The Case for the committed politician*, by Simon Hoggart, *Guardian*, 3 July, 1980.
[15]Letter to the author from Professor J. M. Mitchison, 13 November, 1984.
[16]*The Longest Journey*, by E. M. Forster, edited by Elizabeth Heine, Abinger edition, Edward Arnold, 1985.
[17]Article entitled *The Age of Annan*, *Sunday Telegraph*, 7 March, 1985.
[19]*The Times*, 11 & 25 March, 1982.
[19]Letter from Simon Raven to the author, 27 March, 1985.
[20]*My Cambridge*.
[21]*Ibid.*

## 15 The Restless Sixties
[1]*The Cambridge Mind: Ninety Years of the Cambridge Review 1879-1969*, edited

by Eric Homberger, William Janeway & Simon Schama.
<sup>2</sup>*Social Science & Political Theory*, by the Hon W. G. Runciman, Cambridge University Press.
<sup>3</sup>*A Treatise on Social Theory: vol. i, The Methodology of Social Theory*, the Hon. W. G. Runciman, Cambridge UP.
<sup>4</sup>*Times Literary Supplement*, May, 1974.
<sup>5</sup>Letter to the author from Mr Neal Ascherson, 29 January, 1985.
<sup>6</sup>*My Cambridge.*
<sup>7</sup>Cited in *Vasity Handbook: 1984-85.*
<sup>8</sup>BBC Radio 4 talk, 12 January, 1969.
<sup>9</sup>*The Times*, 20 March, 1969.
<sup>10</sup>Article by Jonathan Miller entitled *Beyond Dispute*, *Times Literary Supplement*, 27 July, 1967.
<sup>11</sup>Article entitled *Sir Andrew Cohen: Personal Portrait*, *London Calling*, 11 February, 1954, by Kenneth Bradley, director of the Imperial Institute.
<sup>12</sup>Interview in the *Daily Mail*, 9 November, 1981, by Harry Longmuir.
<sup>13</sup>*Guy Burgess*, by Tom Driberg, Weidenfeld & Nicolson, London, 1956.
<sup>14</sup>The two letters mentioned are duly signed by the respective members.

## 16  In Pursuit of Truth

<sup>1</sup>Cited in an article entitled *The Conscience of Cambridge*, by Graham Turner, *Sunday Telegraph*, 6 December, 1981.
<sup>2</sup>*Secret Society's veil lifts at meeting*, article by Simon Shaps, *Cambridge Evening News*, 5 October, 1981.
<sup>3</sup>*Ibid.*
<sup>4</sup>*Ibid.*
<sup>5</sup>*Random Variables*, Lord Rothschild.
<sup>6</sup>*Revolution fans the fires of historical scholarship*, news item in *The Times*, 29 August, 1975.
<sup>7</sup>*Cabinet needs a chief scientific adviser*, *The Times*, 2 December, 1975.
<sup>8</sup>Letter to the author from Mr Michael Straight, 28 February, 1985.
<sup>9</sup>*Times Literary Supplement*, 22 December, 1922.
<sup>10</sup>*The Conscience of Cambridge*, article by Graham Turner, *Sunday Telegraph*, 6 December, 1981.
<sup>11</sup>*'Political Apathy' at hard-studying Cambridge*, by John Shaw, *Daily Telegraph*, 15 November, 1984.
<sup>12</sup>*Varsity Handbook*, 1984-5.

# BIBLIOGRAPHY

ALLEN, Peter: *The Cambridge Apostles: The Early Years*, Cambridge University Press, Cambridge, 1978.

ANNAN, Noel Gilroy (Lord Annan): *Leslie Stephen: His Thought & Character in Relation to his Time*, McGibbon & Kee, London, 1951.

BEERBOHM, Max: *Zuleika Dobson*, Heinemann, London, 1911.

BENTLEY, Michael & STEVENSON, John: *High & Low Politics in Modern Britain*, Clarendon Press, Oxford.

BROOKFIELD, Frances: *The Cambridge 'Apostles'*, Sir Isaac Pitman & Sons, London, 1906.

CONNOLLY, Cyril: *The Missing Diplomats*, The Queen Anne Press, London, 1952.

DICKINSON, Goldsworthy Lowes: *The Autobiography of G. Lowes Dickinson & Other Unpublished Writings*, edited by Dennis Proctor, with a foreword by Noel Annan, Duckworth, London, 1973.

FOWLER, Laurence & Helen: *Cambridge Commemorated: An Anthology of University Life*, collected & edited by, Cambridge University Press, Cambridge, 1984.

GOW, A. S. F.: *Letters From Cambridge: 1939-44*, Jonathan Cape, London, 1945.

GREENE, Graham: *Collected Essays*, Bodley Press, London, 1969.

HASSALL, Christopher: *Rupert Brooke: A Biography*, Faber & Faber, London, 1964.
*Edward Marsh: Patron of the Arts*, Longmans, London, 1959.

HAYMAN, Ronald: *My Cambridge*, edited and introduced by, Robson Books, London, 1977.

HODGES, Andrew: *Alan Turing: The Enigma*, Burnett Books, London, 1983.

HOLROYD, Michael: *Lytton Strachey: A Critical Biography*, 2 vols, Heinemann, London, 1967 and 1968.

HOMBERGER, Eric, JANEWAY, William & SCHAMA, Simon: *The Cambridge Mind: Ninety Years of the Cambridge Review 1879-1969* Jonathan Cape, London, 1970.

HOWARTH, T. E. B.: *Cambridge Between the Wars*, Collins, London, 1978.

JOHNSON, Paul: *A History of the Modern World: From 1917 to the*

*1980s*, Weidenfeld & Nicolson, London, 1983.

KEYNES, John Maynard (Lord Keynes): *Essays in Biography*, Macmillan & Co., London, 1933. Also the revised edition of *Essays in Biography*, edited by Geoffrey Keynes, Rupert Hart-Davis, London, 1951.

LEVY, Paul: *G. E. Moore & the Cambridge Apostles*, Weidenfeld & Nicolson, London, 1979.

MARTIN, R. B.: *The Unquiet Heart*, Oxford U. Press, 1984.

NEWSOME, David: *On the Edge of Paradise: A. C. Benson, the Diarist*, John Murray, London, 1980.

ROSE, Jasper, & ZIMAN, John: *Camford Observed*, Gollancz, London, 1964.

ROTHSCHILD, Victor (Lord Rothschild): *Random Variables*, Collins, London, 1984.

RUSSELL, Bertrand (Lord Russell): *The Autobiography of Bertrand Russell*: 2 vols, George Allen & Unwin, London, 1967.

SKIDELSKY, Robert: *Maynard Keynes: 1883-1920*, vol. 1, Macmillan, London, 1983.

STEINER, George: *George Steiner: A Reader*, Penguin Books, London, 1984.

STEPHEN, Leslie: *Some Early Impressions, National Review*, 1903.

STRAIGHT, Michael: *After Long Silence*, Collins, London, 1983.

TENNYSON, Alfred (Lord Tennyson): *The Poems of Tennyson*, edited by Christopher Ricks, London, 1969.

TRILLING, Lionel: *E. M. Forster: A Study*, the Hogarth Press, London, 1967.

WILKINSON, L. P.: *A Century of King's*; Register of Admission to King's: 1919-1958.

WINSTANLEY, D. A.: *Unreformed Cambridge*, Cambridge University Press, 1935.

WITHERS, J. J.: *Register of King's College, 1797-1925*.

WOOLF, Leonard: *Sowing*, Hogarth Press, London, 1960.

Also consulted:
The Tennyson Research Centre, Lincoln; Cambridge University Library; the London Library; *Alumni Cantabrigiensis: A Biographical List of All Known Students, Graduates and Holders of Office at the University of Cambridge, from the Earliest Time to 1900*, 6 vols.; the Papers of W. H. Thompson, Trinity College Cambridge; the Johnson MSS, including the Papers of W. B. Donne; King's College Library, Cambridge; St John's College Library; the *Dictionary of National Biography*; the *Cambridge Review*; *Cantab*; *Stop Press, Broadsheet*; *Granta*; and the archives of *The Times, Daily Telegraph, Sunday Telegraph, Sunday Times, Observer, Cambridge News* and various other newspapers; lists of members of the

Society of Apostles.

Many other sources were also consulted, but these are all cited in the Chapter Notes wherever appropriate.

# MEMBERS OF THE SOCIETY

N.B. Names of members are given in alphabetical order and they include those of many not mentioned in the book. The list is not, of course, complete, nor is it entirely up-to-date. Where possible the exact year of election to the Society is given after each name. Otherwise the decade in which the election took place is indicated thus: '194–' or '195–'.

| | | | |
|---|---|---|---|
| AINGER, Thomas | 1820 | BLAKESLEY, G. H. | 1868 |
| AINSWORTH, Alfred | 1899 | BLAKESLEY, Joseph | 1827 |
| ALFORD, Henry | 1830 | BLISS, Francis | 1912 |
| ANDERSON, Frank | 1867 | BLUNT, Anthony | 1927 |
| ANNAN, Juliet Louise | 197– | BOSANQUET, Richard | |
| ANNAN, Noel Gilroy | | Guy | 1937 |
| (Baron) | 1948 | BOWEN, Edward | 1857 |
| ASCHERSON, Neal | 194– | BOYLAN, Richard D | 1824 |
| | | BRAITHWAITE, | |
| BACON, Francis | 1824 | Richard Bevan | 1921 |
| BAINES, Edward | 1825 | BRANDETH, Henry | 1856 |
| *BALFOUR, Arthur J. | | BRICE, Edward Cowell | 1820 |
| (1st Earl) | 186– | BRICE, Henry Crane | 1821 |
| BALFOUR, Francis | | BROOKE, Rupert | 1908 |
| Maitland | 1875 | BROWNE, Thos. W. W. | 1820 |
| BALFOUR, Gerald | | BROWNING, Oscar | 1858 |
| William (2nd Earl) | 1872 | BRYDEN, Ronald | 196– |
| BARKER, Peter W. | 1838 | BULLER, (Sir) Arthur | 1828 |
| BARNES, R. N. | 1828 | BULLER, Charles | 1826 |
| BATTERSBY, Richard | 1820 | BURDON, W. W. | 1822 |
| BECK, Theodore | 1881 | BURGESS, Guy Francis | |
| BEKASSY, Ferenc Istvèàn | | de Moncy | 192– |
| Denés Gyula | 1912 | BUTCHER, John | |
| BELL, Julian H. | 1928 | (Lord Danesfort) | 1873 |
| BLACKBURN, Hugh | 1844 | BUTCHER, Samuel | |
| | | Henry | 1871 |
| | | BUTLER, Arthur John | 1865 |
| | | BUTLER, | |
| | | Henry Montagu | 1853 |

*A. J. Balfour is an unconfirmed member, but because of the evidence for and against, it seems fitting that his name should be recorded.

| | | | |
|---|---|---|---|
| CANE, Arthur B | 1886 | FISHER, | |
| CARTER (Sir) James | 1824 | Edmund Henry | 1856 |
| CHAMPERNOWNE, | | FORSTER, | |
| David Gawen | 1934 | Edward Morgan | 1901 |
| CHRISTIE, | | FORTESCUE, | |
| William Dougal | 1836 | the Hon. Hugh | |
| CLIFFORD, William K. | 1866 | (3rd Earl Fortescue) | 1837 |
| CLOUGH, Arthur | 1883 | FRY, Roger | 1887 |
| COHEN, | | FURNESS, John M. | 1891 |
| (Sir) Andrew Benjamin | 192– | FURNIVAL, James | 1820 |
| COLBECK, Charles | 1868 | | |
| CONYBEARE, J. W. E. | 1865 | GANDY, Robin | 1947 |
| COOKSLEY, | | GARDEN, Francis | 1830 |
| William Gifford | 1828 | GEDGE, Sydney | 1824 |
| CORY (see JOHNSON) | | GIBBS, Frederick | 1842 |
| COWELL, John Jermyn | 1859 | GLEN, Heather | 197– |
| CRUSOE, Francis J. A. | 1929 | GOODEN, Alexander | |
| CURREY, William | 1861 | Chisholm | 1840 |
| CUST, Henry J. C. | 1883 | GOODHART, | |
| | | Henry Chester | 1880 |
| DARWIN, Erasmus | 1823 | GREEN, Walford Davies | 1892 |
| DAVIES, Hugh Sykes | 193– | GREENWOOD, | |
| DICKINSON, | | Leonard H. | 1902 |
| Goldsworthy Lowes | 1885 | GROSS, John | 196– |
| DODGSON, Walter | 1890 | GUEST, Benjamin | 1820 |
| DOGGART, | | | |
| James Hamilton | 1919 | HALL, Richard | 1826 |
| DONNE, | | HALLAM, | |
| William Bodham | 1827 | Arthur Henry | 1829 |
| DUFF, James Duff | 1884 | HARCOURT, | |
| ELPHINSTONE, | | (Sir) William | 1847 |
| (Sir) Howard | 1851 | HARDCASTLE, Joseph | 1835 |
| EVANS, Charles | 1845 | HARDING, Thomas O. | 1872 |
| EVERETT, William | 1862 | HARDY, | |
| | | Godfrey Harold | 1898 |
| FANE, the Hon. Julian | 1848 | HARFORD, Henry | 1820 |
| FARISH, George | 1830 | HARMER, | |
| FARISH, James | 1825 | (Sir) Frederick Evelyn | 1925 |
| FARRAR, (Rev.) | | HARRISON, | |
| Frederick W. | 1852 | Thomas Wynne | 1824 |
| FENNELL, Samuel | 1821 | HAWKINS, | |
| FESTING, | | Francis Vaughan | 1851 |
| George C. R. | 1821 | HAWTREY, (Sir) Ralph | 1900 |

HEATH,
   Douglas Denon      1831
HEATH, Dunbar Isidore 1835
HEATH, John Moore    1834
HEATHCOTE,
   Charles, G.          1861
HELPS, (Sir) Arthur     1833
HENDERSON, Robert   1820
HIBBERT, Arthur Boyd 1946
HOBHOUSE,
   (Sir) Arthur Lee     1905
HOBSBAWM, Eric     193–
HODGKIN, (Sir) Alan  1936
HOLLAND,
   Bernard Henry     1878
HOLLAND,
   Francis James      1846
HOLSWORTHY,
   Wentworth S.      1836
HOPKINSON, John    1870
HORT,
   Fenton John Anthony  1851
HOWARD, George James
   (9th Earl of Carlisle)  1864

JACKSON, Henry      1863
JAMES, Henry Alfred   1849
JEBB, (Sir) Richard    1859
JOHNSON, Harry G.    194–
JOHNSON,
   Henry Robert     1821
JOHNSON (CORY),
   William          1844
JUDGE, Edward C.     1821

KEMBLE, John Mitchell 1826
KENNEDY,
   Benjamin H.       1824
KETTLE, Arnold      194–
KEYNES, John Maynard
   (1st Lord Keynes)    1903

LAW, Edmund        1836

LAWRENCE, E. J.     1835
LEAF, Walter         1874
LEE-WARNER, Henry  1862
LINTOTT, (Sir) Henry
   John Bevin       1929
LITTLE,
   Thomas Shepherd   1872
LLEWELLYN DAVIES,
   Crompton        1889
LLEWELLYN-DAVIES,
   Richard (Baron)    193–
LLEWELLYN DAVIES,
   Theodore        1889
LLOYD, Geoffrey E. R. 195–
LOCOCK, (Sir) Charles 1849
LONG, Leo          193–
LUCAS, Donald William 1925
LUCAS,
   Frank Lawrence    1914
LUCE,
   Gordon Hannington  1912
LUCE, John Marlowe   1939
LUSHINGTON,
   Edmund         1834
LUSHINGTON,
   (Sir) Franklyn     1842
LUSHINGTON, Henry  1833
LUSHINGTON, Vernon 1854
LYTTELTON,
   the Hon. Alfred    1878
LYTTELTON,
   the Hon. Charles
   (8th Viscount Cobham) 1863
MACARTHY,
   (Sir) Desmond     1896
MACAULAY, Kenneth  1831
MACAULAY, W. H.    1876
MACNAGHTEN,
   the Hon (Sir) Malcolm 1891
MAINE, (Sir) Henry   1843
MAITLAND, F. W.    1873
MAITLAND, J. G.     1839
MALKIN, Frederick   1826

| | | | | |
|---|---|---|---|---|
| MANSFIELD, Horatio | 1841 | NOEL, the Hon. Roden | 1857 |
| MARRIOTT, | | NORTON, Henry J. T. | 1906 |
| (Sir) William | 1823 | NOYCE, Cuthbert | |
| MARSH, | | Wilfred Franics | 1934 |
| Sir Edward Howard | 1894 | | |
| MARSHALL, | | O'BRIEN, Edward | 1828 |
| Maurice Oswald | 1914 | O'BRIEN, | |
| MARTINEAU, Arthur | 1827 | William Smith | 1824 |
| MAURICE, | | OLDFIELD, Edmund | 1836 |
| John Frederick | | OUTRAM, Thomas P. | 1822 |
| Denison | 1823 | | |
| MAXWELL, | | PATTON, George | |
| James Clerk | 1852 | (Lord Glenalmond) | 1823 |
| MAYOR, | | PAYNE, John Burwell | 1863 |
| Robin John Grote | 1889 | PENROSE, | |
| M'CALISTER, | | Alexander P. D. | 1919 |
| (Sir) Donald | 1876 | PENROSE, | |
| MCLEAN, Norman | 1888 | Lionel Sharples | 192– |
| MCTAGGART, | | PICKERING, Percival | 1829 |
| John McTaggart Ellis | 1886 | POLLOCK, | |
| MEREDITH, | | (Sir) Frederick | 1865 |
| Hugh Owen | 1900 | POLLOCK, | |
| MERIVALE, Charles | 1832 | (Sir) William | 1834 |
| MILLER, Jonathan | 195– | POMEROY, Robert H. | 1854 |
| MILLER, Karl | 195– | POWER, Sir Alfred | 1825 |
| MILNES, | | POWER, Joseph | 1821 |
| Richard Monckton | | PRATT, John Henry | 1871 |
| (Lord Houghton) | 1829 | PRINCE, | |
| MITCHISON, | | Peter Derek Vaughan | 1938 |
| John Murdoch | 1949 | PROCTOR, | |
| MONRO, Cecil James | 1854 | (Sir) Philip Dennis | 1927 |
| MONTEITH, R. J. I. | 1830 | PRYOR, M. R. | 1869 |
| MOORE, | | PULLER, Charles | 1855 |
| George Edward | 1894 | PUNNETT, John | 1820 |
| MORRISON, | | | |
| Alexander J. W. | 1829 | RALEIGH, | |
| MORTON, | | (Sir) Walter Alexander | 1882 |
| Edward J. C. | 1878 | RAMSEY, | |
| MORTON, Savile | 1832 | Frank Plumpton | 1921 |
| MOULTON, John Fletcher | | RICHARDSON, | |
| (Lord Moulton | | William | 1825 |
| of Bank) | 1867 | RIVES, George L. | 1871 |
| MYERS, Arthur Thomas | 1872 | ROBERTS, John | 1821 |

ROBERTSON,
(Sir) Dennis H. 192–
ROBINSON, Thomas 1838
ROBY, Henry John 1855
ROLLESTON,
Lancelot Charles 1919
ROMILLY, Edward 1824
ROMILLY, Henry 1826
ROTHSCHILD,
N. M. Victor (3rd Lord) 193–
ROWE, Richard C. 1877
RUNCIMAN,
the Hon. Walter G. 195–
RUSSELL,
the Hon. Bertrand
(3rd Earl Russell) 1892
RYLANDS, George 1922

SANGER, Chas. Percy 1892
SHAW, George H. 1820
SHEPPARD,
(Sir) John Tressider 1902
SHORE, Peter David 1947
SHOVE, Gerald 1909
SIDGWICK, Arthur 1861
SIDGWICK, Henry 1856
SIMPSON, George 1822
SIMPSON, John 1820
SKINNER, Quentin 196–
SMITH, Arthur H. 1882
SMITH,
(Sir) Henry Babington 1885
SMITH, James Parker 1876
SMITH, T. Townsend 1826
SMYTH, A. E. A. W. 1897
SPEDDING, James 1828
SPRING RICE, S. E. 1876
SPRING RICE, Stephen 1833
SPRING RICE, T. C. W. 1837
SPROTT, W. J. H. 192–
STANLEY, the Hon.
Edward (15th Earl
of Derby) 1847

STANNING, John 1861
STANTON, Vincent H. 1872
STEPHEN,
(Sir) James Fitzjames 1847
STEPHEN,
James Kenneth 1879
STERLING, John 1825
STOCK, John S. 1821
STOKES,
Charles Samuel 1838
STRACHEY, (Sir) Arthur 1879
STRACHEY,
Giles Lytton 1902
STRACHEY,
James Beaumont 1906
STRAIGHT, Michael 1936
STUART, James 1865
SUNDERLAND,
Thomas 1826
SYDNEY-TURNER,
Saxon A. 1902
SYMES, J. E. 1870

TALBOT, the Hon. James
(Lord Talbot de
Malahide) 1827
TATHAM, H. F. W. 1885
TAWNEY,
Charles Henry 1858
TAYLOR, Alfred 1822
TAYLOR, Cecil Francis 1910
TAYLOR, Thos. 1840
TENNANT, R. J. 1828
TENNYSON, Alfred
(1st Lord) 1829
THOMPSON,
George Derwent 1923
THOMPSON, Henry 1820
THOMPSON,
Henry Yates 1860
THOMPSON, W. H. 1830
TOMLINSON,
George (Bishop) 1820

| | | | |
|---|---|---|---|
| TOULMIN, | | WATSON, | |
| Stephen Edelston | 1947 | Alister George Douglas | 1927 |
| TOVEY, Duncan | 1865 | WATSON, | |
| TRENCH, | | Henry William | 1848 |
| Richard Trevenix | 1827 | WEDD, Nathaniel | 1888 |
| TREVELYAN, | | WEDGWOOD, | |
| George Macaulay | 1895 | (Sir) Ralph Lewis | 1893 |
| TREVELYAN, | | WHITEHEAD, | |
| (Sir) George Otto | 1859 | Alfred North | 1884 |
| TREVELYAN, | | WHITMORE, C. S. | 1823 |
| Robert Calversley | 1893 | WILKIER, W. C. | 1834 |
| TURNER, Herbert H. | 1880 | WILLIAMS, John Daniel | 1849 |
| | | WILSON, | |
| VAUGHAN, Edward T. | 1835 | George St Vincent | 1825 |
| VEASEY, Alfred | 1821 | WILSON, | |
| VENABLES, | | (Sir) Henry Francis | 1881 |
| George Stovin | 1832 | WISEMAN, Charles | 1820 |
| VERRALL, Arthur W. | 1871 | WITTGENSTEIN, | |
| | | Ludwig | 1912 |
| WALLICH, Walter | 1939 | WOOLF, Leonard | 1902 |
| WALPOLE, Spencer | 1826 | WOOTTON, David | 1974 |
| WALTER, William Grey | 1933 | WRANGHAM, | |
| WARD, James | 1876 | George W. | 1827 |
| WARRE-CORNISH, | | WYSE, William | 1880 |
| Francis | 1860 | | |
| WATKINS, | | YOOL, G. V. | 1848 |
| Arthur Ronald Dare | 1925 | YOUNG, Edward M. | 1860 |

# INDEX